The Down-Deep Delight of Democracy

Antipode Book Series

Series Editors: Vinay Gidwani, University of Minnesota, USA, and Sharad Chari, London School of Economics, UK

Like its parent journal, the Antipode Book Series reflects distinctive new developments in radical geography. It publishes books in a variety of formats—from reference books to works of broad explication to titles that develop and extend the scholarly research base—but the commitment is always the same: to contribute to the praxis of a new and more just society.

Published

Banking Across Boundaries: Placing Finance in Capitalism
Brett Christophers

The Down-Deep Delight of Democracy
Mark Purcell

Gramsci: Space, Nature, Politics
Edited by Michael Ekers, Gillian Hart, Stefan Kipfer and Alex Loftus

Places of Possibility: Property, Nature and Community Land Ownership
A. Fiona D. Mackenzie

The New Carbon Economy: Constitution, Governance and Contestation
Edited by Peter Newell, Max Boykoff and Emily Boyd

Capitalism and Conservation
Edited by Dan Brockington and Rosaleen Duffy

Spaces of Environmental Justice
Edited by Ryan Holifield, Michael Porter and Gordon Walker

The Point is to Change it: Geographies of Hope and Survival in an Age of Crisis
Edited by Noel Castree, Paul Chatterton, Nik Heynen, Wendy Larner and Melissa W. Wright

Privatization: Property and the Remaking of Nature-Society
Edited by Becky Mansfield

Practising Public Scholarship: Experiences and Possibilities Beyond the Academy
Edited by Katharyne Mitchell

Grounding Globalization: Labour in the Age of Insecurity
Edward Webster, Rob Lambert and Andries Bezuidenhout

Privatization: Property and the Remaking of Nature-Society Relations
Edited by Becky Mansfield

Decolonizing Development: Colonial Power and the Maya
Joel Wainwright

Cities of Whiteness
Wendy S. Shaw

Neoliberalization: States, Networks, Peoples
Edited by Kim England and Kevin Ward

The Dirty Work of Neoliberalism: Cleaners in the Global Economy
Edited by Luis L. M. Aguiar and Andrew Herod

David Harvey: A Critical Reader
Edited by Noel Castree and Derek Gregory

Working the Spaces of Neoliberalism: Activism, Professionalisation and Incorporation
Edited by Nina Laurie and Liz Bondi

Threads of Labour: Garment Industry Supply Chains from the Workers' Perspective
Edited by Angela Hale and Jane Wills

Life's Work: Geographies of Social Reproduction
Edited by Katharyne Mitchell, Sallie A. Marston and Cindi Katz

Redundant Masculinities? Employment Change and White Working Class Youth
Linda McDowell

Spaces of Neoliberalism
Edited by Neil Brenner and Nik Theodore

Space, Place and the New Labour Internationalism
Edited by Peter Waterman and Jane Wills

Forthcoming

Fat Bodies, Fat Spaces: Critical Geographies of Obesity
Rachel Colls and Bethan Evans

The Down-Deep Delight of Democracy

Mark Purcell

WILEY-BLACKWELL

A John Wiley & Sons, Ltd., Publication

This edition first published 2013
© 2013 John Wiley & Sons, Ltd

Wiley-Blackwell is an imprint of John Wiley & Sons, formed by the merger of Wiley's global Scientific, Technical and Medical business with Blackwell Publishing.

Registered Office
John Wiley & Sons, Ltd, The Atrium, Southern Gate, Chichester, West Sussex, PO19 8SQ, UK

Editorial Offices
350 Main Street, Malden, MA 02148-5020, USA
9600 Garsington Road, Oxford, OX4 2DQ, UK
The Atrium, Southern Gate, Chichester, West Sussex, PO19 8SQ, UK

For details of our global editorial offices, for customer services, and for information about how to apply for permission to reuse the copyright material in this book please see our website at www.wiley.com/wiley-blackwell.

The right of Mark Purcell to be identified as the author of this work has been asserted in accordance with the UK Copyright, Designs and Patents Act 1988.

Library of Congress Cataloging-in-Publication Data

Purcell, Mark Hamilton.
  The down-deep delight of democracy / Mark Purcell.
    pages   cm
  Includes index.
  ISBN 978-1-4443-4997-9 (cloth) – ISBN 978-1-4443-4998-6 (pbk.)
  1. Democracy–History.
  JC421.P865 2013
  321.8–dc23
                                                    2012045277

A catalogue record for this book is available from the British Library.

Cover image: Viernes 20M_23 By Julio Albarrán
Cover design by www.cyandesign.co.uk

Set in 10.5/12.5pt Sabon by SPi Publisher Services, Pondicherry, India
Printed in Malaysia by Ho Printing (M) Sdn Bhd

1   2013

To the one Forever Overhead.

The board will nod and you will go, and though we grieve we are grateful for these shards of light from the hearts of sad stars.

Contents

Acknowledgments

Like any other book, this one is an assemblage, a rhizome that opens out into the world and connects with many different people, ideas, desires, and energies. It would be impossible to acknowledge them all, and so this is only a partial list. Susan Fainstein, Ananya Roy, Peter Marcuse, David Imbroscio, Byron Miller, Michael Brown, Helga Leitner, Andy Merrifield, Clive Barnett, Nicholas Dahmann, Nathan Clough, Erik Swyngedouw, Nik Heynan, Richard Day, Deborah Martin, Walter Nicholls, Eugene McCann, James deFilippis, Matt Wilson, and Gary Bridge have all contributed to and pushed my thinking in various fruitful directions.

Also incredibly stimulating has been the extraordinary work of bloggers whose active and high-quality thinking and writing are a model we all should aspire to. Among them are Lenin's Tomb, I Cite, ABC Democracy, The Commune, Take the Square, Red Pepper, Ceasefire, Anarchist Without Content, Pop Theory, Cities and Citizenship, No Useless Leniency, Progressive Geographies, and (the former) Infinite Thought.

Among the many at the University of Washington, special thanks go to my students in CEP 301 and CEP 461, who read the classics with me with great effort, patience, and insight. And to Chris Campbell, one of the few administrators who knows the value of scholarship and how to engender it in an institution. And of course to Becoming-Poor, which exists, incredibly, in an academy increasingly cheapened by money, and nevertheless has absolutely no intention of giving in. *Autogestiamo*!

The people at Wiley-Blackwell have been fantastic. Rachel Pain guided the project into existence with grace, and Vinay Gidwani saw it to completion with elegance. Jacqueline Scott and Isobel Bainton were fabulous in every way. And two anonymous reviewers were extraordinary for their supportive, thoughtful, and erudite comments.

I had the good fortune to receive financial support from the College of Built Environments at the University of Washington to hire a copy editor and indexer. I hired Karen Uchic, and I could not be more impressed by her work.

Let's face it, the cover of this book is the best thing about it. The photographer is Julio Albarrán. Find more of his work at http://www. flickr.com/photos/julioalbarran/.

And of course, as always, for everything: Mom, Elham, Roshann, and Neeku.

1

What Is to Be Done?

...be on the watch.
there are ways out.
there is a light somewhere.
it may not be much light but
it beats the
darkness.
be on the watch.
the gods will offer you
chances.
know them, take them...
the more often you
learn to do it,
the more light there will
be...
you are marvelous.
the gods wait to delight
in
you.
　　—"The Laughing Heart,"
　　Charles Bukowski (1993)[1]

In *The Politics*, Aristotle describes how oligarchies fall and give way to democracies: "by concentrating power into ever fewer hands, because of a shameful desire for profit, [the oligarchs] made the multitude stronger,

---

[1] Reprinted from *The Prairie Schooner* 67.3 (Fall 1993) by permission of the University of Nebraska Press. Copyright 1993 by the University of Nebraska Press.

The Down-Deep Delight of Democracy, First Edition. Mark Purcell.
© 2013 John Wiley & Sons, Ltd. Published 2013 by John Wiley & Sons, Ltd.

with the result that it revolted and democracies arose" (Aristotle, 1998b, p. 1286b). As we stagger through the flotsam of the financial crisis and the preposterous proposal of "austerity" as a solution, it is not hard to see ourselves in the first part of Aristotle's account. But in this book, I want to focus on the second part, the part where he suggests that oligarchies tend to "make the multitude stronger," that they awaken and activate a popular power that rises up and expresses its desire for democracy.

Aristotle also reminds us that, in a sense, political questions are always very old ones. He advises that we should "take it, indeed, that pretty well everything...has been discovered many times...in the long course of history....Therefore, one should make adequate use of what has been discovered, but also try to investigate whatever has been overlooked" (Aristotle, 1998b, p. 1329b). Nietzsche displays a similar kind of humility in the face of the long history of political thought, arguing that ideas

> grow up in connection in relationship with each other.... However suddenly and arbitrarily they seem to appear in the history of thought, they [are] nevertheless...far less a discovery than a recognition, of remembering, a return and a homecoming to a remote, primordial, and inclusive household of the soul, out of which those concepts grew originally: philosophizing is to this extent a kind of atavism of the highest order (Nietzsche, 1989a, p. 27).

So asking the question "What is to be done?" is always an atavistic enterprise in a way, a kind of mining of past political action and thought. It is Lenin's old question, but it is no less the question Plato and Aristotle were asking, writing as they were in the wake of the Athenian defeat in the Peloponnesian War and living under a pervasive sense that their society was crumbling. Marx was asking the question too, and Lenin, and Gramsci. In the poem that opens the chapter, Bukowski is also searching for an answer, as are we today. And so in taking up the question of what is to be done, I try to be very much aware of this history, of what has already been discovered, and I try to make adequate use of it. I mine the work of thinkers like Aristotle, Plato, Hobbes, Lefebvre, Deleuze and Guattari, Rancière, Laclau and Mouffe, Gramsci, and others, trying to learn what they have to teach us. At the same time, I do not mean only to retrace the steps of others. I intend to use the political wisdom of the past to cut a path toward a possible future, toward a political community we have not yet realized.

My answer to Lenin's question of "What is to be done?" is: *democracy*. Less concisely, what is to be done, what we all must do together, is to engage in a collective and perpetual struggle to democratize our society and to manage our affairs for ourselves. I do not propose democracy as the Platonic Form of the good community. It is not some end of history we should expect to reach. Rather, my argument is more restrained: perpetual democratization is the best way forward in the current context and for the foreseeable future. What we need in our time is to move politically from oligarchy to democracy, from passivity to activity, and from heteronomy to autonomy.

The Current Context

To understand what it would mean to democratize society in the current context, it helps to have some sense of what that context is. Over the course of the last seventy-five years or so, capitalist social relations of production were extended (if incompletely) to almost all parts of the globe; the dominance of Keynesian and social-democratic thinking was replaced by a neoliberal common sense; attempts to establish a state-socialist alternative to capitalism collapsed in utter failure; the world's population has not only grown rapidly but become predominantly urban; geopolitics moved from the Cold War to a "war on terror" to the current post-terror landscape; and the environment (both the global climate and localized disasters) came to be seen as a central political question at all scales. Like all periods, the current era has also been greatly shaped by recurrent manifestations of popular power, in the form of both intense eruptions and everyday struggles by people to collectively liberate themselves from the various structures that contain them.

Political economy

The recent processes of globalization, through which capitalist production spread to incorporate almost every part of the globe, have been so extremely well documented that I think recounting them at length here is unnecessary (e.g. Dicken, 1998; Brenner and Theodore, 2003; Harvey, 2005). I will therefore offer only a brief review. Although capitalism has been extending itself geographically since its inception, the globalization processes of the twentieth century have greatly speeded up the process by which the entire globe is being integrated into a single capitalist economic machine. How we orient ourselves to this machine is a central political, economic, and cultural question in the current context. State socialism, of the kind that came to power in the Soviet Union, Eastern Europe, and China, among other places, represents a state-led attempt to create a non-capitalist alternative. While these regimes often call themselves communist, they are all more properly socialist societies managed by the state. Another option, what we might call a welfare-state approach, has been to accept capitalism but use the state to actively manage it with an eye toward stability and material redistribution for social justice. Keynesianism and social democracy are the leading models associated with this second option. A third option, generally known as neoliberalism, wants to unleash the capitalist market by reducing the size of the state and its ability to regulate the economy. I argue that each of these options, in its own way, is nothing other than a form of oligarchy. None offers a properly *democratic* response to the question of what is to be done.

The modern welfare-state model was born in the wake of the Great Depression. It typically followed a national-Keynesian approach to economic policy, which is to say it favored a very strong and active central government that carved out an expansive public sphere: strong state authority and generous provision of public goods and services. It was a model in which the state (usually a liberal-democratic one) acted as the primary representative of the public. This association became so ingrained in the culture as to make the state virtually synonymous with the public or the people. In this role as public, the state closely regulated industries and managed the macro economy. It also standardized currencies and ensured relative monetary stability. Government spending was seen as a primary economic variable, a linchpin for ensuring economic growth. Large government bureaucracies were required to carry out this economic management. They employed many people, generally with good wages and benefits. Labor organization was typically strong, and governments participated centrally in creating broad accords between capital and labor that usually secured high wages and good job security for workers. Beyond those accords, government policies tended to favor material redistribution to the less wealthy. Such policies included national social security, high minimum wages, subsidized health care, and the like. In addition, high tax rates enabled governments to provide well-funded and high-quality infrastructure such as public schools and universities, child care, hospitals and clinics, libraries, parks, public transportation, and so on. In the more fully social-democratic regimes, most of which were in Europe, it was common for the state to assume even greater economic control by owning certain enterprises and even monopolizing entire economic sectors like natural resources, telecommunications, or transportation.

Clearly there is a spectrum of possible policy actions within the welfare-state model, and particular policy combinations vary by place and time. However, for the purposes of this brief account, in broad outline what all such regimes share is a commitment to a large and interventionist state that acts on behalf of citizens, usually to create social policies whose goal is some amount of material redistribution for greater equality. The welfare-state model thus occupies the broad middle between the hard-left alternative of state socialism and neoliberalism's free-market fundamentalism. It insists that a liberal-democratic state can and should play a large role in regulating capitalist economic activity so that we can have a stable, prosperous, and incrementally more equal society.

During roughly the same period that the welfare state was the dominant model in the capitalist world, a number of revolutions across the globe created an archipelago of state-socialist regimes that offered a stark alternative to capitalism. The Russian Revolution of 1917 created the Soviet Union, and after World War II Soviet insistence helped install state-socialist regimes in Central and Eastern Europe. Relatively more independent revolutions in Yugoslavia and Cuba produced state socialism there. The Communist victory in the Chinese Civil War in 1949 initiated state socialism in the East Asian sphere, and it spread to places like Korea, Vietnam, Cambodia, and Mongolia. As with the welfare state, state socialism varied in its particulars. In basic outline, it took its agenda from the *Communist Manifesto*, which called for workers' parties to seize the state and use its power to expropriate from the bourgeoisie the privately owned means of production. Such collectivization or nationalization was designed to abolish private property and classes, and thus end capitalist relations of production. The idea was that this socialist phase led by a one-party state would be temporary; once classes were abolished, the state would no longer be necessary, since its purpose was to manage the conflict between the bourgeoisie and the proletariat. The state would wither away in due course and lead to a self-managed and egalitarian communist society. Of course, this transition from state-led socialism to stateless communism did not occur in actual practice. In fact, the opposite tended to happen: as the state bureaucracy took over control of the means of production, it became the new ruling class and ruthlessly intensified the power and scope of the state to the very limits of imagination. Stalinist Russia and Maoist China were the largest-scale disasters, but few state-socialist regimes avoided the horrors of totalitarianism and authoritarianism. Part of the failure was due to the folly of trying to manage national-scale economies through central-state command, and part of it was the ill-conceived attempt to defeat the capitalist West in a race to industrialize. But perhaps an even more fatal flaw of such states was the brutality and terrorism of their totalitarian political regimes. Extraordinary movements in Hungary, Yugoslavia, Poland, Czechoslovakia, China, and Romania, just to name a few, demonstrated that people will not submit to a totalitarian state indefinitely. They will resist, resolutely and creatively, through both small everyday acts and large public spectacles, when the state attempts to control virtually every aspect of their lives.

By 1989, the state-socialist model was largely exhausted. The Soviet Bloc began its rapid collapse and entered a "post-socialist" phase. Today, only China, Laos, Vietnam, North Korea, and Cuba remain as countries with state-socialist regimes.[2] To be clear, the "utter failure" of this model I mentioned is not at all the failure of communism, which was never achieved in almost any sense. It is rather the failure of state socialism: the central management of a national economy by an authoritarian state controlled by a single party nominally allied to the proletariat.

As we saw, during the era when state socialism was at its height, it faced a capitalist world in which the welfare-state model was dominant. But by the early 1970s, the welfare state's dominance had begun to erode. Two main forces precipitated its decline. The first was a sustained ideological assault from the right carried out by neoliberal intellectuals. The second was the emergence of economic problems such as unemployment, inflation, and capital flight that began to intensify in and around 1973. The intellectuals' ideological attacks began to emerge in the late 1940s, when thinkers associated with groups like the Mont Pelerin Society remobilized traditional arguments from liberal economics. Scholars like Friedrich von Hayek, Milton Friedman, Ludwig von Mises, and Karl Popper opposed state intervention in the economy, and they insisted that society is more efficient, wealthier, and more open when capitalist markets are allowed to operate as freely as possible (Popper, 1945; Friedman, 1962; Hayek, 1994). Throughout the 1950s and 1960s, they prosecuted a long war of ideas against Keynesianism and the welfare state and for a neoliberal alternative. Then, in the early 1970s, economic events provided neoliberals with an important opportunity: most economies in the developed world underwent simultaneous and acute stagnation and inflation. It was a clear opportunity to press the case that management by a Keynesian welfare state could not provide economic stability and prosperity. At about the same time, it was becoming increasingly feasible for corporations to relocate their operations, to flee the high wages and benefits won by labor in some parts of the industrialized world for areas with weaker labor organization and lower wages. Some of that flight remained within the industrialized economies, but some left for less industrialized places like Korea and Taiwan and then at different times China, Thailand, Brazil, Malaysia, the Philippines, and Mexico, among others. The flight of capital from Keynesian welfare states made

---

[2] Of course, there are real differences among these regimes. China's economy is rapidly becoming integrated into the world capitalist market, while Cuba's remains much more isolated. But they are all still ruled by an authoritarian state governed by a single communist or socialist party.

such states appear unable to compete effectively in a rapidly globalizing world economy.

The rise of politicians like Reagan and Thatcher in the 1980s helped translate these intellectual and economic trends into concrete policy for the global North. Markets were deregulated, ownership and control of economic enterprise was privatized, and social services were aggressively cut. Such policy initiatives spread insistently, though at different rates, to governments in other wealthy economies, so by the mid-1980s neoliberalism was having great success in its struggle to supplant the Keynesian welfare state. This success was only intensified by the fall of most state-socialist regimes in the late 1980s. As the Soviet Union and its Eastern European satellites collapsed under the weight of their failed totalitarian model, the neoliberalizing West was quick to claim ideological and economic victory, narrating the changes as inevitable, a result of the inherent superiority of free markets and liberal democracy over their "communist" alternative. Francis Fukuyama's thesis about the "end of history" was perhaps the most memorable example (Fukuyama, 1992).

The dominance of neoliberalism extended very much also to the question of economic development in the global South. Over the course of the 1980s and 1990s, a line of thinking known as the "Washington Consensus" came to dominate international economic policy, especially with respect to countries in the global South. The World Bank and the International Monetary Fund (IMF) helped produce a pervasive common sense regarding poorer countries, whereby the only possible path to development was austerity and "structural adjustment," which would drastically reduce state spending and ownership of assets, lower trade barriers, encourage Foreign Direct Investment, and energetically integrate their economies into global commodity flows. The World Bank and IMF induced such policy changes by making them conditions of the loans they offered to developing countries. Throughout this period, more and more Southern countries were integrated into this system whereby the public/state sector was reduced and the economy reoriented toward the production of commodities for the global capitalist market. The fall of the Berlin Wall only accelerated this process, as countries could no longer rely on their position in the Cold War system of satellite or client states to secure resources. They were increasingly forced to participate effectively in the global market.

By the 1990s, neoliberalism had become so taken-for-granted that center-left leaders like Clinton and Blair were unable and/or unwilling to propose either a return to Keynesian welfarism or some other alternative. Or perhaps it is more accurate to say that by the 1990s it had become very hard to imagine anything other than neoliberalism. It was only when the great recession of 2007 hit that the neoliberal consensus began to weaken. The housing sector and its financial markets were widely seen as the leading cause of the crash, and those markets had been subject to the same active deregulation as other markets. It became no longer self-evident that the markets will regulate themselves, that public oversight by the state is superfluous. This new doubt was symbolized by the appearance of Alan Greenspan, a leading light of neoliberal thought, before Congress in October 2008. Greenspan was ashen and penitent. He testified that the crisis had exposed serious flaws in his economic worldview. The Washington Consensus had become open to debate again.

And so we currently occupy a state of uncertainty. The recession of 2007 clearly destabilized neoliberal common sense. But that destabilization was in no way total; much of neoliberalism remains common sense, if only because we have had so few alternatives for thirty years. Recent events only mean that a new battle has been joined over the content of political-economic common sense. There is today an opening, an opportunity, for non-neoliberal alternatives to assert themselves effectively.

One alternative that has already begun to emerge is a reinvigorated Keynesian welfarism. In many ways, President Obama's bailout package in response to the economic crisis in the United States was classically Keynesian, particularly the strategy of government spending as economic stimulus. The US government also took controlling stakes in very large firms crippled by the crisis, such as General Motors and Chrysler (Chang and Gilmore, 2011). The financial regulation bill passed in the United States in 2010 similarly reasserts (albeit weakly) the need for more national-government regulation of market activity. Another alternative is that neoliberalism will stagger on, wounded, but still stronger than any other idea. For example, when Obama took office in the midst of the crisis, one of his first appointments was Laurence Summers as director of the National Economic Council. Summers is an influential neoliberal economist who was Clinton's Treasury Secretary from 1999 to 2001. He was widely thought to have played an important role in deregulating the derivatives market, which helped cause the crash (e.g. Ames, 2008). Yet Obama, even as he explored Keynesian stimulus solutions, also seemed unable (or unwilling) to cast aside the voice of neoliberal orthodoxy, making Summers one of his closest economic advisors in the early days of his presidency.

Since the crash, neoliberals have cast around almost desperately for ways to end the persistent recession. One response, incredibly, has been to remobilize the austerity approach in the global North, which is to say they have tried to solve a crisis precipitated by neoliberal deregulation by pushing neoliberalization still further. Many states in Europe are faced with mounting national debt caused by insufficient tax revenue as a result of the recession, ineffective tax collection systems, and relatively generous welfare spending. The "troika" of the European Union, the European Central Bank, and the IMF has recently been pressing countries such as Greece, Ireland, Portugal, Spain, and Italy to undergo austerity measures, which typically involve cutting all sorts of welfare benefits, reducing the number of public employees, privatizing state-owned assets, and increasing taxes. Architects of austerity claim that reducing the national debt in this way will get economies "back on track" (e.g. Daley, 2011). Austerity for these countries is presented by the Troika and by the mainstream press as the only alternative to their default and the continental economic collapse that would surely follow. Such forced austerity packages have been the stock-in-trade of the Washington Consensus, and they have long been the prevailing wisdom of the World Bank and IMF in dealing with debt-ridden poor countries facing economic crisis. And in fact such austerity measures are not limited to relatively poorer countries. Wealthier governments like the United Kingdom, United States, and Israel are also carrying sovereign debt as a result of the recession and are currently involved in a pitched struggle over how to respond: what public spending to cut and how much, and whether to raise taxes and for whom.

Not surprisingly, coming as they do in the midst of economic recession and high unemployment, austerity measures face vigorous opposition from mobilized populations. Such opposition roiled Greece in 2011–2012, when massive demonstrations destabilized the Greek government to the point of political collapse. Similar uprisings took place in Spain, and there is some indication that something similar is developing in Italy. Even in the United States the Occupy Wall Street movement voiced significant resistance to the current political-economic structure. To some extent, this mobilization is an attempt to defend what remains of the welfare state. Crowds are demanding that the government retain state-sector jobs with good wages and benefits while preserving robust state transfers that support citizens in many different sectors of life. A similar desire can be seen in the anti-cuts movement in the United Kingdom and in the spring 2011 protests in Madison, Wisconsin. Unlike in Greece and Spain, in Wisconsin the attack on state employment and spending was not initiated by supranational monetary institutions but by relatively local political forces. Nevertheless, the mobilized response was similar: massive and strident public demonstrations and occupations to defend established welfare-state goods like public-sector jobs and government service programs. In sum, one important desire that is being expressed in the popular anti-austerity movements is to defend what remains of the welfare state against neoliberal attempts to dismantle it still further.

Each of these uprisings is complex, and the desire to defend the welfare state has been only one among many political demands. I do not want to say we should reject this demand. Defending the welfare state, or even trying to reinvigorate it, is a perfectly understandable way to respond to neoliberalism and austerity (Judt and Snyder, 2012). It is the alternative closest at hand, the non-neoliberal logic we have most recently experienced. Without doubt, a Keynesian welfare state is preferable to its neoliberal alternative. However, I want to argue that we can aim at more; that in terms of democracy, we can do far better than the welfare state. We can aspire to and achieve a much more democratic form of life than the welfare state has to offer.[3] The full weight of this argument will become clear throughout the book as I develop my conception of what democracy means, but here let me sketch the outlines of the Keynesian welfare state's democratic deficit.

As we saw, Keynesianism imagines the state to be essentially the same thing as the public, in the sense that the state stands in for, and acts as though it were, the people. But in fact the state is not the people. Nietzsche's Zarathustra had it right: "State is the name of the coldest of all cold monsters. Coldly it tells lies too; and this lie crawls from its mouth: 'I, the state, am the people'" (2005, p. 44). The state is only ever a very small subset of the people. Democracy means that the people rule themselves. Oligarchy is the term for a regime in which a small subset of the population rules the whole. Insofar as it imagines the state to be the sole, legitimate, and unchallenged representative of the people, the welfare state is much more an oligarchy than it is a democracy.[4] In that way, Keynesianism differs little from state socialism: it accepts that in the everyday functioning of the polity a small cadre of rulers (state officials) will govern a large body of ruled subjects (everyone else). To be sure, Keynesian states have been more democratic than state-socialist ones. In state socialism, the state/public sector aspires to encompass all areas of life, while Keynesianism usually

---

[3] And a desire for this democratic something-more is indeed one of the many desires being expressed in the movements against austerity.

[4] As Aristotle showed, even if we can understand terms like oligarchy and democracy clearly in the abstract, in practice each polity displays some complex mixture of oligarchical, monarchical, and democratic qualities. Polities that we call oligarchies can be relatively more or less democratic depending on their particular institutions and procedures. But the presence of democratic qualities does not mean we cannot still describe a given polity meaningfully as an oligarchy. Therefore, one cannot take the sentence "polity x is an oligarchy" to mean x exhibits *only* oligarchical qualities, that no democratic qualities can be found there. Rather, the sentence must mean something more like "polity x is relatively more oligarchical than it is anything else." It is in that sense that I argue that liberal-democratic states, Keynesian welfare states, and socialist states are oligarchies. Some are more democratic than others, but all are systems in which, in their actual operation, a small subset rules over the many, i.e. an oligarchy.

operates within liberal-democratic governments where the state/public sector is formally limited.[5] Further attenuating Keynesianism's oligarchy is the fact that citizens in liberal democracies have some say in selecting their governors through majority vote. To a limited extent, therefore, state agents are accountable to the people. While this accountability is typically quite weak, it is nevertheless stronger than in a state-socialist regime. Keynesian welfarism thus offers a relatively more democratic version of state socialism in which the state alone embodies the public and acts for the people, but its control is mitigated somewhat by liberal-democratic structures.

Of course, neoliberals have criticized Keynesian welfarism as well. A central tenet of their argument has always been that Keynesianism endangers the liberal qualities of liberal democracy because it advocates a larger state/public role in economic policy, working to enlarge the authority of the state to manage the behavior of people in the private sphere (and particularly the market economy). That is, neoliberals argue, a strong state-public sector restricts the liberty of citizens in the private sector, and such restriction is precisely what liberal democracy, ever since its original formulation in Locke, is designed to prevent. For Locke, tyranny is the greatest of all political dangers, and many neoliberals are quite sincere when they decry high taxes, state regulation of industry, and redistribution policies as tyrannical. Their argument is that a small cadre of state bureaucrats, rather than the free market, is deciding what to do with a significant portion of each citizen's material fortune. The old Republican Party adage that "you know what to do with your money better than the government does" is very much heir to this anti-tyranny legacy.

I do not mean to suggest that neoliberals are offering a more democratic alternative. Not at all. They propose a market of purportedly free individuals as a substitute for state control. Of course, capitalist markets are also highly oligarchical, dominated as they are by a few large corporations that heavily influence how goods are made and distributed.[6] Moreover, it is hard to ignore the less idealistic motivations of neoliberalism. It is also a naked power play to free those large corporations from state interference so they can dominate economic markets and maximize their profit. But still, the kernel of the neoliberal objection to Keynesian welfarism is not wrong: state power, even in a liberal democracy, is

---

[5] Most of what it means for a regime to be "totalitarian" is for it to work to establish a state/public sphere that is in fact total, that absorbs all areas of private/non-state life.

[6] Such markets are technically closer to oligarchy as Plato and Aristotle understand the term. For them, oligarchy requires that one have *wealth* to rule (usually there was a property qualification to be a citizen), and so it results in a regime in which the wealthy few rule the many poor, a regime we usually call plutocracy today.

oligarchic by its very nature.[7] A few state officials must necessarily make decisions for the many. Neoliberalism and the Keynesian welfare state thus offer a choice between one kind of oligarchy and another. We must look elsewhere for a properly democratic alternative.

The continual recurrence of constituent power

Throughout the current era, indeed throughout history, there has been another kind of power at work, a power very different from the one I have been examining. It is a popular power, a power that arises from below, from within the body of society. Michael Hardt and Antonio Negri, in their book *Empire* (2000), offer a useful conceptual framework for understanding this other kind of power. They argue that there is a conflict at the center of modernity. This conflict is "between, on the one hand, the immanent forces of desire and association, the love of community, and on the other, the strong hand of an overarching authority that imposes and enforces an order on the social field" (2000, p. 69). In the Modern age, they argue, the powers of creation that had previously been thought to reside in heaven, in a transcendental sphere, were brought down to earth. The source of all creation is no longer thought to be God, but rather the work of an organized human society. In other words, the power of creation is no longer transcendental, but immanent. This shift resulted in what Hardt and Negri call a crisis of authority: if it is no longer God in heaven that rules the world, if that power is now in the hands of human beings, how can we give form to this immanent authority so that order can be preserved? Hardt and Negri argue that the central project of modern political thought is to imagine this new earthly authority.

Thomas Hobbes' *Leviathan* was the opening salvo. In a world where authority was no longer transcendental, no longer vested in a king by divine right, Hobbes' project was to construct an authority that derived from nothing other than people themselves, an authority those same people would accept as legitimate. He constructed this authority to be supremely powerful, such that "there is no power on earth that can compare to it."[8] He began from the premise that in the state of nature, which is to say in the human condition without a state, immanent power is all that exists. God

---

[7] As I discuss in the chapters to come, the works of Henri Lefebvre (1976–1978; 2009) and Gilles Deleuze and Felix Guattari (1987) offer an extensive development of this argument.

[8] This is the meaning of the Latin verse inscribed in the famous frontispiece to the book: "*Non est potestas Super Terram quae Comparetur ei.*" Alternatively, one could also translate the sentence as "there is no power *above* the earth that can compare to it," which is consistent with the Modern age's shift away from transcendental power, but which in Hobbes' day would have likely subjected him to the serious charge of blasphemy.

does not determine our fate; rather each person has the power to do as he or she pleases. Hobbes thought that in such a state there was nothing to prevent each person from using their own power to make war on everyone else, a situation he famously termed a war of all against all. Hobbes' solution was to invent an originary political contract. This contract had a very specific structure: each person contracts with each of the others individually, and they both agree to give their individual power over to an "artificial person," an entity created by the contract itself. This entity was his Leviathan, or the modern state, an earthly power that serves to overawe the multitude and keep order in society (1996, Chapter 16).

For Hardt and Negri, Hobbes' *Leviathan* initiates the central conflict of modernity, between the power of people to act as they choose, and the power of Leviathan to impose order on them. Hardt and Negri call the power of people to act "constituent power," whereas the power of Leviathan is "constituted power." According to this narrative, constituent power is primary; its origin is in the bodies and minds of all people, in "the multitude" as Hobbes called them. Constituted power is therefore derivative; it is siphoned off from constituent power and turned back onto people in order to control them. This idea of primacy is not Hardt and Negri's invention. It is rather a central tenet of all modern political thought starting with Hobbes: power originates in the bodies of the multitude, and constituted power (Leviathan) is merely an artificial creation, a human contrivance that serves the purpose of establishing societal order.[9] In other words, constituent power is autonomous, it is self-producing. It does not need constituted power to exist. The mass of people, what Hardt and Negri also call "the multitude," can act, create, and produce life on their own. The constituted power of the state (or of capital), on the other hand, depends on constituent power for its very existence.

Constituent power goes by other names. Marx (1994) calls it our "vital powers"; for Spinoza (1996), it is our *conatus*; Deleuze and Guattari (1987) use the term *puissance*; for Nietzsche (1989a) it is our will to power; and Aristotle (1998b) just thought of it as our nature (*physis*), our inner drive to grow into a full-fledged human being. Each retains the idea that this power is somehow our own, that it is different from a power outside ourselves. Thus, the various ideas about constituent power point to the tension between autonomy and heteronomy, between governing oneself and being governed by another.[10] It is the struggle

---

[9] Locke, Rousseau, Marx—this starting assumption is nearly universal. And in fact this line of argument predates modernity. In *Summa Theologica*, Aquinas (1989) argues that the system of human laws (in particular, laws about property and property rights) is not given by God for humans to obey; it is rather a set of practices invented by humans to organize their own power.

[10] *Auto* = self; *Hetero* = other; *Nomos* = law.

between the multitude acting by itself and for itself and the multitude being ruled by an entity outside itself. It is, in short, the struggle between democracy and oligarchy. Hobbes' *Leviathan* is the quintessence of heteronomy. It is when the people give up their own authority to make laws and transfer it to an artificial entity outside of themselves. The modern state is thus founded on the principle of heteronomy, on the multitude being ruled by something beyond them, rather than on autonomy, on the multitude ruling themselves.

The fact that constituent power is the creative force of society, that it produces the world, means that constituent power is always present, always operating, always driving the process of change. We tend to think of this power as weak and fleeting, as flittering at the margins of society, as reacting meekly to the *real* power, to the structures of constituted power like the Keynesian welfare state, or the capitalist market dominated by large corporations, or the totalitarian societies of state socialism. But if constituent power produces the world, if it is the real engine of history, it must also produce constituted power; it must itself create the structures that contain it. This way of thinking, one very much inspired in Hardt and Negri by Deleuze and Guattari (as we will see), repositions constituent power as original, permanent, and primary. Our habit of seeing it as weak is not so much *its* weakness, but ours. If we understand power in this way, then we need to recondition our way of seeing. We must more carefully attend to and learn to better perceive constituent power. Even if power most often manifests as constituted power, we must try to understand how and why constituent power gave rise to the particular structures of constituted power. Moreover, we must also be attentive to constituent power when it emerges and operates on its own terms, as the power of the multitude reclaiming their agency, resolving to act for themselves again.

The Arab Uprisings in Tunisia, Egypt, Libya, Syria, Yemen, Bahrain, and Oman in 2010–2011 are perhaps some of the most spectacular manifestations of raw constituent power in recent memory. Although they are extremely important and worthy of close attention, they are only one in a very long line of such events. In 1871, working class residents all over Paris rose up and took control of the city; they governed it themselves for two months. In 1920 in Turin and Milan, in a wave of factory occupations in Northern Italian industrial towns, workers' councils took control of factories and ran them themselves, without bosses, for extended periods (Anonymous, 1921). In the 1940s, Indians rose up against British domination using a variety of tactics that included mass actions of non-violent refusal. In the 1950s and 1960s, people all over Africa struggled insistently for independence and an end to European colonial domination. In 1956 in Hungary, students, workers, and ordinary people rebelled against a Stalinist bureaucracy and succeeded in controlling the country for several weeks until Soviet troops put down the uprising and reinstalled the former regime. In 1968, again in Paris, students and workers brought off enormous occupations and general strikes that destabilized the government to the point of collapse. Similar upwellings, in Tiananmen in 1989, Chiapas in 1994, Argentina in 2001, Bolivia in 2005, Iran in 2009, and in Portugal, Spain, Greece, the United Kingdom, Chile, Israel, the United States, and Russia in the summer and fall of 2011, teach us that constituent power continues to assert itself, to express its desire, and to shape the course of history. To be sure, a close analysis of each of these events would reveal a complex mixture of constituent and constituted power. The movement for democracy in China, for example, saw a continual struggle between leaders who tried to shape and direct the movement and the mass of participants who repeatedly refused to be ruled (Zhao 2004). All such events are marked by intricate ebbs and flows between constituent and constituted power, between autonomy and heteronomy. All I want to do here is to give a name to constituent power, to understand it as fundamentally different from constituted power, and to make clear that it has been a vibrant and important force in the politics of the current context.

Rapid urbanization

One particularly prominent feature of the political-economic shifts of the last forty years has been the rapid urbanization of the globe, a process driven almost entirely by urbanization in the global South (e.g. Davis, 2006; Roy and Ong, 2011). As cities in the global North deindustrialized, some manufacturing production has moved to other cities and towns in the North, but much of it moved to cities in the global South. Those cities began to attract migrants to the new factories, and rural-to-urban migration intensified. This process has been particularly strong in newly industrializing countries like China, Thailand, Malaysia, the Philippines, Indonesia, and Vietnam, but it is common in other places as well. Often this urbanization develops fitfully, as firms like Nike contract to make products in a certain place for a time, but then move their operations elsewhere in search of cheaper labor. Thus, urbanization as a result of industrialization in the South has been very uneven, and it is often characterized by rapid boom-and-bust cycles.

But industrialization and pull factors are not the only, or even primary, force driving Southern urbanization. Also key have been push factors in the countryside. As the capitalist market has increasingly penetrated all parts of the globe, large sections of the rural areas of the South have been industrialized, and production has shifted from food for local consumption to cash crops for global markets. This shift has been accompanied by changes in land tenure, as small holdings have been consolidated into large ones that are more able to carry out the mass production of cash crops necessary to compete in the global market. While this process of rural land consolidation and market integration is not new, having begun in most places during the colonial era, it has intensified in recent decades, especially in Africa and Asia, as the global market has become increasingly integrated.[11] As we saw, structural adjustment policies actively encouraged countries to integrate themselves into the global market and to encourage Foreign Direct Investment, and so those policies made rural restructuring even more acute. As a result, an increasing number of peasants and small holders have been displaced from their land. While not all have immediately migrated to cities, that has been the most common outcome. In countries with primate cities, like Nigeria, Thailand, or the Philippines, these migrants overwhelmingly flock to just one city, causing astronomical growth. Thus, places like Lagos, Nigeria, and Dhaka, Bangladesh, have taken over the mantle of "shock city" from Manchester and Chicago, whose rapid urbanization in the nineteenth century now seems stately by comparison.

In addition to industrialization, new international free trade agreements have also promoted the consolidation of rural land holdings. Free-trade agreements like NAFTA and ASEAN prohibit national governments from engaging in protectionism for their own agricultural products. As a result, in many places, local markets for agricultural products have been flooded with cheaper replacements from abroad, driving down prices and making it difficult for local small-holder growers to compete. When they are unable to sell their crops, they can go into debt and eventually lose their land. Periodic drought and infestation can of course make this situation worse. Again, the result is the creation of new migrants, many of whom float into cities.

Still another factor causing migration out of rural areas is conflict and civil war that creates large numbers of refugees in places like Sudan, Somalia, Congo, Sri Lanka, Palestine, and Lebanon. Some are resettled in camps, but many end up in cities like Khartoum, Mogadishu, and Kinshasa.

And so many, and sometimes the majority, of rural-to-urban migrants are not being drawn to cities so much by the economic opportunities they offer, but rather because diverse push factors mean they can no

---

[11] As always, such a general account hides much variation. Places with a history of growing cash crops, such as Ghana with cocoa, and places with valuable natural resources, like Nigeria, will be subjected much more intensely to this process.

longer make a living or live securely in the countryside. Thus, frequently there are more migrants to cities than the urban economy can employ. Moreover, because the process is usually so rapid, cities often cannot provide adequate housing, services, or infrastructure for the new migrants either. Thus, we see the well-known phenomenon of informal settlements or "slums" that characterize almost all rapidly growing cities in the global South. Though exact figures are difficult to know reliably, a majority of urban dwellers in the South will soon be slum dwellers, if that is not already the case (Davis, 2006). Informal settlements are of course places of great hardship, poverty, disease, crime, and unemployment, but they are also, in a way, places off the grid, places where people are able to experiment with possible alternatives. They are huge concentrations of people that in large part operate beyond the formal institutions of capital and the state. Houses are often built by people themselves rather than the building industry; services are provided by local arrangements rather than municipal authorities; goods are exchanged in markets not legally sanctioned by the state; public order is sometimes secured by local gangs rather than by the police. By no means should we think of informal settlements as models for future cities and societies. But if democracy means that people manage their affairs for themselves, and informal settlements are the places where people are increasingly living out their daily lives, then we must be keenly aware of efforts in these places to create something different, something other than Fukuyama's end of history.

Shifting geopolitics

In addition to the broad political-economic trends discussed in the previous sections, the current context has also seen significant geopolitical shifts. Much of this history is well known. The period from World War II to the fall of the Berlin Wall was dominated by the Cold War, a conflict between state socialism and liberal-democratic capitalism (in both its welfare-state and neoliberal forms). The "New World Order" ushered in by George H.W. Bush, in which the United States aspired to play the role of global hegemon in a shifting strategic alliance among powerful countries, lasted only about ten years. The attacks of September 11, 2001 began a new era in which the United States prosecuted a "war on terror," which was in fact a guerrilla war against Islamic radicalism, waged in various places around the globe. Gone were the diplomacy and multilateralism of the New World Order, replaced by the US government's willingness to act unilaterally in pursuit of its security interests as it understood them.

Two recent events promise to bring great changes to existing arrangements associated with the "war on terror." The killing of Osama bin Laden and several of his aides by US Special Forces seemed to punctuate the declining geopolitical relevance of *al-Qa'ida*. It was an important symbolic event, in the sense that part of bin Laden's mystique had always been that the United States couldn't seem to capture him and bring him to justice. He seemed to have carried off the September 11 attacks with impunity. However, the strategic importance of the killing is less clear. *Al-Qa'ida* is a global and relatively decentered network, and so the operational importance of one leader, even the most important one, is relatively small. There are cells in many different places, such as *al-Qa'ida* in the Arabian Peninsula, and most think these cells operate relatively autonomously. Still another reason is that *al-Qa'ida* is by no means the only radical Islamist organization in the world, and those other organizations figure to operate very much as before.

I think it is important not to dwell on the killing of bin Laden. In fact, I think we should understand the Arab Uprising to have killed bin Laden long before the United States did. That is because a central tenet of bin Laden's opposition to the United States was always its support for secular dictators in the Islamic world, such as Hosni Mubarak, King Saud, or Bashar al-Assad, who intimidated and humiliated their people. One of *al-Qa'ida's* primary political goals was to depose those US-backed dictators and replace them with governments based on Islamic law. The Arab Uprising showed that, at least in Tunisia and Egypt, Muslims don't need *al-Qa'ida* and bin Laden to liberate them from their dictators. They showed the world, and themselves, that they can do it on their own. Moreover, it was all too clear during the uprisings that the United States was in no rush to side with the people in the streets of Tunis and Cairo. It was even less willing to support those in Bahrain, where the Saudis hold greater sway and the uprising was quashed with their assistance. And the US response to the Syrian government shooting its own unarmed people has been inert. As a result, not only did the uprisings teach Arabs that they can depose their own dictators, but that they can do it without any kind of positive support from the United States and other Western governments. What need then for *al-Qa'ida*, which has spent ten years engaging in horrific acts that have done very little to change the everyday political and economic fortunes of people in the Arab and Muslim world? And *al-Qa'ida* looks especially impotent and cruel when compared to the peaceful, joyful, and entirely revolutionary achievements of people in Egypt and Tunisia, or to the great bravery of people in Syria, Bahrain, and Libya in opposing their murderous governments.

It is of course too soon to know precisely what kind of new geopolitical order will emerge from these events. Obviously, radical Islam will continue to exist, and it will still play an important role in the politics of the region. For example, there is no doubt the Muslim Brotherhood will continue to be an important factor in Egypt. But it seems safe to predict that most people in the region will judge al-Qa'ida's violent attacks against civilians to be a means of struggle that is largely exhausted. A whole new option has been opened up: it is now perfectly reasonable for people to believe that they can achieve their political goals themselves. And this belief has spread so quickly through the Arab world, and then through Europe and on to North America as well, that there is no reason to believe it won't continue its momentum. The "war on terror" is waning, and it may well be giving way to a new geopolitical zeitgeist of continual democratic awakening.

Ecological collapse and environmental disasters

In addition to these political-economic and geopolitical factors, the question of the non-human world and our relation to it has become increasingly urgent in recent years. It has become clear that anthropogenic changes to the global climate are real, and they will significantly alter weather systems and climate zones, which will, at the least, require whole societies to undertake an extensive process of "adaptation." These changes also introduce the possibility of global environmental collapse if strong enough positive feedback processes (through which warming causes more warming) bring us to a point of no return (Kolbert, 2006; Foster, Clark and York, 2010; see also Urry, 2011). Climate change is a global process that necessitates global policy solutions, which require the formation of a global political community to discuss and develop those solutions. So far, only an international community exists, made up of nation-states concerned with their local—not global—interests, and that has been one factor preventing the creation of adequate responses to the problem. Also central of course has been the desire for continued economic growth, and this has highlighted the contradiction between the needs of capitalism and the ecological well-being of the planet. While these contradictions have long existed, the emergence of the specter of global ecological collapse has introduced a new urgency to the need to form a functional global community that can invent and implement a sustainable way of life for the entire human population.

In addition to this global problem, the current context has also witnessed what appear to be increasingly frequent and intense instances of more local environmental disasters. The two most recent large events were the near-total devastation of New Orleans in 2005 by hurricane and flood and the ravaging of parts of Japan in 2011 by earthquake, tsunami, and radiation leaks. As with climate change, such disasters are at least as much a political and social event as they are natural. In New Orleans, the existence and path of Hurricane Katrina was determined by non-human forces (although most now think the number and intensity of hurricanes will be increased by global warming), but the social, ecological, and engineering systems it fell upon were largely anthropogenic. The erosion of the coastal wetlands buffer, the engineering and economics of levee construction, the ongoing sinking of the city due to the river's channelization, the uneven and inadequate response of government emergency management agencies, and an urban geography of poverty and racial segregation were all crucial to producing the disaster. The hurricane on its own would have done relatively little damage. The same kind of analysis can be made in the Japanese case.

Of course, the United States and Japan are two of the world's wealthier countries, and they are relatively well equipped to prepare for and respond to such events. Similar events in less wealthy places—such as Haiti in 2010—produce far more suffering. The stakes are incredibly high. Therefore, even though this book does not focus its attention on issues of environment and ecology, I want to acknowledge that they are an absolutely central feature of the contemporary context. Moreover, I think such issues are no less a question of politics than are more conventionally political-economic or geopolitical issues. As a result, the question of "What is to be done" applies just as much to global warming and Hurricane Katrina as it does to neoliberalism and the "war on terror." For all these questions, I argue, democracy should figure prominently in any answer.

A Methodology of Thought and Practice: Transduction

Of course, saying democracy is the answer to the question raises some questions of its own. An obvious one is, "What is democracy?" I have already intimated that I understand democracy quite radically, as a way of living together in which people rule themselves. I will develop this radical understanding further in the chapters that follow. Another question, given that radical understanding of democracy, is "How can we achieve it?" This question is less troubling for a liberal democrat, since there are many examples of actually existing liberal democracies to point to. But radical democracy is rarer. Some would even say it is a utopian fantasy, a nice thought but impossible to achieve. And so I think some explanation is in order as to the particular political method by which we might defend democracy as an answer.

Drawing from the work of Henri Lefebvre (1996; 2003b), I want to proceed by a method he called transduction, by which he means a way to cut a path that leads beyond the actual world already realized and toward a possible world yet to come. Perhaps the best way to explain what that involves is to start with Italo Calvino and his novel, *Invisible Cities*. In the book, Kublai Khan sends Marco Polo on numerous expeditions to cities around the world. The book is taken up primarily with Marco's descriptions of those cities. At the end of the book, having listened to all of Marco's descriptions, Kublai Khan realizes that each city is marked by a serious flaw. He despairs of ever finding the perfect city, or even a good one. "It is all useless," he says, "if the last landing place can only be the infernal city, and it is there that, in ever-narrowing circles, the current is drawing us." But in his response, in the words that close the book, Marco offers us both hope and a specific way to approach change in the world. "The inferno of the living," he tells Kublai Khan,

> is not something that will be. If there is one, it is that which is already here, the inferno that we inhabit every day, that we create by being together. There are two ways to escape suffering it. The first is easy for most: accept the inferno and become such a complete part of it that you no longer know it is there. The second is risky and requires vigilance and continuous attention: seek and learn to recognize who and what, in the midst of inferno, are not inferno, and help them endure, give them space (1993, my translation).

Another author, David Foster Wallace, in articulating his own project as a writer, lays out something very similar to Marco. He says

> Look man, we'd probably most of us agree that these are dark times, and stupid ones, but do we need fiction that does nothing but dramatize how dark and stupid everything is?[12] In dark times, the definition of good art would seem to be art that locates and applies CPR to those elements of what's human and magical that still live and glow despite the times' darkness. Really good fiction could have as dark a worldview as it wished, but it'd find a way both to depict this world and to illuminate the possibilities for being alive and human in it (McCaffrey, 2012, p. 26).

Both Marco and Wallace are saying that there is something already here, something good, breathing in the midst of human society. This good is

---

[12] Lewis Hyde makes a similar point about poetry and prose. The critical detachment of irony, he says, "has only emergency use. Carried over time, it is the voice of the trapped who have come to enjoy their cage" (quoted in Wallace, 1997, p. 67).

not transcendent, or an ideal to come. It is immanent, incipient, coming. Marco Polo calls it that which is "not inferno." For Wallace, it is those elements of "what's human and magical" in the world, elements that illuminate the "possibilities for being alive." Even though we are surrounded by the actual world of the inferno, we can seek out the not-inferno and help it to grow. In a similar way, Lefebvre's transduction argues that this possible world is not "out there," beyond our current situation, but rather it is already here, even if it remains inchoate.[13] Our task as political thinkers and actors, Lefebvre argues, is to discover this good, this other world, to remove the barriers that prevent its growth, and to nurture it as best we can.

Lefebvre works out the concept of transduction most fully in *The Urban Revolution* (1970; 2003b), where he says it is a methodology for "research involving a virtual object, which attempts to define and realize that object as part of an ongoing project...[it] reflects an intellectual approach toward a possible object" (2003b, p. 5). To understand what he means by a "virtual object," we have to begin by understanding his concepts of "the industrial city" and "urban society." The industrial city for Lefebvre is not the historical industrial city of Fordist factory production. Rather, it is the many manifestations of the capitalist city in the industrial era. It is the Paris he inhabited in 1970, or the Seattle I inhabit today: a city in which private property and exchange value are the dominant ways to organize urban space. It is a city in which the dominant socio-spatial processes separate and segregate people from one another, and those separated parts are homogenized and made equivalent so they can be exchanged on the market (1991, p. 9; 2003b, p. 176). In the industrial city, urban inhabitants are rendered politically passive, and they function primarily as consumers rather than citizens. These inactive inhabitants are warehoused in sterilized urban spaces he calls "habitat." The industrial city is a city reduced to the narrow function of ensuring economic growth through the production of standardized commodities. It is, in short, an oligarchy, a city managed by an elite few state and corporate administrators. Today we would call this the neoliberal city. Lefebvre's contemporary, Guy Debord (1983), called it "the society of the spectacle."

Lefebvre contrasts the industrial city to "urban society." In urban society, urban space is not controlled by property rights and exchange value but by inhabitants who appropriate space, make it their own, and

---

[13] It is worth mentioning that Calvino's *Invisible Cities* was originally published in 1972, two years after Lefebvre published *The Urban Revolution*. I have not yet found hard evidence that Calvino was specifically influenced by Lefebvre, but it seems very likely.

use it to meet their needs. Urban society draws inhabitants into the center, into vital urban spaces where they encounter each other and engage in collective and meaningful negotiations about what kind of city they desire (1991, p. 149; 2003b, pp. 117–118). These encounters build a shared sense of common purpose and solidarity among inhabitants, but they also cause inhabitants to become aware of the substantive differences among them, and they are forced to confront and manage these differences together (2003b, p. 96). This effective engagement with one's fellows is what Lefebvre calls *l'inhabiter*,[14] an active and fecund life-in-space he contrasts with the sterile space of habitat. The connections inhabitants make with each other nourish their creative potential and encourage them to create *œuvres*, which for Lefebvre are unique works owned by the producer rather than standardized commodities for sale on a market. In urban society, the purpose of the city is the development of human potential[15] rather than capitalist accumulation. Urban society is, in short, a city in which urban inhabitants manage the space of the city for themselves.

It is important to understand that for Lefebvre these two concepts are of different kinds. The industrial city is what he calls "actual": it is "a clearly defined, definitive object" that has in fact been realized. It is realized both as a concrete, built form and as a set of normalized social relations, habits of action, thought, and common sense. Urban society, on the other hand, has mostly not been realized. It is what he calls a "virtual or possible object" (2003b, p. 16). It is a horizon toward which we can move. It is a possible way of living together. For Lefebvre, a virtual object is *not* a utopia, a no-place, an ideal imagined out of the ether that can never exist. It is rather an extrapolation or amplification in thought of practices and ideas that are *already taking place* in the city, practices and ideas that are inchoate, that have not yet come to full maturity, but are nevertheless being expressed, if only hesitantly, fleetingly, or inarticulately (2003b, p. 17). This act of thought imagines these inchoate practices in their fully realized form, as a whole urban world beyond the industrial city (1996, p. 103). So, the virtual object is in no sense idle daydreaming that ignores the reality on the ground, but

---

[14] The French literally means "the to inhabit." The strange noun-infinitive construction is derived from Heidegger's concept of dwelling (*das Wohnen*) (Lefebvre, 2003b, see translator's note 2, p. 189). There is also quite a lot of resonance here with Lewis Mumford's (1937) idea of "effective social intercourse."

[15] This concept of development is not precisely defined in the book. It can be read as the Aristotelian idea of the full development of each inhabitant's natural human potential, or it can be read as a Marxist idea of humans flourishing in an association in which the free development of each is the condition for the free development of all. I think the two interpretations have much more in common than we tend to think (see also Lefebvre, 1991, pp. 137–138).

rather it pays very close attention to that reality and tries to extend existing practices of urban society, to project them out into the future. Urban society as a virtual object therefore always has a direction; it always moves toward a horizon. But a horizon is never an endpoint, never a destination we can arrive at. Though we set out down a path toward a virtual object, it will always recede into the distance as we come near to it.[16]

For Lefebvre, virtual objects are not merely philosophical exercises. They are intended to be practical tools for political action. Once a virtual object has been extrapolated from actual practices, it becomes a powerful lens through which we can view the world. This lens helps us better perceive the elements of the virtual object that already exist (2003b, p. 23). In Lefebvre's terms, when we extrapolate urban society as a virtual object, it can help us see incipient elements of urban society that already exist in the body of the industrial city.[17] These elements of urban society are difficult to see because they are emergent and ephemeral; they exist amid the overwhelming light and noise of the industrial city. We can be looking right at urban society,

> but we see it with eyes, with concepts, that were shaped by the practices and theories of industrialization, with a fragmentary analytic tool that was designed during the industrial period and is therefore reductive of the emerging reality....It [is] simply that our eye has been shaped (misshaped) by the earlier landscape...(2003b, p. 29).

Urban society thus remains a "kernel and virtuality. What the eyes and analysis perceive on the ground can at best pass for the shadow of a future object in the light of the rising sun" (1996, p. 148).[18] So, a virtual object is a kind of corrective lens for eyes misshapen by life in the industrial city. The industrial city teaches us to see urban space as property, inhabitants as consumers, and the city as a capitalist economic engine (2003b, p. 29). Constructing urban society as a virtual object is a way of retraining ourselves to see urban society. Lefebvre thus sees a

---

[16] It is important to be clear that a horizon is not a limit. A limit is a fixed edge that we approach asymptotically, such that our movement toward it decreases as we get closer. A horizon always moves away from us as we move toward it, and so while it suggests a direction it does not ever restrict our movement toward it. My thanks to Susmita Rishi and James Thompson for helping me think this difference through.

[17] In *The Production of Space* (1991, p. 52), he articulates this relationship more generally: "differential space" waits, inchoate, to emerge from the dominant "abstract space."

[18] Iranians have an expression that captures a similar idea. In the context of a polity in which periodic uprisings punctuate a regime of broad repression, they talk of the desire for democracy as an ember that continues to glow underneath the ashes of a fire that seems extinguished (Astor, 2011).

virtual object as a "conceptual instrument" that helps us seek and learn to recognize, in the midst of inferno, that which is not inferno (2003b, p. 68).

Of course, as we get better at seeing the incipient virtual in the midst of the actual, we begin to see it everywhere. The more we see it, the more experience we gain with it, the more material we have to extrapolate from, to build an even more robust virtual object in thought. Thus, a system of positive feedback can develop, a process of continual mutual strengthening between virtual urban society and its emerging manifestations in the industrial city. Lefebvre insists on the importance of such "incessant feedback" between the virtual object and actual practice (1996, p. 151). His goal is to construct a powerful enough tool with which we chart a course out of the present condition, through the myriad obstacles that the industrial city throws up, and move toward the horizon of urban society. He wants "to open a path to the possible, to explore and delineate a landscape that is not merely part of the 'real,' the accomplished, occupied by existing social, political, and economic forces" (2003b, p. 7).[19] He sees this approach as an alternative to both abstract, impractical utopianism, on the one hand, and short-term, visionless pragmatism, on the other (2003b, p. 75). He wants to avoid what Laclau and Mouffe (1985, p. 190) call "the two extremes represented by the totalitarian myth of the Ideal City, and the positivist pragmatism of reformists without a project." Lefebvre says that exploring virtual objects through transduction is a way to "step back from the real," to refuse to accept what already is, but also to never lose sight of that real, to always begin from the activity people are already engaging in.

Transduction therefore offers a practicable approach to political action, a concrete plan for moving forward, even though it also demands significant and rigorous philosophical reflection.[20] Lefebvre intends for transduction to cut a path out of the industrial city and toward the virtual object of urban society (2003b, p. 76). As I pursue it, transduction is an attempt to cut a path out of oligarchy and toward the virtual object of democracy. As the following chapters will make clear, our society is dominated by a condition of *passive heteronomous oligarchy*, and the virtual object I develop is something we might call *active democratic autonomy*. My project parallels Lefebvre's closely; for him,

---

[19] Murray Bookchin (2002) articulates a similar idea when he argues that a demand that appears reformist, e.g. for public rather than private ownership of railroads, can open "*pathways*, politically, to revolutionary forms of ownership and operation."

[20] For a similar approach to political praxis, inspired instead by the work of Jean-Paul Sartre, see Merrifield (2011, pp. 139–144).

urban society is characterized by active citizens who commit to managing themselves and their space autonomously, which is quite similar to democracy as I understand it.

And so the larger theoretical and practical project that the book proposes is to extrapolate, extend, cultivate, and nourish the democracy that currently exists in the midst of our oligarchic society. This democracy exists in both thought and action, and there is a rich tradition in both. My focus will be mostly on the former, on the intellectual tradition of democracy, rather than on concrete practices for democracy. I don't think this distinction should concern us overly. The theoretical texts that I focus on are themselves deeply shaped by political action and are in constant conversation with it. Gramsci's thought grew out of a life of communist activism in Italy after World War I. Rancière's work tries to make sense of politics in the wake of the promise and failures of the 1968 uprising. Such theoretical writing is always deeply bound up with action. Moreover, action is always inspired and informed by theory. So while this book extrapolates democracy from theoretical texts, matters of everyday life and concrete political struggle are not at all absent from the discussion. They are always present in the body of such theory, even as the theory is always present in the body of action. Moreover, everyday practices and political action will very much play a role in my analysis, especially the democratic uprisings that swept across the Middle East, Europe, and North America in 2011.

Extrapolating democracy as a virtual object requires much effort because we live in a world that equates democracy with a liberal-democratic state, which is a form of oligarchy that sets severe limits on democracy and insists that anything beyond those limits is impossible.[21] We need to become better at seeing democracy through the haze, to develop the tools to cut a path beyond the present oligarchy and toward the horizon of a possible democracy. My focus in the book will be mostly on this task of extrapolating democracy as a virtual object, on building a new lens. But I will also indicate some ways we might *use* that lens to seek and recognize democracy as it exists, and to help it flourish.

Let me end this section with one last quality of transduction. In the long quotes at the beginning of this section, both Calvino and Wallace imply a very particular way to see political practice, one that I think transduction shares. Calvino enjoins us, once we have found those that

---

[21] Consider, for example, the multiple commentators, including Barack Obama and Hillary Clinton, who talked about "a transition to democracy" as the next step to be taken after the Arab Uprising, equating democracy with a stable liberal-democratic state and devaluing the uprising as something that is not-yet democracy (see also, e.g. Stepan, 2011).

are not inferno, to "help them endure, give them space."[22] The not-inferno already exists; we need only allow it to flourish. Wallace casts the artist as an emergency medical technician, as one who applies CPR to an injured, but nevertheless alive, human potential. For Wallace, the artist does not *create* life; he only discovers it and helps it survive. Similarly, transduction cannot cause democracy to come into existence. Democracy already lives in the body of our current society. It produces itself. It possesses what Spinoza (1996) calls a *conatus*, the drive to continue living, to grow, to flourish. The project of transduction is merely to give democracy space, to shelter it from threat, to provide it with the nourishment it needs to flourish. There are of course very important implications to this approach to politics. Vanguards, leaderships, parties, organizers, activists, planners, experts: none of these are the agents of politics. None of these make democracy happen. Instead, the agents of democracy are everyone and anyone at all. Anyone at all can choose, is already choosing, to take up the project of governing him- or herself. Anyone at all is qualified to rule (a particular emphasis of Rancière, e.g. 2001). Calvino, Wallace, and Lefebvre are not talking to activists or organizers or party leaders or any subset of the population. They are talking to everyone. Transduction is a project that we all take up together.

Plan of the Book

Given that methodological agenda, the rest of the book proceeds as follows. Chapter 2 examines the work of several radical political theorists. They are from different places and different generations and shaped by different political experiences, but I argue that we can understand them all to be aiming at a project of democracy. Moreover, their ideas about what democracy is are far more similar than they are different. Chapter 3 then addresses the question of the end of politics. It is tempting to see democracy as an end point beyond politics, in which people govern themselves in harmony. Instead, the chapter argues for a democracy that is thoroughly political, democracy as a perpetual movement

---

[22] I should note here that I have translated Calvino differently than does William Weaver in the standard edition of the book (Calvino, 1974, p. 209). The Italian is *"farlo durare, e dargli spazio."* Weaver renders this as *"make* them endure, give them space." The verb *fare* in Italian, like *faire* in French, has a wide range of meanings. It certainly could mean "make" as Weaver has it. I have rendered it as "help," which is taking a bit of liberty with the Italian, since "help" is not a standard translation for *fare*. But what I'm trying to capture here is closer to *"make it so that they can* endure," which is more elegantly phrased as *"help them* endure." I am trying to get as close as possible in English to the meaning most consistent with what I think Marco is trying to say. I hope that I have not done too much disservice to either language, or to Calvino.

toward the horizon of democracy, as a perpetual struggle by people and communities to become autonomous, active, and democratic. Chapter 4 confronts perhaps the most pressing political question associated with this view of democracy: How can people become active, aware, awake, alive, and how can they take control again of the conditions of their own existence? It is a Herculean task, but it is one everyone can achieve. Chapter 5 then takes up another critical problem: not only must each person become active, but they must do so together with others. The chapter explores the nature of the *connections* among people who have taken up the democratic project of ruling themselves. It also considers how those connections might proliferate to the point where they can create a tipping point, a flood, a generalized explosion of autonomous and democratic practices. This tipping point, this "breakthrough" as Deleuze and Guattari call it, would cast us into a world where democracy pervades the social field, even if it never becomes total. In the conclusion, Chapter 6, I consider some implications for political practice that this understanding of democracy has in the contemporary context. The chapter indicates some ways democracy as a virtual object can serve as a powerful practical tool that helps us seek and learn to recognize democracy, to help it endure, and to give it space.

2

What Democracy Means

In 2010, a virtual who's who of left intellectuals (Agamben, Badiou, Rancière, Nancy, Brown, Zizek, etc.) came together in a collection of essays called *Democracy in What State?* to answer the question of whether democracy is still a viable way to think about politics in the contemporary era (Agamben, 2011). Most agreed that there was still something to save in the term, but also that we have a very long way to go because democracy has been almost entirely swallowed by the liberal-democratic state in alliance with neoliberal capital. The prevailing mood of all the authors is one of great pessimism about democracy. In *Recapturing Democracy* (2008), I made a very similar argument: that we can recapture democracy from the powers that be but that it will be a difficult struggle—not only because neoliberals have co-opted it, but also because neoconservatives (Bush, Wolfowitz, Cheney, Pearle, etc.) are waving the banner as they pursue a new kind of American empire around the world.

At the end of 2011, both books seemed badly out of date. The messianic crusade of the neoconservatives has been left by the wayside, the neoliberal consensus has been greatly unsettled, and a chain reaction of democratic popular movements has swept across the world. It is almost embarrassing, knowing what we know now, how unseeing the great thinkers in the Agamben collection are in their pessimism. Of course, it is not a reflection on them really: almost no one saw this coming. But it came anyway. What in 2010 seemed a dying flame being faithfully tended by a clutch of celebrated intellectuals became a crackling fire near the end of 2011. Democracy, the democracy in which people struggle together to take control again over their own lives, is back on the agenda.

The Down-Deep Delight of Democracy, First Edition. Mark Purcell.
© 2013 John Wiley & Sons, Ltd. Published 2013 by John Wiley & Sons, Ltd.

A Social Order of Many Souls

As we try to make sense of 2011, to understand just what sort of democracy is emerging here, I think it is extremely valuable to ask just what democracy means. There are countless ways to approach that question. My method in this chapter is to weave together an account of democracy from strands taken from a range of different political thinkers: Gramsci, Lefebvre, Deleuze and Guattari, Hardt and Negri, Laclau and Mouffe, and Rancière. I argue that it is possible to discover in their work a shared and deep desire for democracy.

Before I make that argument, it is important to say a word about how I conceive of an exercise like this, a close reading and analysis of a set of works of political theory. I approach it from a very particular assumption: each theorist is multiple. This is how Deleuze and Guattari think of it too. They open *A Thousand Plateaus* with the line, "The two of us wrote *Anti-Oedipus* [their first book] together. Since each of us was several, there was already quite a crowd" (1987, p. 3). This perhaps appears to be grandstanding, but it turns out to be an important core of their thought, that those entities we think of as singular, like individuals, are in fact multiple. They are not self-contained monads. They are better conceived of as assemblages that open out into the world. They are something more akin to a particularly concentrated knot of connections in a vast network of social relations. By this thinking, each seeming individual is in fact made up of a multitude of people, events, ideas, relations, places, and experiences, each of which is connected to multiple other such people, events, and so on. The primary source of Deleuze and Guattari's thinking here is Nietzsche, who offers a compelling argument on the matter. In *Beyond Good and Evil*, he insists that we must

> give the finishing stroke to that...calamitous atomism which Christianity has taught best and longest, the *soul* atomism...the belief which regards the soul as something indestructible, eternal, indivisible, as a monad, as an *atomon*: this belief ought to be expelled from science!...The way is open for new versions and refinements of the soul-hypothesis; and such conceptions as "mortal soul," and "soul as subjective multiplicity," and "soul as social structure of the drives and affects," want henceforth to have citizens' rights in science (1989a, p. 20).

A bit later he argues that "our body is but a social structure composed of many souls" (Nietzsche, 1989a, p. 26). Deleuze and Guattari's claim—"each of us was several"—is a direct heir to Nietzsche's idea of the soul as social structure. Nietzsche is railing here against the Christian conception of the monadic soul, one he thinks has been the default conception for as long as anyone can remember. But the idea of a multiple soul actually has quite a tradition. It goes back all the way to Plato, who is, it is fair to say, obsessed by the problem. In *The Republic*, he argues that the soul is tripartite, made up of reason, spirit, and desire. A central argument of the book is that in a good soul, reason must rule over spirit and desire. He returns to this question continually, articulating it in many different forms, perhaps the most evocative of which is when he represents reason as a human, spirit as a lion, and desire as a many-headed beast (Plato, 2008, p. 588c).[1] It is a matter of vital importance for Plato that reason is able to impose order on this soul composed of many souls. For his part, Aristotle accepted this multiple soul also, as well as the idea that reason should rule, although in the *Ethics* and *Politics* he usually presents the soul as having two parts rather than three (e.g. 1998a, pp. 1102a–1103a). While we should reject, with Nietzsche, the hierarchy of the soul that places reason at the top,[2] nevertheless Plato and Aristotle demonstrate that the idea of soul as a multiplicity turns out to be quite an old idea that was very much assumed as a starting point by the seminal political theorists.

Thinking about individuals this way allows us to see each theorist as multiple. Doing so leads us to also think of each piece of a theorist's *work* as multiple as well. Each essay or book is driven by many desires, drives, and wills, some of which contradict others. And of course each thinker's whole body of work isn't a coherent *body* at all, but many different discrete pieces of work, written over decades. And yet—and perhaps this now seems strange—we tend to think of each essay or book and each theorist's body of work as a coherent and internally consistent mass.[3] Or at least we seem to want each theorist's work to have that kind of coherence. We argue over the underlying and most-important theoretical or political desire, the single soul of the work. This tendency leads us to ask unproductive questions like, "was Lefebvre a Marxist?" or "are Laclau and Mouffe post-Marxists?" If we follow Nietzsche and give the finishing stroke to the soul atomism, if we think of each theorist and their work not as integral monads but as teeming multitudes, then such attempts to attach a singular label become pointless. Lefebvre was very much a Marxist. He was also very much an anarchist. But he was not only one or the other, and the terms are not at all mutually exclusive.

---

[1] Nietzsche of course picks up the image of the lion, which Plato uses often, and runs with it. It becomes his "blonde beast" (1989b, First Essay, Section 11, see also Nietzsche, 2005) and serves as the standard for his mission to rediscover and champion, almost verbatim, the argument of the sophist Callicles in Gorgias (Plato, 1998).

[2] For more on which see the section on Deleuze and Guattari in this chapter.

[3] The case of Marx, in which there is extensive scholarly debate about the possibility that there are different Marxes, is perhaps an exception.

Figure 2.1 Jackson Pollock, *Summertime: Number 9A*, 1948, Tate Modern, London. Credit: © 2012 The Pollock-Krasner Foundation/Artists Rights Society (ARS), New York.

Figure 2.2 Photo credit: European People's Party.

There is a powerful strain of explicit Marxism in much of Lefebvre's work; there is also a strong element of what looks quite a lot more like Bakunin than Marx.

What I am doing here, following Deleuze and Guattari (esp. 1987, Chapters 6, 7, and 10), is taking my own default conception of each thinker as a coherent body and trying to pull it apart, to prise open the seeming unity of its structure, and think of each more as a loose cluster of multiple wills, each of which is in motion and continually connecting with other wills in other agglomerations. I am trying, in short, to imagine each theorist as a figure in the Jackson Pollack painting *Summertime Number 9A*, as a wild tangle of many wills, always moving, almost dancing, always sending out connecting tendrils into other tangles (see Figure 2.1). I am imagining the Pollack figures rather than the figures in the photograph in Figure 2.2, each of whom appears to be a discrete body.

But notice that the Pollack painting is not one of his abstracts. It is not a seemingly random tangle that extends fairly uniformly across the canvas (e.g. *One: Number 31*). Rather, in this Pollack there are brush or knife strokes and blocks of paint that indicate discernible figures amid the wild tangles. These figures may be faint, you may have to squint a bit to see them, but they are there. We could walk up to the painting and point this one out, or that one, and our companion would likely agree with our assessment. But at the same time, each figure is not *clearly* distinguishable; there could be some debate over which is a figure and which is not, or where one figure ends and another begins. Along these lines, I am not saying that each thinker I examine is entirely formless, utterly random, or a collection of every human thought or impulse in history. Even if the work of each is not a perfectly coherent body, even if it is stuffed with contradictory desires, nevertheless each thinker does have some sort of consistency, each is a particular cluster of wills or qualities that distinguishes him or her from other thinkers. And each also has boundaries to their thought, even if those are often fuzzy. Lefebvre was an anarchist, a Marxist, and probably a libertarian, but he wasn't really a Maoist, and he definitely was not a liberal or (even less) a Stalinist. Even if each author is a teeming multitude, that multitude is not infinite, and it does take on a perceptible form, a discernible consistency, that gives his or her thought a character we can identify and communicate to others.

So if we imagine each thinker as a figure in *Summertime Number 9A*, as a discernible cluster of wills linked in complex ways to a multitude of others, it becomes possible for us to makes choices, to engage with some wills and not with others. We can latch on to some of a thinker's wills and desires, we can worry them out of the tangle of other wills and desires, and we can connect them up with other wills and desires from other authors, other strands from other traditions. And as we do so, we should not imagine each will as a fixed point that we connect to other fixed points in a static net or mesh. Rather, each will is like one of the wild loops in the painting: a moving vector, an energy following a line. We should think of each will as a flow that we can stream together with other flows, increasing their overall speed, stoking their revolutionary force. In this approach, we seek out desires and wills in an author's work that resonate with our own, wills we think can augment the flow of our own ongoing project to the point where we have enough energy and speed to achieve a breakthrough.

So that is my project here, to draw out strands from various theorists of whom I have made a close study, to stream together the desire for democracy in each. My aim is to produce a strong flow, an overstuffed concept of democracy that can serve as a virtual object with which we can cut a path out of the present context and toward the possible. I will not claim that democracy is the predominant or defining desire in any one of these theorists, that they are not *really* Marxists or anarchists or liberals but rather democrats. I will only insist that the work of each exhibits a strong will to democracy, and it is that will I try to draw out. My approach here accords with Deleuze and Guattari, who argue that

> reading the text is never a scholarly exercise in search of what is signified, still less a highly textual exercise in search of the signifier. Rather it is a productive use of the literary machine, a montage of desiring machines, the schizoid exercise that extracts from the text its revolutionary force (1977, p. 106).

Of course, I take seriously the responsibility of developing a rigorous understanding of each text, but my analysis of each text is not intended to be a thorough exposition of the true meaning of the work-as-a-whole. Rather, it is intended as an act of extrapolation, of exegesis that can draw force from the text, force I can stream into my concept of democracy.

Let me offer just one last word about my selection process. At various points throughout the book, I examine the work of Lefebvre, Laclau and Mouffe, Rancière, Gramsci, Foucault, Deleuze and Guattari, Hardt and Negri, Nietzsche, Hobbes, Aristotle, Plato, Italo Calvino, and David Foster Wallace (I know, that last one pops out—see Chapter 4). That is already quite an extensive list, perhaps overly so. Nevertheless, each reader no doubt will have in mind one or more theorists that I leave out but who are nevertheless critical to the argument. Those readers will very likely be right. People like Marcuse, Habermas, Benjamin, Arendt, Jameson, Butler, Badiou, Nancy, Derrida, Lefort, Tronti, Agamben, Debord, Vaneigem, Virilio, Castoriadis, Fraser, Wolin, and Young receive only passing mention or do not appear at all. I could certainly have drawn on their work to augment the force of my conception of democracy. I do not exclude these thinkers because I think they are less relevant, or of lesser quality. Rather it is because a serious study of work like this requires considerable time and effort, and I have not yet spent sufficient time with these thinkers to properly mine their work in the depth it deserves.

Democratic Desires

The rest of the chapter draws out the will to democracy present in several different thinkers: Lefebvre, Deleuze and Guattari, Hardt and Negri, Laclau and Mouffe, and Rancière. They are certainly important political and generational differences among these theorists, but they do all share some contextual characteristics. First, and perhaps most importantly, they are all writing in the wake of the disaster of state socialism. They are searching for a way to reinvigorate the project of developing critical alternatives to capitalism, even as they categorically reject the state-socialist alternative, particularly its Stalinist variant. Second, they all share an experience with the uprisings in 1968, especially those in Paris, and see them as a pivotal moment, not least because they established clearly that (1) the state is primarily an agent of repression rather than liberation and (2) class is only one of many axes around which people can mobilize. Thus, these thinkers are among the first to operate in a definitively post-state-socialist era (even if the socialist states still existed), and they are among the first to start from the assumption that we must reject class reductionism.

However, even though these thinkers are engaged with projects beyond Marxism (feminism, anti-colonialism, anti-racism, etc.), each is also very serious about Marx and the Marxist project. And in fact it is in Marx that we can usually find the root of their commitment to democracy. Each is inspired, to a different degree, by Marx and Engels' society to come, by the communist society that was supposed to have come after the transitional phase of socialism. Of course, in practice actually existing socialism bogged down in the state-socialist phase, but still, each of these thinkers retains a hope that there might be a way to think about and move toward a communist society. It is a society Marx never explicated very well or very fully, but there is broad agreement that communism connotes a society without a state or capitalist classes, in which people manage together and for themselves the conditions of their own existence. It is, in short, democracy. Of course, Marx and communism are not the only source for the democratic ideas of these theorists—anarchism and syndicalism, for example, are important as well. But Marx is an important source they all share, and that is worth making clear at the outset.

Lefebvre and autogestion

Lefebvre is perhaps best known for his writings on space and the city, but his work ranged quite widely. He also wrote texts on rural sociology, everyday life, philosophy, the state, and globalization. He was inspired by many different thinkers—Hegel, Heidegger, Lenin, and Nietzsche—but it is likely Marx that made the deepest imprint on his thought (Elden, 2004). Therefore, it is probably most apt to call Lefebvre a Marxist thinker. But he is more than just that, and in no way was he orthodox or dogmatic about his Marxism. Lefebvre's many works gather around a deep commitment to a project of the radical transformation of society. As a Marxist, even a heterodox one, he understood radical transformation to mean a move beyond capitalist society. He imagined that society beyond to be socialist, but we should never confuse Lefebvre's socialism with the actually existing socialism in societies like the Soviet Union or China. Lefebvre lived through the Stalinist era, and he was deeply critical of the totalitarian state socialism that came to dominate the period.[4] Lefebvre was also very involved in the Paris uprisings in 1968, and that experience reinforced his conviction that the state could not be a viable ally in the struggle for radical liberation.

In 1990, very near the end of his life, Lefebvre proposed something he called a "new contract of citizenship," which he presented as the core of his political vision for the future (original, 1990; translation, 2003a). He enumerates a suite of new rights to be included in the new contract, such as the right to difference, the right to information, the right to auto-gestion, and the right to the city. On its surface, the contract could easily be interpreted as an addendum to the Bill of Rights, and it seems to fit firmly within a tradition of liberal-democratic rights. But the agenda of formal juridical rights guaranteed by the liberal-democratic state is not at all Lefebvre's agenda. His new contract of citizenship is aiming at a much more politically revolutionary change that cannot in any sense be contained within the state.

Lefebvre does not intend the new contract of citizenship to be a political end goal. He does not imagine that once we are granted these rights we

---

[4] This position was shared by still other radical thinkers in France during the 1960s and 1970s. Cornelius Castoriadis (1988), Guy Debord (1983), and Michel Foucault (1980), among others, were equally appalled by Stalinism, and their work became as much a reaction against state and bureaucratic domination as it was against capitalism.

will have achieved our goal of a better society. Instead, he thinks of the rights in the contract as a kind of political opening statement, as a point of departure from which we begin a broad struggle for a thoroughgoing renewal of political life. When people claim the rights in the contract, he imagines, they are not appealing to a liberal-democratic state for concessions. Instead they are rousing themselves, they are touching off a political awakening, and they are shaking off a torpor. Claiming the new contract is for Lefebvre a way for people to become active, to struggle to take control over the conditions of their existence, and to begin to manage those conditions for themselves. Their political awakening prompts them to discover and reappropriate their own power, power that has been expropriated by the state and by capitalist institutions. Lefebvre uses the term "autogestion" to mean this struggle whereby people actively take up the project of managing their own affairs for themselves.

In many ways, the concept of autogestion holds the key for understanding Lefebvre's wider political project. His political writing works very closely with Marx and Lenin, and he retains much of their terminology and concepts. Three such ideas occupy a prominent place in his politics: the dictatorship of the proletariat, the deepening of democracy, and the withering away of the state. Lefebvre insisted on holding fast to the idea of a dictatorship of the proletariat, through which the overwhelming majority of society comes to control the decisions that determine that society. "Today, as a Marxist," he declares, "I FULLY RECOGNIZE the necessity of the dictatorship of the proletariat" (2009, p. 87). However, prompted by his critique of Stalinism, Lefebvre is adamant that this dictatorship cannot be imposed by a vanguard party that has seized the state; rather, it must emerge spontaneously from below. For that reason, even though he retains the term, he is talking less about dictatorship and more about a situation in which the emergent power of the proletariat comes to pervade society and displace the oligarchy of bourgeois rule. He argues that, imagined this way, the dictatorship of the proletariat will constitute a deepening of democracy, because it means the large majority of society assumes control from the small minority of oligarchs that had previously governed (2009, p. 157).

For Lefebvre that small minority has two aspects, capital and the state. With respect to capital, Lefebvre understands the deepening of democracy through the idea of alienation.[5] He argues that the productive power of labor is expropriated by capitalists in order to transform the work of laborers into capital. Capital thus can exist only by alienating workers

---

[5] While he acknowledges Marxism's many wrong turns (e.g. philosophism, historicism, and economism), he very much thinks we should retain the concept of alienation, arguing it has enjoyed a brilliant career as a truly enlightening notion (Lefebvre, 1991, p. 343).

from their labor and siphoning off the value they produce.[6] That is because the power to create, to produce value or even life itself, inheres in the bodies of workers. This power is proper to them, it is their own, originally theirs. As a result, the political task of deepening democracy in a capitalist political economy is simply for workers to reclaim what belongs to them, to reappropriate their own power to produce value (Lefebvre, 2009, p. 146). This reappropriation will of course directly challenge capitalist relations of production, and the extent to which it is successful is the extent to which capitalism will wither away. The other aspect of the minority group is the state. Here Lefebvre draws on Lenin's *State and Revolution* (2009) and the early Marx to argue that state power is power that has been alienated from its original locus in the bodies of people. As autogestion develops and people rouse themselves to become active, as they demonstrate to themselves that they are capable of managing their own affairs, the state apparatus begins to appear increasingly less necessary, and it too progressively withers away (1991, p. 279; 2003b, p. 180).

As we saw in Chapter 1, this second claim about the alienation of the state is a very old ontological understanding of the state that goes back at least to Hobbes. Recall that Hobbes very much wants state power to be legitimate, despite the fact that it derives from an alienation of popular power. Lefebvre, on the other hand, follows the early Marx and his critique of the bourgeois state. He rejects the idea that people are better off being ruled by the state. In his analysis of Marx's essay "On the Jewish Question," Lefebvre makes the point quite starkly: "Man realizes himself not at the level of the State, nor in the State, nor in that which depends on the State, but in freeing himself from the State" (2009, p. 73, original 1964). He thus insists that people must reappropriate their power from the state. He argues that "only when there is nothing more outside him, beyond him, raised above him, in the form and the force of the political: the state, but he has recovered the alienated forces in his politics, in political life, 'it is only then that he accomplishes human emancipation'" (Lefebvre, 2009, p. 79; see also Merrifield, 2011, p. 122).[7] This human emancipation,[8] for Marx as well as for Lefebvre, comes only in a real democracy. In his "Critique of Hegel's Philosophy of Right," Marx argues that

> Democracy is human existence, while in the other political forms man has only legal existence. That is the fundamental difference of democracy....

---

[6] As Marx put it, "Capital is dead labor, that, vampire-like, only lives by sucking living labor, and lives the more, the more labor it sucks" (1993a, Chapter 10, Section 1).

[7] The quote at the end of the passage is from "On the Jewish Question."

[8] As opposed to *political* emancipation, a distinction Marx works out in "On the Jewish Question."

Furthermore it is evident that all forms of the state have democracy for their truth, and for that reason are false to the extent that they are not democracy (Marx, 1970, Part 2).

But unlike Marx and Engels, Lefebvre had the benefit of the lessons taught by Stalinism. As a result, his idea about how we move toward and achieve a society without a state is very different from that found in *The Communist Manifesto*. Unlike Marx and Engels, who favored using the state apparatus to bring about the abolition of classes and private property (Lefebvre, 2009, p. 85), Lefebvre is hostile to the idea that we can use the state itself to create the conditions that will cause it to wither away. Instead, he envisions an ongoing process whereby people take up the responsibility of governing themselves. He thus advocates what he calls "autogestion." The word literally means "self-management," but it has a much richer meaning that is rooted in the long history of workers' actions in which they appropriate their factory and begin managing it themselves.[9] There are many historical examples of such actions, including those in Russia during the revolution, Germany in 1914–1918, Italy in 1919–1920, Spain in 1936–1937, Indonesia 1945–1946, Hungary in the 1950s, Yugoslavia under Tito, France in the 1970s, Portugal in 1974–1975, Britain in 1981, and Argentina in the decade after 2001.[10] Typically the factory is run either by the body of workers as a whole, or by workers' councils chosen by the workers. In the latter case, positions on the council are usually filled on a rotating basis. The idea is for the worker-run factory to produce goods as well as or better than the manager-run factory.[11] In that way, workers demonstrate—to the bosses and to themselves—that they are able to manage the factory on their own. They show by their success that bosses are unnecessary and that workers' self-management is possible. And so, embedded in economic autogestion is an idea of an awakening among workers, a growing realization that they are more capable than anyone thought.

Lefebvre develops the idea of autogestion most fully in the collected volume *State, Space, World* (2009). There he argues that autogestion can go beyond mere *workers'* self-management. He says we should generalize the idea beyond the factory and into all institutions and spheres of human life: the state, the family, neighborhood, the school, and so on (1991, pp. 378, 416; 2009, pp. 148–149).[12] This spreading out beyond

---

[9] This usage makes sense, because the noun *gestion* (as well as *gérer*, the verb) is typically used in French to mean "management," in the sense of the act of managing a business or a factory.

[10] For a comprehensive collection on the topic, see Ness and Azzellini (2011).

[11] Accordingly, one autogestion factory in Argentina is called *Fábrica Sin Patrones* (FASINPAT), or Factory without Bosses.

[12] Neil Brenner and Stuart Elden edited the collection and did much of the translation. Their work on both counts is an important part of why the volume is such a great help in understanding Lefebvre's wider project.

the factory is what Raoul Vaneigem, a contemporary of Lefebvre and well-known member of the Situationist International, referred to as *autogestion généralisée*, generalized autogestion (1974, esp. Chapter 3). We must pursue autogestion in every sphere of life, build it from below, encourage it to emerge spontaneously out of the everyday practice of people. Because it is by definition a process whereby people govern themselves, autogestion cannot be brought about intentionally by a vanguard. It cannot be organized by a cadre of activists, nor can it be prompted by a party leadership. That approach would be something we would have to call "heterogestion," or management by others. Autogestion means people making decisions for themselves, as opposed to giving those decisions over to a power beyond themselves (2009, p. 150).[13] Lefebvre says that "each time a social group...refuses to accept passively its conditions of existence, of life, or of survival, each time such a group forces itself not only to understand but to master its own condi- tions of existence, autogestion is occurring" (2009, p. 135).

Certainly it is possible—perhaps even desirable—for some measure of organization and even quasi-institutions to emerge in the context of a struggle for autogestion. For instance, we might imagine a workers' council managing a factory in Turin, or a neighborhood assembly managing a barrio in Buenos Aires, or a popular assembly managing a camp of activists in Madrid in 2011. But in autogestion this organiza- tion must emerge from within the group rather than being imposed by an outside entity. Members of a self-managed community would con- tinue to actively participate in these institutions. They would use the institutions as a tool to arrive at decisions and manage the community, but the institutions would not form into durable bureaucracies. They would not become detached from the community, take up a position above it, and begin to govern it as an outside force. Within autogestion, any institutions would be continually undone, remade, and resubjected to control from the mass of people in the community (see Hardt and Negri, 2011, Part 6).

Of course, the modern state is very different from autogestion. It is precisely a bureaucratized outside force that is separate from people and sovereign over them (2003b, p. 101). "Whether bourgeois or not," Lefebvre writes, "the State in essence opposes a centralizing principle to the decentralizing principle of autogestion..." (2009, pp. 147–148). The struggle for autogestion is a struggle from below by people who

---

[13] Because "self-management" is vague and appears bureaucratic and apolitical in English, throughout the book I leave the word *autogestion* untranslated, in order to preserve Lefebvre's specific and political meaning of the term. Actually, more accurately, I simply adopt it as an English word: autogestion. The word is virtually the same in Italian (*autogestione*) and Spanish (*autogestión*), and so I just take it up into English as well.

have decided to take on the responsibility of governing themselves, who gain confidence through their successes, and who are able to demonstrate, bit by bit, that the state is no longer necessary. To the extent they demonstrate this, Lefebvre argues, the state will wither away. Autogestion thus obviates Hobbes' old blackmail that without the state there will be a war of all against all. In autogestion, we do not smash the state and then begin managing our own affairs. Rather we manage our own affairs, we work hard at it, and we get to the point where it is evident that we can govern ourselves. Only then does the withering of the state truly kick in. Autogestion thus offers the possibility of a withering from below. It is a clear alternative to a failed model of a vanguard party seizing the state in order to impose conditions that will cause the state to wither away.

I think we need not stretch too far to see Lefebvre's desire for autogestion as a desire for democracy. In autogestion, people reject the oligarchy and heteronomy of capitalism and the modern state. Instead they govern themselves directly. It is economic democracy, it is political democracy—it is democracy in all spheres of life. Moreover, there is evidence that Lefebvre also equated the two, even if he more often spoke in terms of autogestion than democracy. Neil Brenner and Stuart Elden (2009, pp. 37, 124), for example, argue that autogestion necessarily involves radical democracy from the grassroots. In an interview in 1976, in response to the question of whether or not autogestion can be found in Marx, Lefebvre responds that Marx did not write about autogestion per se, but "there is no doubt that there is [in Marx] an idea of grass-roots democracy, of a bottom-up democracy that rises from the base to summit. Nor is there any doubt that he had a notion of workers' and producers' associations…" (Lefebvre, 2009, p. 160). Two years later, in Volume 4 of *De l'État*, Lefebvre argues that autogestion works by confronting the administrative rationality of the state with the pressure of a direct and actualized democracy (2009, pp. 250–251). Clearly, Lefebvre saw a deep connection between autogestion and democracy. I merely propose to draw that connection out, to understand his call for autogestion in terms of a call for democracy and popular autonomy.

For Lefebvre, this political project of autogestion and democracy is also a project to transform the way we produce and use space. Recall how he imagines transduction spatially, in terms of a transition from the industrial city to urban society. In *The Production of Space*, he sets out the more general project of moving from "abstract space" to "differential space" (see also 2003b, pp. 37, 125–127). The former is a space "determined economically by capital, dominated socially by the bourgeoisie, and ruled politically by the state" (1991, p. 227). It is a space of domination that has been expropriated and alienated from users and is controlled by a heteronomous elite. Abstract space reduces space to its economic function as either a means of production or an exchangeable commodity. What he says we need to do is to undermine abstract space and enable "the production of a space that is *other*," a differential space (1991, p. 391). Differential space would involve restoring the fullness of space

> whereby living labor can produce something that is no longer a thing... needs and desires can reappear as such, informing both the act of producing and its products. There still exist—and there may exist in the future— spaces for play, spaces for enjoyment, architectures of wisdom or pleasure. In and by means of [differential] space, the work may shine through the product, use value may gain the upper hand over exchange value: appropriation...may (virtually) achieve domination over domination, as the imaginary and the utopian incorporate (or are incorporated into) the real...(1991, p. 348).

The project of differential space is a project of reappropriation. Our thinking about space, what he calls a "science of space," must "be viewed as a science of use" that would "accord *appropriation* a special practical and theoretical status. *For* appropriation and for use...and *against* exchange and domination" (1991, p. 368). "Any revolutionary project today," he declares (1991, pp. 166–167), "whether utopian or realistic, must, if it is to avoid hopeless banality, make the reappropriation of the body, in association with the reappropriation of space, into a non-negotiable part of its agenda." "Revolution," he goes on to say,

> was long defined either in terms of a political change at the level of the state or else in terms of the collective or state ownership of the means of production....Today such limited definitions of revolution will no longer suffice. The transformation of society presupposes a collective ownership and *management of space* founded on the permanent participation of the 'interested parties,' with their multiple, varied and even contradictory interests (1991, p. 422, emphasis added).

Those "interested parties" are the users of space, those who actively *inhabit* space in the course of their daily lives. It is they who must reappropriate space by wresting its control away from its owners and from the state. Democracy and autogestion, for Lefebvre, are thus always spatial projects; they are always struggles by users and inhabitants of space to collectively manage that space in a way that meets their needs and satisfies their desires.

Deleuze, Guattari, and desire

Like Lefebvre, Deleuze and Guattari wrote in the wake of Stalinism and the era of state socialism. They were younger than Lefebvre in 1968, but they were similarly impacted by the experience of that struggle against the French state. Partly as a result, their political theory is designed to ward off heteronomy and pursue autonomy. Michel Foucault, in his insightful preface to Deleuze and Guattari's *Anti-Oedipus* (1977, p. xiii), suggests that the book "is an *Introduction to the Non-Fascist Life.*" He goes on to explain that it advocates a struggle against both national-scale state fascism and the personal-scale fascisms that live within each of us. By fascism here, he means the general desire to surrender ourselves to another, to let ourselves be ruled by the state and its leaders. But Foucault says Deleuze and Guattari's project is also something more. It is not only a negative project against fascism; it is an alternative, he says, to the "sad militants" who despise the current system and think only of smashing it (1977, p. xii). Deleuze and Guattari are in effect taking up Nietzsche's exhortation (1989b) that we move beyond *ressentiment*, beyond simply stewing in our own bile at the injustice of the system created by the powerful to benefit only themselves. Instead, Deleuze and Guattari are offering us a positive politics, a politics of affirmation and joy. Although they do detail the repressive power of the system, their primary project is to emphasize, seek out, and celebrate our own creative and productive capabilities.

That positive project proceeds by staging a morality play whose hero is desire. To understand what that play entails, we have to examine the central role of psychology and psychoanalysis in Deleuze and Guattari's thought. In *Anti-Oedipus*, they develop a sustained attack on Freud and Oedipal psychoanalysis. That attack is complex, as is Freud's work, but we can simplify both, usefully I hope, by understanding Freud's deep roots in Plato's thought. As we saw, Plato conceived of the soul in three parts, rational, spirited, and desiring. These are conceived hierarchically: the rational is superior to the spirited, which is itself superior to the desiring. Across his works, Plato argues that justice at the scale of the person is achieved when the rational part of the soul is able to govern or rule over the other parts. The other parts have their specific role to play, but that role is subordinate to the governing role of reason. It is a view of justice that is aristocratic in the ancient Greek sense of the term. In ancient Greek, *aristoi* means "the good," those who possess *arête* or "excellence." Aristocracy therefore proposes that those who are excellent should rule over those who are not. Freud adapts this aristocratic framework into his concept of the id, the ego, and the superego. He argues the ego, in partnership with the superego, should govern the desiring impulses thrown up by the id. It is in this sense that Freud is relevantly Platonic: like Plato, he casts desire as untamed and dangerous, as something that must be subordinated, controlled, ruled. Desire must be contained in and tamed by the family structure, which for Freud is governed by the logic of Oedipus. Deleuze and Guattari stridently object to this capturing of desire within social structures, both in Freud's Oedipus and in society in general.

The source of their critique can also be found in Plato's work, specifically in Callicles, one of the characters in the dialogue *Gorgias*. Nietzsche had a great affinity for Callicles, and Deleuze and Guattari are in turn inspired by Nietzsche's adaptation of Callicles' argument. So who is Callicles? Typically in Plato's dialogues, Socrates refutes the arguments of a series of interlocutors. There is always one interlocutor that stands out, whose arguments Plato clearly takes more seriously and feels the need to explore at greater length in order to thoroughly refute. In *The Republic*, it is Thrasymachus, in the *Gorgias*, it is Callicles. The subject of the *Gorgias* is the nature of the good. Callicles argues that the good is to be found in desire. He says that in order to achieve the good we must cultivate our desire, intensify it, and then use the other parts of the soul—reason and spirit—as means to satisfy our desire. He says to Socrates:

> I tell you frankly that natural good consists in this, that the man who is going to live as a man ought to encourage his appetites to be as strong as possible instead of repressing them, and be able by means of his courage and intelligence to satisfy them in all their intensity by providing them with whatever they happen to desire (Plato, 1998, pp. 491–492).

Callicles thus inverts Plato's hierarchy of the just soul, setting desire *above* reason and spirit. Socrates responds by arguing for temperance. He says we must use reason to control our desires so that we indulge them only in moderation. Callicles scoffs at this. He says the existence of the temperate person, who lets reason rule desire, "is the existence of a stone" (Plato, 1998, p. 494). It is Callicles' standing Plato on his head by posing desire as the soul's leading element that Nietzsche is so enamored of, especially in *Beyond Good and Evil* and *On the Genealogy of Morality*. Nietzsche's entire thrust is to invert traditional Platonic (and Christian) morality, to argue that temperance's denial of desire is a denial of *life*, of our best selves, of all that which is good in us. Nietzsche argues that we are creatures who desire, who have a will to discharge our strength into the world, a will to act upon and shape our surroundings (1989a, p. 21). But our moral rules tell us that such action is wrong, that we should restrain ourselves from desiring and acting boldly into the world.[14] He thinks these moral rules are tantamount to telling birds of prey they are wrong to kill other creatures. He argues that these moral rules make us a "sick animal" (1989b, p. 121). We are imprisoned like a beast that can only rub itself raw against the bars of its cage, even if it is a cage we ourselves have created (1989b, p. 85).

It is against this lineage that we can properly understand Deleuze and Guattari's politics. Like Callicles and Nietzsche, they seek to invert Plato and Freud, to insist that desire is primary and should receive first consideration among the human faculties. It should not be controlled and managed; it should be set free and allowed to create and produce according to its will. For Deleuze and Guattari, desire is ontologically primary, it is the source of our creativity, and it produces all things in human society. Accordingly, they usually use the term "desiring-production" rather than simply "desire." In that term, there is more than an echo of Marx, of his idea that labor is the source of all economic production. Just as the power of labor is captured by capital, or popular power is captured by the state, so too in *Anti-Oedipus* desire is captured by Oedipal psychoanalysis (Deleuze and Guattari, 1977). In fact, Deleuze and Guattari (1987) suggest that there are in society a whole series of "apparatuses of capture," structures that contain desire, channel its flow, and cause it to work for purposes alien to its own. In addition to psychoanalysis and capitalist relations of production, these apparatuses of capture include the state, the organism, the concept of individual identity, the semiotic conventions of language, and the musical refrain. For Deleuze and Guattari, these apparatuses are unproductive structures, structures that only work by feeding off the productive force of desire. Desire is thus the only *autopoietic* entity, the only one that can produce itself, and so it is the only entity fully capable of autonomy. The ethical and political mission of Deleuze and Guattari's work is to help desiring-production escape these apparatuses, to help it flee along paths it chooses, and to help it regain its original autonomy.

Against the apparatus of psychoanalysis, for example, they pose the curative and liberating process of schizoanalysis, through which we can come to understand how our desiring-production works. Schizoanalysis helps us understand how desiring-production "invests the social field," which is to say how it produces the social relations that structure our everyday lives (1977, p. 174). Schizoanalysis can thus make clear how desiring-production creates the apparatuses of capture that confine it. Deleuze and Guattari argue that if we can become more familiar with apparatuses of capture, we will be able to more effectively escape them.

---

[14] One can also see Arendt's insistence on action (1998, esp. Section V) in this line of thinking.

Indeed, they make clear that this is their model of praxis. One should become familiar with an apparatus,

> experiment with the opportunities it offers, find an advantageous place on it, find potential movements of deterritorialization, possible lines of flight, experience them, produce flow conjunctions here and there, try out continuums of intensities segment by segment, have a small plot of new land at all times (1987, p. 161, see also p. 188).

These "lines of flight" are for Deleuze and Guattari the primary act of a liberatory politics. Once we become more familiar with how desiring-production works and with the apparatuses it has built, we will be much better able to help desire flee. Even then, escape will not be easy. The apparatuses of capture establish social norms that are extremely difficult to contravene and live outside of. For example, those who refuse the Oedipalization of psychoanalysis are subject to a whole series of disciplinary measures, including physical removal from society to a mental institution. It is similarly challenging to produce goods outside of capitalist relations of production, to inhabit urban society outside of the industrial city, to act politically outside of the control of state sovereignty. A line of flight therefore faces overwhelming odds when it is undertaken by a single element of desire. The most likely outcome is recapture and reintegration into the system of apparatuses. More disturbingly, in its frenzy to remain free desire can struggle to exhaustion, burn itself out, or even careen off into death (1987, p. 229). Of course, neither recapture nor death is acceptable to Deleuze and Guattari, even if those outcomes are the most common. In order to avoid them, escaped elements of desire must not flee alone. Rather they must continually seek out other escapees and try to connect up with them, to stream together their energy, to make common cause in their escape. "Connection," Deleuze and Guattari write, "indicates the way in which decoded and deterritorialized flows boost one another, accelerate their shared escape, and augment or stoke their quanta" (1987, p. 220). It is precisely when a line of flight fails to augment its valence by connecting with other lines that it will be recaptured or killed (1987, p. 229).

Though flight may seem a risky game, Deleuze and Guattari offer a very specific cause for hope. They argue that one of the most basic qualities of desiring-production is that it almost compulsively produces connections (1977, p. 181). An escaped element of desire will obsessively seek out connections with other escapees. For example, when they are discussing lines of flight from capitalism, Deleuze and Guattari say that initially capitalism will attempt to recapture the escaped flows, to conjugate them back into its system. But this attempted conjugation, even though it will succeed in recapturing most escaped flows, will inevitably miss some, and it will also force the ones it misses further ahead. Those accelerated flows, still on the run, will seek out other such flows and enter into connections with them. In the best case, as escaped flows succeed in producing more and more connections, they will begin to produce large aggregates of free connected desire, and those aggregates, as they grow, will begin to trace out something they call "a new land" (1987, p. 472). For Deleuze and Guattari, this new land is more metaphorical than physical. It is a land composed of flights; it is made up of flows of desire that have set themselves free from the apparatuses, have evaded recapture, and have connected to each other.

It is in this idea of a new land that it becomes most clear that Deleuze and Guattari are proposing not merely incremental change or political reform, but revolution. They aim at "revolutionary movement" and "the becoming-minoritarian of everybody/everything" (1987, pp. 472–473). They hope every escaped element of desire, pursuing its line of flight, will construct "revolutionary connections" so that they can resist recapture, ward off the apparatuses, and begin to delineate, through their connected lines, a new land.[15] Deleuze and Guattari thus hope to "tip the assemblage," to bring about a thoroughgoing sea change that revolutionizes society and creates a new land where flight pervades and apparatuses of capture begin to wither away (1987, p. 161). And the specific word "pervade" is important here. Flight *pervades* the new land; it does not *predominate* in it. "Pervade" comes from the Latin *per+vadere*, which means to "to go through," or a bit more evocatively, "to spread throughout." "Predominate" comes from the Latin *dominus*, which means "master" and connotes a hierarchical relation in which a master rules a household.[16] For Deleuze and Guattari, flight grows and spreads to the point where it fills up a territory, much like a spreading rhizome in a garden. It is not a force that dominates and subordinates others. Flight is by definition an escape from domination, and so it can only pervade, rather than predominate, in the new land.[17]

Deleuze and Guattari use this more general vision of flight, desire, and revolution to understand the more specific relation between people and the state. With respect to that relation, the new land they advocate is what they call a "smooth space," a space beyond or outside or other than

---

[15] Also see Andy Merrifield's similar conception of a "Great Escape" (2011, p. 108). Or see the Invisible Committee's notion of a territory so thick with communes that it becomes opaque or unreadable to structures of authority. "We don't want to occupy territory," they say, "we want to *be* the territory" (2009, p. 72).

[16] "Domicile" and "domestic" share the same root.

[17] Laclau and Mouffe, as we will see later, would likely be more comfortable with the idea that democracy should "predominate."

the "striated space" of the state (1987, esp. Chapter 14). In smooth space, desire is relatively free from the apparatuses of capture and can produce according to its will. In other words, desire's inherent autonomy, its original power of self-production, is rediscovered outside the state in smooth space. However, when people take up the project of governing themselves, when they escape into a new land or succeed in producing smooth space, the forces of state heteronomy can be expected to reassert themselves. The state will pursue escaped elements into smooth space and attempt to reimpose striated space on them. As a result, even in a new land we must always be vigilant; it is necessary to continually ward off the reimposition of apparatuses of capture.[18]

To an extent, in Deleuze and Guattari smooth space is a conceptual or metaphorical space, but they also intimate it can be a physical space as well. To the extent it is concrete, smooth space is not necessarily a space "out there," beyond the frontiers of the state's striated space. Smooth space can also emerge inside the body of striated space; glimmers of a new land can appear inside the old. Thus, for example, when workers occupy an abandoned factory and begin producing again, they create, at least for a time, a smooth space that is not striated by private property, market exchange, capital–labor relations, or by the state's policing of those relations. This space is governed differently, managed collectively by the factory's workers. Or when squatters occupy abandoned housing and begin living there, they create smooth space in a very similar way. Thus, smooth space very much can be realized in concrete situations. The result is what Lefebvre (1991) would call *differential spaces*, spaces that function differently from the dominant norms of abstract space. Of course, eventually the state, usually in the form of the police, will arrive to evict the workers or the squatters in order to return the space to its legal owners and reimpose the striated system of property rights and state law. This forced reimposition often results in pitched physical confrontations, most of which are won, eventually, by the better-armed police.

Like Lefebvre, Deleuze and Guattari are rejecting categorically any lingering idea that people might seize the state in order to achieve their liberation. While Lefebvre is willing to engage with and be inspired by a Marxist-Leninist approach in his attempt to chart a path beyond it, Deleuze and Guattari will not even go that far. They want no intimation of working-class hegemony, or of replacing one form of heteronomy with another. They insist on a flight from heteronomy in general, from the state in general, in an effort to rediscover and reactivate the autonomy

---

[18] Hence Deleuze's great line, from the dialogues with Clare Parnet: "Flee, but while fleeing grab a weapon" (quoted in and translated by Hardt and Negri, 2004, p. 342).

of desiring-production. To be sure, fleeing heteronomy is extremely difficult, more difficult than simply seizing the state. However, Deleuze and Guattari again offer us a very specific reason for hope: desire is the source of all production, the source of all power. Desire produces itself as well as the apparatuses that capture it. It is therefore perfectly capable of realizing its own autonomy and resisting the reimposition of heteronomy. Whether it will actually achieve those feats is another question, but the new land, for Deleuze and Guattari, is entirely possible.

Unlike Lefebvre, Deleuze and Guattari almost never refer explicitly to democracy.[19] However, it is not at all a stretch to see clearly in their political vision democracy as we have been imagining it. They want desiring-production to be able to rule itself, rather than be ruled by apparatuses of capture like psychoanalysis, capital, and the state. At the individual level, they imagine each person engaging in schizoanalysis so that desiring-production can reclaim its autonomy from Oedipal psychoanalysis and create as it sees fit. On a larger scale, in the political sphere they imagine people struggling to free themselves from the state apparatus so that they can govern themselves. And in the economic sphere, they imagine producers fleeing capitalist economic relations and managing production on their own terms. Deleuze and Guattari's new land beyond capitalism, as well as their idea of smooth space beyond (and also within the body of) the state, are essentially visions of the desiring demos fleeing control by oligarchy and governing themselves together in smooth space. People escape the heteronomous apparatuses of psychoanalysis, the state, and capital, they discover their own power already within, and they connect with others undertaking a similar flight. Together, these people-in-flight engage in an active struggle to flee from heteronomy and reclaim autonomy. Deleuze and Guattari's vision is thus a deeply anti-oligarchic and anti-heteronomic one in which people take control again over the conditions of their own existence. It is, in so many ways, democracy.

Hardt, Negri, and the multitude

To a great extent, it is possible to read Hardt and Negri as carrying forward Deleuze and Guattari's analysis into the contemporary era. They are both closely connected to Deleuze and Guattari: Negri worked with

---

[19] One can find a few commentators (e.g. Krause and Rolli, 2008; Patton, 2005; Patton, 2008) who make much of Deleuze and Guattari's extremely fleeting mention of "becoming-democratic" in *What is Philosophy?* (1994, p. 113). However, the discussion of democracy there is very much in passing and refers almost exclusively to democracy negatively, as an existing form of government.

both (Deleuze and Negri, 1990; Guattari and Negri, 1990), and Hardt (1993) has undertaken detailed studies of Deleuze's political philosophy. Of course, Hardt and Negri's work builds upon other influences as well, Italian autonomism and Foucault prominent among them. But their central thesis—that modern sovereignty is being replaced by Empire—owes a great debt to Deleuze and Guattari's arguments about the difference between the "barbarian despotic machine" and the "civilized capitalist machine" (1977, pp. 139–271). And so, in order to understand Hardt and Negri's argument about Empire and democracy, we need to start with Deleuze and Guattari's machines.

These machines are two kinds of what Deleuze and Guattari call a "socius," which is a generalized logic that governs social relations. In the despotic machine, the state-form predominates over other forms of social organization, such as kinship or market. One element of society is singled out and raised above the rest; it becomes transcendent and assumes the role of the sovereign.[20] This state works by "overcoding" all elements of society, subordinating them hierarchically to the ultimate authority of the sovereign. It controls by territorializing, by partitioning and striating space, by defining space as subject to state authority, and arranging subjects within it.[21] This system is quite rigid in the sense that it must capture everything in society within its hierarchical determination. Nothing is allowed to escape, everything must be contained within the body of the despot (1977, pp. 211, 213). When elements of desire escape along lines of flight, the despot must respond through recapture and reterritorialization. A historical example of an element escaping the despotic machine is private property. During the seventeenth century, English nobles and merchants were vigorously claiming rights to private (rather than royal) ownership of land. They were challenging the despot's control over his realm. That challenge was successful, of course. The king was unable to recapture and recode the escaped elements, and the capitalist political economy and its liberal-democratic state supplanted royal authority. The new liberal state was limited in its authority by a broad conception of the private (i.e. non-state) realm. This is precisely the political project John Locke is providing theoretical support for in the *Second Treatise*.

For Deleuze and Guattari, this was an important moment, when the state began the process of transition from being a transcendent, absolute authority to being only one authority among many, immanent to the

---

[20] Deleuze and Guattari are very much working straight from Hobbes' *Leviathan* here, and I think the famous image of the Leviathan from the frontispiece is a good way to imagine the despot they are describing.

[21] An idea that resonates with Rancière's idea of the *partage du sensible*.

relations of capital (1994, p. 106). Locke's intervention is thus a key event in a long history of transition from the despotic machine, modeled on the state, to the civilized capitalist machine, modeled on capitalist production. For Deleuze and Guattari, capitalism worked very differently from the state. Instead of a comprehensive territorialization in which everything is assigned a specific place, capitalism began by deterritorializing. It first decoded the codes of the despot, liberating elements to flow freely, beyond the reach of the *ancien regime*. The despotic machine scrambled to reterritorialize, recode, and recapture these flows, but it was not able to do so. It was overwhelmed by the flows decoded by capitalism, and it lost its predominant position in the socius.

However, for Deleuze and Guattari capitalism does not only deterritorialize and decode, leaving liberated elements to flow where they will. It incorporates those elements into its own ruling logic. The classic example of this is the private property we have seen, which was deterritorialized as King's realm and reincorporated into a capitalist system of property rights. In a similar way, the European peasantry was uprooted from a feudal way of life,[22] a life embedded in the agricultural land of rural estates, and reinscribed in a new capitalist system of production as workers in urban factories (Hardt, n.d.; Deleuze and Guattari, 1994, p. 97).[23] Thus, we should not make the mistake of reading Deleuze and Guattari as speaking only in metaphors here. The deterritorialization achieved by capitalism very much involved a transformation of *actual territory*, a radical reordering of the feudal system of land tenure and the social relations that system required. The rapid and thoroughgoing urbanization of Europe's rural population, out of the rural peasant way of life and into the urban slums and factories, was only the most dramatic of the many spatial transformations wrought by this process.

For Deleuze and Guattari, the way capitalism reinscribes the elements it deterritorializes takes a particular form. Unlike the despotic machine, the capitalist machine does not *recode* the decoded flows. Rather, it absorbs them into what Deleuze and Guattari call the capitalist *axiomatic*. There is an important difference for them between recoding and axiomatizing. Whereas the body of the despot-state and its codes were fixed, the capitalist axiomatic is able to expand itself, to grow and adapt to changing conditions by adding new elements to its logic as they arise (1994, pp. 97, 106). Because capitalism functions by decoding and deterritorializing, it requires an extremely effective system for reincorporating what it sets

---

[22] This example is likely the source of their term "deterritorialization." It is used both as a broad metaphor and in its quite literal meaning.

[23] Of course, a very similar process is also happening today, only at much greater speed and with far greater numbers of people, in places like Brazil, India, China, and sub-Saharan Africa, resulting in the megacities and sprawling informal settlements that so typify contemporary urbanization.

free. It cannot be unchanging and rigid. It must be "always ready to widen its own limits so as to add a new axiom to a previously saturated system" (1977, p. 238). For example, in early capitalism each worker was considered to contract independently with management. As workers formed into unions and articulated themselves in a collective voice, the capitalist axiomatic expanded to include rules and institutions for collective bargaining that effectively preserve the fundamental relations between capital and labor.[24] For its part, the state, which is no longer transcendent, now functions immanently as part of the capitalist axiomatic. It serves as an assistant, helping to axiomatize what capital sets free (Deleuze and Guattari, 1994, p. 106). Because of this robust capacity to incorporate liberated flows by expanding itself, the capitalist axiomatic poses a particularly challenging problem for Deleuze and Guattari, whose primary political instinct, as we have seen, is to liberate desiring-production from the apparatuses that capture it.

Hardt and Negri explicitly take up that problem in their work (2000; 2004; 2011). At the core of their analysis is an argument that mirrors Deleuze and Guattari's distinction between the barbarian despotic machine and the civilized capitalist machine. They contend that in the contemporary world (roughly 1989 to the present), sovereignty is changing. The old system, modern sovereignty, is progressively giving way to a new form of sovereignty, Empire. Recalling their distinction between constituent power and constituted power,[25] we can understand the old system of modern sovereignty as an attempt to use a transcendent constituted power to impose order on an immanent constituent power (2000, p. 74). The modern state presided over this kind of sovereignty, producing a relatively more rigid and hierarchical system of control. This system was territorial in the political sense, as each state was considered by all the others to be sovereign within its own territory, and within each territory the state's sovereignty was absolute. That is, the authority of the state within its territory transcended all other forms of power. For Hardt and Negri, modern sovereignty is thus very much rooted in a Hobbesian model of transcendent state power. But as Deleuze and Guattari suggest, that model was under attack almost from its very inception. The bourgeoisie quickly began to carve out arenas (e.g. territory, freedoms, and new conceptions of private property) not subject to state control, or at least only partly subject to its control. Hardt and Negri suggest that the attack took time, and the process of

---

[24] This process of "subjectivization," through which, for example, workers become aware of their own collective existence and articulate themselves as speaking subjects, is central to Rancière's politics (see Rancière, 1999, p. 51), as I discuss in the section on Rancière in this chapter.
[25] Presented in Chapter 1.

moving from the despotic machine and its Hobbesian state to the capitalist machine and its Lockean state was a long one. The French Revolution did not sweep away the despotic machine; it merely helped advance its long decline.

That long decline paralleled the long rise of what Hardt and Negri call "Empire." It was only in the twentieth century that imperial sovereignty (i.e. sovereignty in the form of Empire) manifested itself fully. For Hardt and Negri (2000), we today find ourselves primarily under the sway of the civilized capitalist machine of Empire. Imperial sovereignty is not modeled on the transcendent state, but rather on the immanent power of capitalism (see also Deleuze and Guattari, 1994, p. 97). Empire does not establish a fixed territorial center of power. Rather it operates through flows across space, and by connecting flows into particular networked arrangements. It does not rule by territorializing, but by deterritorializing, by uprooting previous arrangements of power (such as nation-states) and reintegrating their elements into its own imperial relations of power and imperial spatial networks, which it administers by means of an ever-expanding capitalist axiomatic. Imperial sovereignty does not limit itself to the national scale, but rather continually expands its limits toward the global scale. The attendant story of the restructuring of the global political-economic geography is familiar: since the 1970s, capital has been vigorously globalizing its production process, and nation-states have become increasingly unable to contain and regulate its flows. Hardt and Negri theorize that imperial sovereignty has developed at the global scale to manage this new global system. It does so through a complex arrangement of networked national and supranational entities, which include nation-states, multinational corporations, non-governmental organizations, supranational governing bodies (EU, UN, etc.), and international regulatory agencies (IMF, WTO, etc.). Hardt and Negri argue that Empire's network is decentered and distributed rather than nested and hierarchical. It is flexible and expandable. It is able to incorporate into its ruling system new territories beyond its limit and new social forces when they arise. It is what Deleuze and Guattari call an axiomatic, rather than a coding. But despite that great flexibility, Hardt and Negri do argue that Empire has a single logic of rule, which is to establish a perpetual and universal peace as a condition for the effective functioning of the capitalist world economy (Hardt and Negri, 2000, pp. xv, 198). Moreover, as with the capitalist machine, Hardt and Negri aver that the flexibility of Empire's networks is not infinite. The possibility does exist that the axiomatic can be overwhelmed. A breakthrough is possible.

So as a mirror of Deleuze and Guattari's capitalist axiomatic, Empire poses the same challenging problem that the capitalist axiomatic does: we seek to liberate desiring-production and constituent power, but Empire itself works by liberating, and then feeding off of, these popular forces. It is not so simple to flee from a system of control that is built to absorb escapes. For their part, Deleuze and Guattari propose, with Nietzsche, that what is required is not to oppose capitalism's incessant decoding and deterritorialization, but to speed it up, to "accelerate the process," to push capitalism beyond the wall, beyond its absolute limit, to achieve a breakthrough (Deleuze and Guattari, 1977, pp. 239–240). Coming from a similar understanding of the problem, Hardt and Negri nevertheless articulate a somewhat different political alternative. They stress that as Empire globalized its network of rule, it also globalized the population that is subject to its rule. That population of global imperial subjects is what Hardt and Negri call "the multitude." They argue that what Empire has done is to produce "the people" at a global scale for the first time in history. But this multitude, Hardt and Negri argue, is the source of all economic production and political power (a conviction Deleuze and Guattari very much share). It is therefore perfectly capable of achieving whatever it desires. It is able, if it wishes, to produce an alternative to Empire in which the multitude rules itself, in which it manages global flows and exchanges without Empire. The multitude is very much capable of inventing new democratic forms in which its own power, constituent power, becomes active, reclaims its autonomy, and causes Empire to wither away.

For Hardt and Negri, in order to reclaim its autonomy and propose a new alternative, the multitude must "create a new social body" (2000, p. 208, see also p. 214). It must become aware of itself, develop itself politically, and mature into a collective subject capable of reappropriating its own power. It must discover how to increase its own capacities for democracy, to develop those capacities into effective abilities (Hardt and Negri, 2011, esp. Parts 1 and 6). Hardt and Negri conceptualize this process of political awakening and reappropriation explicitly in terms of democracy. They envision the "organization of productive and political power as a biopolitical unity managed by the multitude, organized by the multitude, directed by the multitude—absolute democracy in action" (2000, p. 410). They take the term "absolute democracy" from Spinoza's *Political Treatise* (2000 [1677], Chapter XI). For Hardt and Negri, absolute democracy is the first great modern innovation of democracy, and it functions to radically extend the ancient concept. For ancients such as Aristotle, the *demos* did not mean the people as a whole. Rather, it referred only to the many poor who were not members of the elite classes. Aristotle assumed that these poor were always the majority, but they never constituted everyone in society. Thus *demo-cracy*, the rule of the *demos*, was for Aristotle the rule of the many poor over everyone else. The modern innovation, for Hardt and Negri, was to extend absolutely this concept of the *demos* from the many poor to everyone (2004, p. 240). As a result, modern democracy becomes the rule of everyone over everyone, or absolute democracy.[26]

What Hardt and Negri call the second great modern innovation of democracy addresses the question of scale. Rather than the polis-sized community of ancient democracy, modern states were national in scale. Even so, they still aspired to be democratic, and so they needed to invent a notion of democracy that was feasible at that larger scale. Representation was the solution: everyone participates in selecting a few representatives, and those few govern in the place of everyone; they represent the whole. Representative democracy thus connects people to their rulers through elections. But it also separates people from their rulers because it opens a gap between "those who govern" and "everyone," between rulers and ruled. The representatives *stand for* everyone, but they can never *be* everyone. But the first modern innovation imagines democracy to be absolute. It imagines that in a democracy everyone governs everyone. And so, Hardt and Negri argue, modern democracy cannot tolerate the gap between representatives and everyone. Representative democracy is therefore a contradiction. Hardt and Negri write that "democracy and representation stand at odds with one another. When our power [the power of everyone] is transferred to a group of rulers, then we all no longer rule, we are separated from power and government." However, they continue, "despite this contradiction...representation came to define modern democracy to such an extent that...it has become practically impossible to think democracy without also thinking some form of representation" (2004, p. 244). That association has become so taken-for-granted that in 2002 Joseph Nye, a leading liberal political thinker, asserted that "democracy is government by officials who are accountable and removable by the majority of people in a jurisdiction" (Nye, 2002, p. 109, quoted in Hardt and Negri, 2004, p. 245). Representation and democracy contradict each other, and yet the two have become synonymous.

Hardt and Negri suggest the solution to this tortured state of affairs is not to accept liberal democracy and its contradictions, but to recommit ourselves to absolute democracy. That would mean the multitude reclaiming its own political power and managing its affairs for itself. In an absolute democracy, the multitude is everyone. And in Empire that everyone is now global; it means every human being. Absolute democracy in the context of Empire, therefore, would mean all human beings governing themselves collectively. Before we dismiss that vision as

---

[26] I should mention that Hardt and Negri are probably extending Spinoza beyond where he was willing to go. He imagined absolute democracy to be a form of absolute *state* (Tucker, 2012), whereas in Hardt and Negri it is conceived of quite differently, as being beyond the state.

impractical, it is worth recalling that Hardt and Negri locate this project, whereby the multitude takes up the task of governing themselves, in the multitude's own activity, in the everyday practices they are already engaged in. For Hardt and Negri, the multitude need only to reappropriate their own power (2000, p. 66). They are not expropriating the power of another, and they are certainly not seizing the state. They would need simply to nullify Hobbes' old contract, voiding the terms by which they surrendered their power to Leviathan in the first place. Or perhaps better, since Hobbes' state works because we act *as if* the contract existed, they are proposing simply that the multitude decide to act *as if* they never gave their power to a sovereign in the first place. Hardt and Negri (2000, p. 204) quote Étienne de La Boétie (1975, pp. 52–53):

> Resolve to serve no more, and you are at once freed. I do not ask that you place hands upon the tyrant to topple him over, but simply that you support him no longer; then you will behold him, like a great Colossus whose pedestal has been pulled away, fall of his own weight and break into pieces.

For Hardt and Negri, this refusal, this secession from the arrangements of sovereign power, is only part of what is needed. As the multitude beholds the colossus collapsing, they are also beholding their own power. For Hardt and Negri that power is quite real; it is rooted in their common experience as producers, as the creative force that generates both wealth and political power in the world. The multitude must come to believe, through experience, that they are capable of using this power to manage their affairs for themselves. That is what Hardt and Negri mean by creating a new social body (2000, p. 204). The multitude must produce, by themselves and for themselves, a positive alternative to Empire at the global scale. Beyond simple refusal, the multitude must construct a new mode of life, a new community, a new social force.

That feat is also not impossible. Recall that for Deleuze and Guattari, desiring-production operates by connecting, by proliferating connections among lines of flight. So too, for Hardt and Negri, one of the multitude's signature abilities in the current era is to produce *affects*, which is to say it works by generating connections, solidarities, and community bonds. In the current world economy, Hardt and Negri argue, the leading edge of labor, its most important productive potential, is its ability to produce such affects (2000, p. 293). Cooperation, collaboration, and communication are precisely the activities that most define the current regime of accumulation. But they are also the activities that produce community, that generate what Hardt and Negri call "the common." That common, the common-wealth, must form the basis of any alternative to Empire.

In short, Hardt and Negri are suggesting that the multitude, working away under Empire's control, is already training itself to produce this common, this global community to come.[27] That community is not merely Empire seized and controlled by the working class. It is the dissolution of Empire and the radical reimagining of the global common. Hardt and Negri insist that this is what the project of absolute democracy is: the multitude constructing for themselves the community to come. A new land. Autogestion on a global scale.

Laclau, Mouffe, and hegemony

While Hardt and Negri take their principal cue from Deleuze and Guattari, Ernesto Laclau and Chantal Mouffe root themselves in the thought of Antonio Gramsci. Like Hardt and Negri, they have other influences as well (e.g. Lacan, Derrida), but Gramsci's concept of hegemony occupies a particularly central place in their thought. On its face, this approach seems to be at odds with the insistence on autonomy and self-management I have been emphasizing so far. Hegemony, with its twin aspects of coercion and consent, is typically understood to involve some element of hierarchy and domination, an acceptance of categories of rulers and ruled. Moreover, Gramsci was deeply involved with communist party politics. He devoted much of his energies to the project of building a workers' party capable of seizing the state and using its power to collectivize property and abolish classes. That agenda seems to be precisely what Lefebvre wants to move beyond, and what Deleuze and Guattari have broken with decisively. It appears on its face to be an "old left" way of thinking.

None of those concerns is necessarily wrong. However, there are more layers to the story, enough that I think it is worth paying careful attention to Laclau and Mouffe's arguments. The first layer is that Gramsci himself was very much more than a crude vanguardist. For example, he was deeply involved with the workers' councils that occupied factories in Turin and Milan in 1920 (Anonymous, 1921; Hoare and Smith, 1971; Forgacs, 2000; Kohn, 2003). The occupations were largely a spontaneous uprising by autonomous organizations, rather than a planned and party-led action. Indeed, Gramsci was greatly occupied by the question of what the right relationship should be between such councils and the party (see in particular 1971, pp. 125–205; 2000, pp. 79–109). Second, some of Gramsci's particular

---

[27] This line of analysis very much echoes Giorgio Agamben's "coming community" (1993). Hardt was the translator for the English edition.

power as a thinker is that he continually pushed beyond the old-left common sense of his time. As a Marxist thinker, for example, he argued forcefully against economism and reductionism. Within the Italian Communist Party, he fought against the vanguardism of leaders like Amadeo Bordiga. He maintained instead that parties must consist of *both* an incisive leadership and an active base. He embraced the concept of "democratic centralism," in which there is

> a continual adaptation of the [party] organization to the real movement [of the membership], a matching of thrusts from below with orders from above, a continuous insertion of elements thrown up from the depths of the rank and file into the solid framework of the leadership apparatus which ensures continuity and the regular accumulation of experience (1971, pp. 188–189).

This "real movement" does not come from the will of party leaders. It arises from a democratic desire, an active energy that flows from workers themselves. Of course, there is also centralism here, a party leadership that can guide and plan for the base. But we must read this in Gramsci's context, where the prevailing model of successful revolution was the vanguardism of 1917. What is remarkable is that he recognizes and emphasizes—from Marx, from Lenin, from the experience of the workers soviets in Russia and factory councils in Italy—the vital importance of an active popular struggle, of a spontaneous energy from below that he takes to be the real motor of history.[28]

The second layer of complexity is that Laclau and Mouffe are not bound by Gramsci's context or his thought. Like Lefebvre and Deleuze and Guattari, they are writing in the wake of Stalinism and the disaster of state-led revolution. They understand clearly the horrors that a "leadership apparatus" can inflict. As a result, they take up the democratic aspect of Gramsci's democratic centralism, and they systematically pursue it further. More generally, their project is very much to move beyond Gramsci. While they take their cue from him, their political thought is also very much a creature of their post-Stalinist context.

In their preface to the second edition of *Hegemony and Socialist Strategy*, Laclau and Mouffe explicitly address the question of what is to be done in the context of a thoroughly neoliberal political economy (Laclau and Mouffe, 2000). They argue that the answer lies not in the state, but in civil society, where there are multiple struggles for democracy already underway. They urge us to link those struggles into a broader movement for radical democracy.

---

[28] Obviously Rosa Luxemburg is also a key figure in arguing for the importance of spontaneity, and Gramsci was very much aware of and influenced by her arguments.

If one is to build a chain of equivalences among democratic struggles, one needs to establish a frontier and define an adversary, but this is not enough. One also needs to know for what one is fighting, what kind of society one wants to establish. This requires from the Left an adequate grasp of the nature of power relations, and the dynamics of politics. What is at stake is the building of a new hegemony. So our motto is: 'Back to the hegemonic struggle' (2000, p. xix).

So, they clearly frame their approach in terms of hegemony. But to understand why, we must examine what they mean by "power relations" and "the dynamics of politics." They understand power and politics in the context of a particular ontological assumption: the political field is irreducibly plural. That is, the observed political pluralism in society cannot be resolved into a homogenous social whole. A seamless whole can never be established, they argue, because there exists a permanent possibility that political conflict will emerge. They understand this conflict in terms of "antagonism," which arises when a relation of social difference—an "us" distinguished from a "them"—is transformed into a relation of political conflict: a "friend" confronting an "enemy" (Mouffe, 2002, p. 7). They stress that these definitions are never predetermined or fixed. They are always defined through political interaction. As a result, the possibility always exists that one group will redefine another group as an enemy that has wronged them and with whom they are now in conflict. This ever-present possibility for antagonism is what Mouffe (1993) will later call the potential for the "return of the political." As a result, it is impossible to "suture" the political field once and for all into a seamless unity (Laclau and Mouffe, 1985, p. 88). Rather, that field necessarily remains open, plural, and marked by conflict. As they put it, "the central role that the notion of antagonism plays in our work forecloses any possibility of a final reconciliation, of any kind of rational consensus, of a fully inclusive 'we'" (2000, p. xvii).[29] That is why they vehemently reject contemporary declarations that we are in a "post-political" condition, that we have moved beyond all significant conflict about how to organize political and economic life, that we have reached the "end of history," a stable world of liberal-democratic states and free-market capitalism. Such a putative consensus is always a lie for Laclau and Mouffe. That lie is why they "stress that it is vital for democratic politics to acknowledge that any form of consensus is the result of a hegemonic articulation, and that it always has an 'outside' that impedes its full realization" (2000, p. xviii).

For Laclau and Mouffe, that irreducible pluralism is important, because it means that all politics *necessarily* take the form of hegemonic struggle.

---

[29] Rancière harbors the same hostility for the notion of political consensus, as we will see in the next section.

Even though the social body cannot be sutured into a whole, nevertheless such wholes are constantly being claimed and accepted as real. But, they argue, all such declarations are false. They are in fact one part of the political body claiming to be the same thing as the whole: a particular interest presenting itself as a universal one. Any such assertion of universality can never be true. All interests are necessarily partial, localized in a particular place, in a certain territory. The field of politics is irreducibly plural. Hegemonic struggle, Laclau and Mouffe argue, is the struggle to have an assertion of universality be *believed*, to have one's partial interest be taken as a universal one. Thus, for example, the public must believe that what's good for General Motors is good for America, in Charles Wilson's famous line. Laclau and Mouffe call such claims "contaminated universality"; they are claims to universality that are contaminated by the fact that they are made by interests that are necessarily particular, situated, and local (Laclau and Mouffe, 2000, p. xiii; see also Laclau, 2000). Contaminated universality, for Laclau and Mouffe, is the very content of hegemonic politics.

To understand how a particular group successfully claims universality, Laclau and Mouffe rely again on Gramsci, who insisted that society is too fragmented for one class or group to rule by itself (1971, pp. 52–120).[30] In order to rule society, he argued, a particular class, like the bourgeoisie or the proletariat, must form *alliances* that can bring together a large bloc of particular interests. That process requires groups to construct what Laclau and Mouffe (1985, p. 129) call a "chain of equivalences" among themselves, which is to say they define themselves as equivalently antagonistic to some other set of interests in society. For example, Gramsci hoped the Italian proletariat would join with Southern peasants, soldiers, and petty bourgeois to define themselves as equivalently disadvantaged by a capitalist-Catholic hegemony. He felt the proletariat could not engage in hegemonic struggle merely by pursuing its narrow class interests. Rather, it needed to "widen itself out towards a whole social grouping," progressively "propagating itself throughout society" by connecting with other groups to define a frontier of antagonism against capitalist hegemony.

For Gramsci, such hegemonic struggle involves relations of both coercion and consent (1971, pp. 34, 80; 2000, pp. 170, 289, 401). Between the hegemonic bloc and those outside it, there is an important measure of consent, as almost everyone in society must accept that the interests of the dominant bloc are the same as those of society as a whole. But, of course, where consent is not enough, the hegemonic bloc must use coercion and even violence to maintain its position. Within the hegemonic bloc there are

[30] Gramsci's argument here relies mostly on his analysis of Italian society. However, based on his close reading of other European Marxists, he concluded that other European national societies were similarly fragmented. Much of his argument about how a hegemonic class must partner with other groups, for example, is drawn from the experience of the French bourgeoisie during the French Revolution.

relations of consent, as when groups ally voluntarily with other groups for whom they feel a political affinity. But coercion can be present here as well. It is often necessary to threaten punishment for any who leave the bloc or act contrary to its interests. Thus, Gramsci offers us a very nuanced account of political relations. He is clearly much more willing to admit and use relations of control, domination, and force than any of the thinkers we have considered so far. And because of their ontological assumptions about politics, Laclau and Mouffe accept that some element of coercion, control, and domination will be part of any hegemonic project. They maintain that such conflictual relations, relations that are nonconsensual, can never be eliminated from the political field because it is always possible that antagonism will emerge, that the political will return. Because we can never achieve a final, all-encompassing consensus—a society beyond conflict—control and domination must always be part of political relations.

For Laclau and Mouffe, the hegemonic struggle, pursued through relations of coercion and consent, is undertaken by multiple groups in many different spheres, such as a workers' struggle in the context of capitalist relations, a feminist struggle in the context of patriarchy, or an anti-racist struggle in the context of racism. In order to establish a hegemonic articulation, these struggles must begin to form links with each other. As they do so, they can come to decide they are equivalently disadvantaged by the current hegemonic order and that a new hegemonic order is necessary. Laclau and Mouffe propose that the content of that new hegemonic order should be democracy. They advocate a hegemonic struggle to move us toward the goal of a "radical and plural democracy" (2000, p. xviii). This democracy is radical in the sense that it seeks to radically deepen and extend current forms and values of liberal democracy. "The alternative of the Left should consist of locating itself fully in the field of the democratic revolution...[it] *cannot be to renounce liberal-democratic ideology, but on the contrary, to deepen and expand it in the direction of a radical and plural democracy*" (1985, p. 176). For Laclau and Mouffe, radicalizing democracy involves the extension of democratic practices to locations and arenas that are not now democratic, both within the state and in civil society. Of course, the factory is one of those locations, and radical democracy would necessarily involve "a socialist dimension, as it is necessary to put an end to capitalist relations of production, which are at the root of numerous relations of subordination" (1985, p. 178, see also p. 192).[31] However,

---

[31] The unequivocal understanding across all these theorists that democracy by definition means the end of capitalist social relations helps us begin to see just how badly many on the left today underestimate democracy's potential. For example, John Holloway recently argued that "it is important to think of our movement as a movement of rupture against capitalism and not just as a movement for democracy" (2011).

socialism is merely one of the components of their project of radical democracy. Other arenas, such as the home, the school, the environment, and the bureaucracy must also be democratized. Very much echoing the *autogestion généralisée* of Lefebvre and Vaneigem, Laclau and Mouffe insist that radical democracy

> cannot mean only *workers'* self-management...what is at stake is true participation by all subjects in decisions about what is to be produced, how it is to be produced, and the forms in which the product is to be distributed. Only in such conditions can there be social appropriation of production (1985, p. 178).

For Laclau and Mouffe, economic production is bound up with social reproduction, and the economic sphere is bound up with a variety of other spheres such that the "true participation" by ordinary people in decisions must be generalized beyond the economy. It is along these lines that their democracy is *plural* as well as radical. It involves "the multiplication of political spaces and the preventing of the concentration of power in one point" (1985, p. 178). It embraces the irreducibly plural nature of the political field and pushes it further in an effort to decentralize and disperse power. That dispersal is meant to limit the centralization of power in the state. But radical pluralism is also meant to militate against economism, to dismantle the idea that economic class is the only, or even primary, basis for political struggle. Laclau and Mouffe insist that hegemonic struggle must arise out of many different spheres across the social field. This point may seem self-evident to some readers, but unfortunately class reductionism remains, even today, a bad habit of thought among many on the left.

But because for Laclau and Mouffe all politics are hegemonic politics, their radical and plural democracy must be pursued through hegemonic struggle. Unlike Deleuze and Guattari's multiple flights, for Laclau and Mouffe the struggle must be to confront and unseat the current neoliberal hegemonic order and to replace it with the hegemony of radical democracy. That new hegemony would operate both by struggling for the radical democratization of society and by defending democratic gains through a rearguard action that prevents the reimposition of structures like an authoritarian state, an oligarchic capitalist market, or a patriarchal family. Clearly, there is a tension here: Laclau and Mouffe want both hegemony *and* democracy. To some degree they are thus at odds with Deleuze and Guattari's approach, which is to flee from all forms of hegemony and control. For Deleuze and Guattari, the project is not to impose a new hegemony, a becoming-majoritarian as they sometimes call it, but to accomplish a breakthrough: to achieve a generalized flight that overwhelms the ability of the capitalist axiomatic to reabsorb it, that creates a new land, and that then actively wards off the reimposition of the apparatuses. For Laclau and Mouffe, the project must be a hegemonic one, for that is the nature of politics, but it is a hegemonic project to maximize democracy, autonomy, participation, and the active nature of political subjects (1985, p. 167). While I don't think we can wish this significant difference away, I also think we should be attentive to an important overlap between Laclau and Mouffe and Deleuze and Guattari: both pairs of scholars advocate a sea change, a breakthrough, a tipping over into a new, generalized condition in which heteronomy and oligarchy are resisted, and autonomy and democracy pervade the political community. Both understand that this new generalized democratic condition would be neither total nor final. Democracy will never *entirely* crowd out all other forms of political relation, nor will its preeminence be permanent, an end-state for humanity. Both say that the forces of heteronomy and oligarchy will reassert themselves, that there will always be the need to prevent their reemergence. For Deleuze and Guattari, this means "warding off" those forces, while Laclau and Mouffe might be more comfortable with "suppressing" or "coercing" such forces. So again, I want to acknowledge the real differences between Deleuze and Guattari's non-hegemonic politics and Laclau and Mouffe's hegemonic approach, but I also want to stress that the differences are quite a lot more subtle, and the overlaps greater, than those binary terms would lead us to believe.

Rancière and politics

Unlike either Laclau and Mouffe or Deleuze and Guattari, Jacques Rancière is not a thinker of political sea change. Like Laclau and Mouffe, however, he places democracy at the center of his political theory. He shares with them a strident opposition to consensus—to the idea that we can reach a generalized state of agreement in which meaningful debate has ended and conflict has been resolved, in which the only questions that remain are technical questions about *how* to achieve what we have all agreed we must achieve. Instead, for Rancière, democracy is disruption; it is an unsettling of existing assumptions, norms, and practices, an interruption of the perpetual articulation of social order. But his democracy is not really a way to break through. He does not offer us hope that we can move beyond that social order and into a new land.

For their democratic theory, Laclau and Mouffe look to the modern bourgeois revolution in democracy. Rancière instead casts his eye back to the ancient Greeks and works closely, even obsessively, with Plato and

Aristotle. He reads their work against an even older tradition, Athenian democracy, which proposed what for Rancière is the most radical of political ideas: everyone is equally qualified to rule. Rancière says this proposition has very important implications. If everyone comes to the political community as equals, then there is no natural social order that pre-exists such communities. What Athenian democracy is proposing, therefore, is that all social orders are constructed by humans and laid down on top of that original equality. If "no social order is based on nature, no divine law regulates human society" (Rancière, 1999, p. 16), then every order is "artificial" in Hobbes' sense, which is to say it is not given by nature but produced by human artifice. Every social order is therefore contingent, erected on top of a foundational equality, and so every order can always be different than it is now. The Greeks, Rancière tells us, called that social order *arkhê*, a word which denotes a relation of those who lead and those who are led, an arrangement in which some walk at the head of the line and others trail along behind (Rancière, 2001). If there is no natural or transcendent *arkhê* that underlies all social orders, then the only thing down there, the only thing that underlies all political communities, is *an-arkhê*. In that way, for Rancière, democracy's basic assumption, "the equality of anyone at all with anyone else" (Rancière, 1999, p. 15), is a form of *an-arkhê*. Democracy presupposes anarchy.

This idea of *an-arkhê* echoes Nietzsche's idea of "the Dionysian" (1999).[32] He suggests that existence is in fact made up of a meaningless swirl of random events, the Dionysian. We cannot look fully into the face of this swirl because to do so would overwhelm us, and so we construct filters of meaning and order, which he calls "the Apollonian." These filters are necessary artifices; we need them in order to go on living, but they nevertheless alienate us from the energy, the life force, of the Dionysian. Nietzsche's line of thinking here goes back to Hobbes, who says that in the state of nature there is no order, and everyone is equal to everyone else (Hobbes, 1996, Chapter 15). For Hobbes, that condition produces chaos and war, and so as we saw previously, he invents an imagined social contract through which authority and order are vested and become legitimate. And Rancière shows how this destabilizing idea of original equality goes back even further than Hobbes, to the Athenian democrats. As a result, it is also present in Plato, who wrote in the shadow of that democracy. It is even fair to say that Plato's politics are *driven* by the need to address the problem of original equality. For Plato, the good political community is a well-ordered one in which

---

[32] See also Lefebvre's (1991, pp. 117, 130) discussion of Heraclitus, who proposed "an ever-new universal flux that carries 'beings' along and in which all stability is merely appearance."

all members of the community understand their proper place in the order and remain in that place faithfully. In the good *polis*, the guardian class assigns "each individual to the one task he is naturally fitted for, so that by applying himself to his own one task each may become a single person rather than many people, and in this way the entire city may grow to be a single city rather than many cities" (2008, p. 423d).[33] Plato greatly feared the "desires of the ordinary majority" (2008, p. 431d) because those desires lead them in all sorts of different directions, beyond the particular roles assigned to them. Plato says that democratic man, "the man who puts equality before everything," is unable to regulate himself, and he gives free rein to his desires. Democratic man assumes that

> all desires are equal.... And so he lives out his life from day to day, gratifying the desire of the moment. One day he drinks himself under the table to the sound of the pipes, the next day he is on a diet of plain water. Now he is taking exercise, but at other times he is lazing around and taking no interest in anything. And sometimes he passes the time in what he calls philosophy. Much of his time is spent in politics, where he leaps to his feet and says and does whatever comes into his head...there is no controlling order or necessity in his life (2008, pp. 561c–d).

For Plato, democracy—a political community in which everyone is considered equally qualified to rule—would be a disaster, as his characterization of democratic man suggests. He abhors this notion of equality and insists instead that there are better and worse people, superior and inferior members of the polity, some more qualified to rule than others. In Plato's good political community, those who are more qualified rule those who are less qualified. The less qualified should rightly follow. That order of leaders and followers is maintained by a carefully designed and hierarchical structure of rule in the community, a structure Rancière labels Plato's "archipolitics." This structure "reveals in all its radicality the project of a community based on the complete realization of the *arkhê* of community, total awareness...with nothing left over" (Rancière, 1999, p. 65), in other words, the polar opposite of *an-arkhê*.

Plato's archipolitics are important because they become the model for Rancière's concept of the *partage du sensible*,[34] an idea he also sometimes renders as "the police" (1999, pp. 21–42; 2001, Thesis 7; 2004). Rancière

---

[33] Recall Plato's other obsession, with the multiple soul.
[34] This phrase is typically translated as "the partition of the sensible," which in English seems clunky and vague. *Partage* definitely refers to a partitioning, a dividing up into parts and then placing those parts in a particular arrangement. *Sensible*, as in English, means both that which can be perceived by the senses and that which "makes sense" to think or to do.

here means the set of procedures whereby power is institutionalized, places and roles in society are distributed, and the entirety of the system is legitimized. It is a general order that arranges bodies into a particular distribution within the political community (Rancière, 1999, p. 28).[35] It is a *partage du sensible* insofar as it defines what is visible and what is sayable, what bodies can be seen and what voices can be understood. It is a partitioning that purports to be total, to take account of all parts in society. As in Plato's archipolitics, the *partage du sensible* is assumed to leave nothing out, to define all bodies and acts and utterances in its system of classification.

However, and in strong agreement with Mouffe's concept of the return of the political, Rancière argues that the police order is always unable to take account of all elements of society. He says every order will have a remainder, an overflow: what he calls "the part of those who have no part" (1999, p. 30). Here he is working closely with Aristotle's *Politics*, and particularly the way Aristotle separates the polis into groups he considers full "parts" of the polis and those that are not parts but merely necessary conditions: groups the polis needs in order to exist (Aristotle, 1998b, pp. 1278a, 1328a–b, 1329a). For Aristotle, the nature of the polis was to bring people together to engage in discussions about the just political community. Those who carried out such work, the citizens of the polis, "took part" in its affairs; they were fully "parts" of the polis. Non-citizens—women, workers, and slaves—did not carry out the work of politics. They were thus not integral parts of the polis. Nevertheless, they were necessary conditions for the existence of the polis, because they did all the other work (farming, child care, construction, cooking, etc.) so that citizens would be free to do the political work. Obviously women, workers, and slaves formed a real, material "part" of the population of the polis. But they were unable to take part in the activities of citizenship. They were thus, for Rancière, the original "part of those that had no part." Rancière poses this problem of the part of those who have no part as a general problem that all political communities face. The police order will always claim to offer a complete accounting of all parts, but there will always be an overflow. There will always be parts of the community that have not been assigned a part in the *partage du sensible*, but that nevertheless exist, play a role, constitute a part.

Politics, as Rancière defines them, happen when the police order is disrupted. It occurs when those who have no part in the *partage du sensible* develop an awareness of themselves as being, in fact, part of

---

[35] An idea that echoes the way that Lefebvre (1991, pp. 32–33) talks about the difference between "social space," which assigns everything its proper place (Rancière's "police"), and "representational spaces," which operate outside of and in spite of the norms of social space (Rancière's "politics").

society, but as having no part in the existing order. This process of becoming aware is what Rancière calls "subjectification": the part of those who have no part begins to think, to act, and to speak *as though it were* a part of society just like any other (1999, p. 35; 2000, pp. 11–12, 20; 2001, Thesis 8). In other words, it begins to "take part" in both senses of the term, to partake in politics and to claim its rightful part in the order of things. The most important way it takes part, for Rancière, is to speak, to engage others in a discussion about the affairs of the polis. Here again, Aristotle is key for Rancière. For Aristotle, citizens work out for themselves what constitutes the good political community by using *logos*, a word that means both speech and reason (e.g. Aristotle, 1998b, p. 1260a). Aristotle is saying that the act of citizenship is the act of speech-reason, of rational discourse with one's fellow citizens about public affairs. That act, the concrete practice of speech-reason, was for Aristotle the very definition of what it meant to be a citizen and act politically. For him, it then follows that those without a voice, without the ability to engage in speech-reason, cannot be integral parts of the polis. *Logos* requires the capacity to speak, to make conscious vocalizations. It also requires an audience that is attentive to and affected by that voice. Even more, it requires the ability to reason, to formulate rational, or *sensible*, arguments about what justice means, arguments that have the potential to convince others.

Rancière provides a few examples in which we can see this particularly Aristotelian way of conceiving of political subjectification. One instance, taken from ancient Rome, involves an encounter between plebeians and patricians on the Aventine Hill (1999, pp. 23–26). The plebeians revolt and declare their secession from Rome. The patricians respond that there can be no discussion with the plebs—the plebs do not speak. It is not that they do not have tongues and vocal chords, but that they do not have *logos*, they are not able to take part in a proper discussion about the affairs of Rome. Like the women, workers, and slaves of Greece, they lead a purely private existence consumed entirely with the reproduction of life (Arendt, 1998). They have nothing to do with *sensible* discussions about public affairs. As a result, when the plebs speak, the patricians hear only noise, a kind of bovine lowing. The struggle of politics, for Rancière, is the struggle over whether a discussion between parties is even possible, over whether the plebs can speak, be understood, and convince others—over whether or not they can take part. The response of the plebs on the Aventine is simply to press on, to speak *as if* the patricians were able to make sense of their words, as if they had a legitimate place in the *partage du sensible*, as if they were equal. That assumption of equality, that acting *as if* one were equal, is for Rancière the critical act of politics, and of democracy. It is an act that disrupts the assumptions of the established order, an act by which the part of those who have no part claim and demonstrate with their voices and their bodies that they are indeed capable of *logos*, that they can very well take part, that they can assume an active role in the affairs of the polis. This assumption of equality is thus a reassertion of democracy's foundational *an-arkhê*: the assumption that anyone at all is capable of taking part.

Rancière grounds his assumption that the plebs are capable of *logos* in the writing of a French educator named Joseph Jacotot. Jacotot began his pedagogy from the assumption of equal intelligence (Rancière, 1991). This idea, which is central to Rancière's work, is that everyone learns in the same way, by comparing propositions to experience, and so everyone has an equal capacity to gain new knowledge (1991; 2009, p. 10). If we are all capable of engaging in *logos*, then it is just a question of adopting the assumption of equal intelligence and acting as if it were true. Rancière finds the seeds of this idea buried in Aristotle. The latter worried greatly about the role of *logos* in the relationship between master and slave. For Aristotle, the master is master because he has *logos*; the slave is a slave because he does not (Aristotle, 1998b, pp. 1254a–1255a, 1259b–1260b). But, Rancière points out, even Aristotle sees the problem: the slave must understand a command when it is issued. He must understand that he is obligated to obey that command. He therefore must be able to take part in an exchange using *logos*, which is to say he must already in some sense be equal-in-*logos* to the person who is giving the commands (Rancière, 1999, p. 16). It is in that primary contradiction of politics, one that presents itself almost from the outset of *The Politics*, that Rancière sees irrefutable evidence of the contingent and constructed nature of all social orders, of the Hobbesian base condition of human society, which is that everyone is equal to everyone else.[36]

For Rancière then, politics is defined as the moment when this base condition bubbles again to the surface, when the logic of the current order is destabilized and it becomes clear that the current *partage du sensible* has not really taken account of everything.[37] For Rancière, that moment of politics is also the moment of democracy. For him, democracy is not a set of institutions; it is not one kind of police regime among others. Rather democracy is "the way for politics to be" (1999, p. 99). "Democracy is, in

---

[36] Indeed, when Hobbes declares the original equality of all people (in Chapter 15), he does so in direct (and withering) opposition to Aristotle: "I know that *Aristotle*...maketh men by nature, some more worthy to command...others to serve...as if master and servant were not introduced by consent of men, but by difference of wit: which is not only against reason; but also against experience. For there are very few so foolish, that they had not rather govern themselves, than be governed by others...."

[37] Lefebvre's idea of "produced difference" is very similar. It "presupposes the shattering of a system; it is born of an explosion; it emerges from the chasm opened up when a closed universe ruptures" (1991, p. 372).

general, politics' mode of subjectification." It is a singular disruption of the *partage du sensible*, an interruption in the smooth operation of order that works by a process of subjectification, through which a part that has no part comes into awareness and claims its place in the community (1999, p. 99). Democracy is thus an event during which the people make themselves apparent.[38] He doesn't mean so much that everyone appears all at once in the public square, but rather that the subjectification of the part of those who have no part, their appearance on the stage, and their articulation of their claim that they have been left out of the *partage du sensible*, exposes the fact that the *partage du sensible* does not (and cannot) take account of the *whole* community. Democracy is thus the event that makes this mis-fit apparent; it makes it clear that the *partage du sensible* is always a lie and that it can never fully take everyone into account.

Some contemporary geographers have attempted to read a spatial logic into Rancière's conception of the *partage du sensible* and its disruption by democracy (e.g. Dikeç, 2005). They argue that *partage du sensible* is a spatial ordering, a way of assigning to everything and everyone its proper place. But I think that attempt is overreaching. Rancière is really far more interested in the *partage du sensible* as an ordering of *logos*, as a way to define who can speak and who cannot, who can participate in the affairs of the polis and who cannot.[39] But there is no need to force a spatial sensibility into Rancière. That is because Lefebvre's concept of abstract space does the same theoretical work, and it is explicitly a spatial concept (Lefebvre, 1991, esp. Chapter 4). Abstract space, for Lefebvre, is a gener- alized set of procedures, institutions, and norms that arranges actual bodies in a concrete spatial order. It says where things can be and where they can't be, and it imposes norms that legitimate that spatial order. It is in effect an explicitly spatial *partage du sensible*. What is more, Lefebvre also offers a spatialized concept of Rancière's politics, an idea he calls differential space (Lefebvre, 1991, esp. Chapters 6 and 7). Differential space introduces a practice that destabilizes abstract space, that refuses its spatial ordering and proposes different spaces, different locations for things, different spatial relations. So even though Rancière does not imagine his idea of democracy spatially, it phases quite closely with Lefebvre's more explicitly spatial imagination.

Among the theorists I have considered so far, Rancière is also distinctive for how he theorizes the outcome of politics. For Rancière, the democratic

---

[38] This idea, of course, resonates with theorists such as Badiou (2006), who insist that democracy is not a set of institutions but an event.
[39] He is also interested in the aesthetic and the visual, and so the *partage du sensible* is also a regime of what is seeable and what is not.

eruption of the people that destabilizes the *partage du sensible* can never be a breakthrough, as in Deleuze and Guattari, nor a generalization of autogestion, as in Lefebvre, nor a hegemonic shift, as in Laclau and Mouffe. Rather, the outcome is always a resettling, an institution of a new police order, of a reworked *partage du sensible* that assigns a place in the new order to the insurgent part. The part that formerly had no part can now take part in the new *partage du sensible*. The archetypical example, for Rancière, is the working class. In early capitalism, the *partage du sensible* defined workers not as a class, but as a multitude of individuals, each of whom contracted separately with an employer to sell his labor. But organization and mobilization by workers achieved a subjectification that created a new part, a class called "the proletariat." The existing police order took no account of that class of people. The proletariat did not have a part in the police order. Bosses wanted to continue to define workers not as a class, but as an aggregate of individuals. They thus saw confrontational actions by workers as riots, as criminal behavior by individuals. Workers had to struggle to invent the subject of the proletariat as a viable interlocutor, as a partner that could negotiate on an equal footing with capital. This is a classic example of politics in Rancière's terms: a part with no part becomes a subject and exposes the lie of the existing police order. The struggles of the labor movement resulted in the collective subject "labor" becoming real, becoming recognized as a counted part in the account of the *partage du sensible*. Perhaps the apogee of this recognition is the U.S. Taft–Hartley Act of 1947, whose official name is the "Labor–Management Relations Act." The official police order has recognized two official subjects, "labor" and "management," and it expects them to engage in relations.

To be sure, the new *partage du sensible* is distinctly different, expanded, more complex than the previous one (1995, pp. 85–86). Rancière insists that some police orders are better than others (1999, pp. 30–31), and the better ones are those that have been most often jolted out of their routine, the ones whose legitimacy has been most often destabilized by the eruption of democracy. But even the better police orders are still police orders. For Rancière, we cannot move beyond the condition of a police order because, he says, society and equality work at opposite purposes. Drawing again on Joseph Jacotot, he argues that there is "an inegalitarian logic inherent in the social bond" (Rancière, 1995, p. 81). That is, it is impossible to extend the community of equals to the entire social field, to achieve a society without inequality. For Jacotot and Rancière, this project is a contradiction in terms. The social body operates according to an inegalitarian principle. Therefore, when politics-democracy gives voice to an egalitarian logic, it "can never achieve substantial form as a social institution." He argues that "no matter how many individuals become emancipated, society can never be emancipated...the community of equals can never become coextensive with a society of the unequal" (1995, p. 84). All that democracy can produce is "an insubstantial community of individuals engaged in the ongoing creation of equality" (1995, p. 84).

So Rancière rejects the possibility of absolute democracy, of a society without inequality. But that claim is more or less made by the other theorists as well. What sets Rancière apart is that he does not really even countenance the possibility of a breakthrough or a sea change through which democracy is generalized in society. His vision for what democracy can do is therefore relatively limited. He thinks that the most we can aim at is to create what he calls a "community of sharing." This community is marked by division, and its parts are unequally related. But it is a community that shares a particular rationality, which is a shared obligation to hear, to be affected by the speech of others (1995, p. 87). That obligation allows as much room as we can expect for democracy, for the eruption of equality in the midst of the inequality of the *partage du sensible*. But democracy, when it emerges, rarely makes a very large change in the *partage du sensible*. He says democracy only "occasionally finds the wherewithal to imprint the surface of the social body with the traces of its actual effects" (1995, p. 87). So while he insists democracy will always return to disrupt the social order, it can never transform our world into something we might call a democratic society, into a world where democracy pervades, even if it is not absolute.

Conclusion

My working title for this chapter was "The Democratic Unconscious." I am tempted to end it with a kind of psychoanalytic interpretation of the desires of the left after Stalinism. It would be an argument that what all these theorists—Lefebvre, Deleuze and Guattari, Hardt and Negri, Laclau and Mouffe, Rancière—are *really* doing, whether they know it or not, is aiming at some form of democracy. Deep in their psyche lies the true nature of their thought, the spine of their politics, and it is absolute democracy. But the approach I have taken points to a different claim. Each of them is multiple. The work of each is an endlessly complex tangle of desires, wills, and affects. Some of these wills desire democracy, others desire other political values. Democracy may or may not lie at the heart of their thought. We may not even be able to say that their thought has a "heart" at all. Nevertheless, there is no doubt that for each theorist the desire for democracy is very much there. All I have done in this chapter is to pick out the will of each for democracy and try to present it coherently. What remains now, according to the method of transduction, is to stream those wills together, to get their flows moving in the same direction, so that we can begin to see the outline of democracy as a virtual object, as a horizon toward which we can move, and as a lens that can help us see the democracy that is already here.

The underlying assumption of so many of the arguments we have seen is the idea that political power has a proper place, that it originates in the bodies and minds of people. This is one sense in which some speak of "radical" democracy: the root of political power can be found in the people, and so all other power is derivative of or expropriated from this original, root source (the best example is Lummis, 1997). One is tempted to find the origin of this line of thinking in Marx, in his twin arguments that (1) labor is the source of all economic value and capital lives vampire-like off the value labor produces, and (2) the state and its formal citizenship is an impediment to, not the realization of, human freedom. That attribution would not be wrong. As I say at the outset of the chapter, each of the authors I examine in this chapter has a great intellectual affinity for Marx. Going deeper still, we could even trace this line of thinking to Feuerbach (2008), who argued that God is an alienated representation of man's own qualities and powers. Alternatively, we could point to the anarchist tradition through Bakunin, who enthusiastically applied this idea of alienation to all three arenas: capitalism, the state, and religion (Bakunin, 1972; 1973).

However, that genealogy does not yet go far enough, because the idea of alienated power is as old as modern political theory itself. As we have seen, it is as old as Hobbes, whose entire problematic is based on the assumption that in the state of nature people are the original source of all power. That is precisely the problem for Hobbes. He thought that if left to their own devices, people will use their power to destroy each other. Therefore, he argued, they must agree to surrender their power, to alienate it to a state, which will then use that power to keep the peace. Leviathan doesn't have any power of its own; it can only have the power people grant to it through the contract. Even though Locke has a less authoritarian view of the state and a subtly different idea about the relationship between people and the state, nevertheless he very much retains Hobbes' assumption that in the absence of a state people have a natural right to discharge their own power. For Locke also, the political contract involves people giving up some of their power in order to create the state. Locke is very concerned to establish how the people might take *back* that power should the state do wrong by them, but that idea can only exist because he begins from the assumption that state power is alienated popular power. Rousseau has a still different imagination of the relationship between people and state, but he

WHAT DEMOCRACY MEANS   73

nevertheless retains the model in which people enter into a social contract by surrendering the power they originally held in the state of nature. In fact, all modern political theory can be seen as an attempt to argue for the legitimacy of a situation in which people's own proper power has been given over to the state, and the state in turn uses people's own power to rule them. Marx and Bakunin by no means invented this idea of alienated popular power; they merely (1) rejected the argument of the previous theorists that the alienation is legitimate and (2) applied the analysis of alienation to capitalism as well as to the state.

And so this is the deep agreement about the proper place of power that all the theorists in this chapter share. They agree that labor is the source of all economic value, and the people are the source of all political power. This agreement can be attributed most immediately to their affinity for Marx, but it is an understanding that pervades all modern political theory. Moreover, that agreement is so fundamental, it is rooted so deeply, that it even survives into post-modernity, into arguments about the death of modern sovereignty. First Deleuze and Guattari (1977, pp. 222–262), then Foucault (esp. 1990, pp. 81–91), and then Hardt and Negri (2000, pp. 325–350) announced the end of modern sovereign power and its transcendent, centralized authority. They spoke of the rise of an immanent power, modeled on capitalism, and distributed in networks throughout the social body. But even after theorizing this shift, even though power is now understood to be distributed and immanent rather than centralized and transcendent, Deleuze and Guattari still hypothesize an original, primary productive power (desiring-production) and a secondary, derivative power that feeds off and controls the original (apparatuses of capture). For Hardt and Negri, even in the distributed networks of Empire, all production and political power depends on the constituent, popular power of the multitude. The constituted power of Empire is merely an alienated remobilization of the multitude's own power.

In short, there exists a shared idea among these theorists that the question of democracy is the question of the relationship between the proper power of people—all people—and the entities that have expropriated and organized that power into routinized institutions like the state, the corporation, the party, the union, the church, the family, and so on. If the gist of modern political theory is an effort to legitimate the transfer of popular power to these institutions, democracy is then simply the struggle of people to take up that power again. Democracy is the act of voiding the social contract, or more accurately, resolving to act as if the contract never existed in the first place. In the absence of the contract, organs of power try to justify their existence by pointing to a fiction. From the perspective of democracy, such organs are necessarily illegitimate expropriations of popular power. They are oligarchs. They arrange the polis such that a few rule the rest. State officials rule the citizenry, managers rule workers, school administrators rule teachers and students, party officials rule the rank and file. Democracy struggles against oligarchy, against the formation of organs of power, against the rule of the few over the many. It is the struggle of everyone, of all people, to reappropriate their own power, to refuse to be ruled by an organ and its few, to identify oligarchy and to denounce it as something the demos, the everyone, never agreed to.

Folded into this struggle against oligarchy is also a struggle against heteronomy and for autonomy. Heteronomy means to be ruled by another, whereas autonomy means to rule oneself. Oligarchy necessarily institutes a heteronomic relation, because the few (others) rule the rest. Democracy instead constitutes autonomy: everyone rules themselves. Heteronomy is a condition in which the power of everyone to govern themselves has been alienated, expropriated to an organ, a few, an-other. Autonomy is a condition in which that power is not alienated, in which people retain their own power for themselves. Democracy insists that people never agreed to surrender their power in the first place, and so achieving autonomy requires only that people discover and reassert the ruling and law-giving power that is already theirs.

Despite the elaborate discourse that has grown up around it, I want to suggest that democracy is not actually all that complicated. It is simply the act of governing ourselves together in the polis. In a democratic polis, there are no states, no elections, no parties, no representatives. There are no organs of power like corporations, or churches, or unions. There is only us, each the equal of every other. We declare our intention to govern ourselves, to keep our own power for ourselves, to give the laws to ourselves, to manage our community, our city, and our affairs for ourselves. We refuse to be ruled by another, by the few, or by the one. We do not yet know what we can do, but we have decided to find out.

3

Becoming Democratic

> I saw a man pursuing the horizon;
> Round and round they sped.
> I was disturbed at this;
> I accosted the man.
> "It is futile," I said,
> "You can never"—
> "You lie," he cried,
> And ran on.
>   —Steven Crane (1972 [1905])

Perpetual Struggle

Since the end of the Cold War, there has been much talk about "the end of history," about the idea that liberal democracy and free-market capitalism have proven themselves, through competition, to be the best possible way to organize human society. That proof is supposed to mean that the big ideological struggles are over, that whatever problems remain—inequality, poverty, sexism, racism, and so on—are technical ones, to be addressed within the confines of the liberal-capitalist system that everyone agrees is best. It proposes that politics, real politics, are a thing of the past. We are now "post-political." This argument comes largely from an ascendant right, a neoliberal hegemony hoping to solidify its position. Many on the left have been largely reduced to arguing the obvious: that history has not, in fact, ended.

The Down-Deep Delight of Democracy, First Edition. Mark Purcell.
© 2013 John Wiley & Sons, Ltd. Published 2013 by John Wiley & Sons, Ltd.

Obvious though the argument may be, the left itself has only recently accepted it. That is because utopianism and ideas about an eventual end of history are a rich part of the tradition of the left as well. In the *Communist Manifesto*, we are presented with the possibility that we can move beyond politics, that the class conflict of the capitalist era can be dissolved; or, in fact, that it is already being tendentially dissolved by the real movement of history. Even earlier (in 1844) Marx proposes that true communism is "the riddle of history solved and knows itself as this solution" (1994, p. 71). And in the preface to the German edition of *The Communist Manifesto*, published in 1883, Engels argues that the proletariat cannot liberate itself "without at the same time *forever freeing the whole of society* from exploitation, oppression and class struggles" (Simon, 1994, p. 157, emphasis added). "This basic thought," he insists, "belongs solely and exclusively to Marx." To achieve this final freedom, they imagine, a workers party must seize the bourgeois state, collectivize property, and thereby eliminate the existence of both the bourgeoisie and the proletariat as classes. The state will be no longer necessary, since its primary function is to manage class conflict, and it will wither away. Marx and Engels say less about the resulting communist society than one would like, but it is clear that communism would be egalitarian, cooperative, and would lack class conflict. Since class conflict is the motor of history, this communist society must be the ultimate one, the end of history (see also Marx, 1976, p. 212).[1]

What actually ended up happening in places like the Soviet Union and China, of course, was that after proletarian hegemony was established by seizing the state, a new ruling class formed, a party-bureaucratic class. The state did not wither; it became totalitarian. The bureaucratic class ruled society with "iron discipline" because the expected end of history never came: these regimes spent all their energy suppressing the reconstitution of capitalist social relations (Badiou, 2008, p. 36). As I said in Chapter 2, the spectacular failure of this end-of-history politics made a big impression on almost every left intellectual that lived through it. Lefebvre, Deleuze and Guattari, Hardt and Negri, Laclau and Mouffe, Rancière: each of them interpreted the lesson of state socialism to be that we must abandon the idea of the end of history, that we should not expect to achieve a final society without conflict. We must instead think differently about politics. We must conceive of our project as a politics without end, an ongoing process, a perpetual struggle. Of course, we can still have a direction, a horizon, a set of values and goals toward which we move, but we can no longer posit a full realization for politics, a final victory, an end of history.

[1] Clearly other readings of these texts are possible. I only want to suggest that this reading is both plausible and in fact quite a common one.

Gramsci's pluralism

Even if the post-war experience of state socialism marked the decisive break for most, it is actually Gramsci that begins to move us away from the end-of-history imagination. He spent much time and effort rejecting the historical determinism of many Marxists of his day, who believed that capitalism was increasingly resolving itself into just two classes, bourgeoisie and proletariat (e.g. Bukharin and Preobrazhensky, 2007; Kautsky, 2010). In this line of thinking, the uncompetitive members of both the petit bourgeoisie and bourgeoisie increasingly drop down into the proletariat, while the peasants are increasingly incorporated into capitalism as workers. That process produces an expanding proletariat that stands starkly against the remaining bourgeoisie, which controls an increasing share of the wealth. As the forces of history cause the proletariat to become ever larger and poorer, to be dominated by an ever smaller and richer bourgeoisie, revolution becomes almost inevitable.

That account may resonate greatly today in 2011, as the Occupy movement lambasts the stark inequality of wealth: the 1% of haves and the 99% of have-nots. However, Gramsci helps us see the current moment in broader historical context. He insisted that there is not just one process at work, one historical tendency that increases inequality and sharpens class conflict. Rather there are many processes; some tend toward proletarianization, but others redistribute and equalize (e.g. Keynesianism), and others fragment classes into a whole array of class fragments (e.g. financial, industrial, and property capital or lumpenproletariat and labor aristocracy). Moreover, non-class identities have proven durable in their political importance (e.g. religion, region, gender, urban–rural, etc.). Gramsci saw that these multiple processes make pluralism a durable feature of politics. His concept of hegemony is therefore designed to take account of this pluralism. Given that pluralism is permanent and capitalism is not tending toward a resolution into two unequal classes, then politics must necessarily operate through complex alliances, by which some parts of society come to rule the rest through coercion and consent. For Gramsci, this coercion and consent is present in all political relations, between the hegemonic bloc and those outside, among groups within the hegemonic bloc, and between leaders of each group and its membership. In short, Gramsci accepts that relations between rulers and ruled are a necessary part of the political field.[2] Politics

---

[2] To be clear, Gramsci does not think political relations are *only* competitive and conflictual. Of course, solidarity and cooperation are also an important part of politics for Gramsci. It is just that he thought cooperation could never be the *only* relation in the polis.

always establishes an order, a relation between leaders and led. As a result, it involves an ongoing contestation, a perpetual struggle for control. Those not part of the hegemonic alliance will always reassert themselves in an attempt to establish a new hegemony. Hegemony is never total or final. Gramsci thus insists that we need to let go of the idea that we can move beyond pluralism and its attendant antagonism, that we can resolve conflict and achieve a society beyond class and beyond politics.

Laclau, Mouffe, and the agon

Laclau and Mouffe, and particularly Mouffe in her own work, draw on Gramsci's vision of ineradicable conflict and develop it radically, to the point where they think of it as an ontological starting point that frames all politics. Among the theorists considered here, they are the strongest bulwark against any foreclosure of the political, any thoughts of a final society without inequality or conflict. For Laclau and Mouffe, political struggle never ends. As we saw in Chapter 2, they argue that relations of difference (us vs. them) always have the potential to turn into relations of conflict (friend vs. enemy). That potential is the ever-present possibility of antagonism in the community, the permanent potential for what Mouffe calls "the political" to return.

Mouffe's analysis draws on Carl Schmitt and his insistence on the centrality of the friend–enemy relation in politics (2002, p. 6). She argues that this relation must be the starting point for thinking properly about democracy. As Laclau and Mouffe (2000, p. xviii) put it, "to believe that a final resolution of conflicts is eventually possible...far from providing the necessary horizon for the democratic project, is to put it at risk." Like Rancière, Mouffe argues that every supposed resolution or "consensus exists as a temporary result of a provisional hegemony, as a stabilization of power...that always entails some form of exclusion" (Mouffe, 1999, p. 756). She lambastes champions of consensus who posit the possibility of creating win-win scenarios, positive-sum games in which everyone benefits. She insists instead that all outcomes are the result of a political struggle that produces both winners and losers. To be clear, in rejecting a final resolution of conflict she does not therefore posit a politics of pure antagonism. What democracy is, for Mouffe, is the *domestication* of antagonism. It is a way to transform antagonism into what she calls "agonism." Antagonism is a relation of hostility in which one party tries to destroy another, to eradicate it from the community. Agonism, which derives from the

Greek *agon*, meaning contest,[3] denotes a relation of adversaries, of two groups whose interests can never be reconciled, whose conflict can never be resolved, but who accept the existence of the other, who in fact *need* each other for the contest to continue. Through this model of the *agon*, politics becomes something like a chess match, and so it makes absurd both consensual and antagonistic approaches to politics. It would make no sense in chess to collaborate with one's opponent to achieve a win-win outcome. The adversarial relation in an *agon* is not a problem for which we must find a solution. It is instead the very purpose of our being together. Similarly, it would be senseless to destroy one's opponent, to eliminate his presence in the game, for that too would make the game impossible.

Imagined this way, as a contest between adversaries, democracy can only be perpetually ongoing. It can only be a struggle that admits no final solution, neither a rational consensus nor a violent purge. To be sure, there will be temporary victories and defeats (i.e. each game in a long series of chess matches), but the *agon* will continue without end. Therefore, Laclau and Mouffe's hegemonic project for democracy is a project to move decisively toward greater democracy, but it never expects to reach absolute democracy as a stable end state. They understand that other hegemonic projects—such as for oligarchy or for heteronomy—will continue to emerge and struggle against democracy. For Laclau and Mouffe, there must always be a lively tension between adversaries, between oligarchy and democracy, between leaders and masses, between hegemony and freedom, between organization and spontaneity. The hegemonic struggle that they urge us to return to does have a direction: it moves toward democracy. But it can never arrive there. It is necessarily a perpetual struggle, a politics without end.

Rancière: recurrent eruptions

Rancière joins Laclau and Mouffe in an energetic critique of consensus, of the idea that we can move beyond conflict and politics. Democracy and consensus are, for Rancière (1999, p. 95), a contradiction in terms. As we saw in Chapter 2, for Rancière all social orders are founded on insubstantial ground; they operate without a pre-given, natural order to the world. Therefore, every order is constructed, it is contingent and always subject to change. At the same time, the *partage du sensible* presents itself as having taken full account of society, as having placed every part into an order that encompasses everything. In *On the Shores of*

---

[3] Nietzsche was also keenly interested in this concept (e.g. "Homer's Contest" in Nietzsche, 1954).

Politics (1995, pp. 1–4), Rancière invokes Plato's image of the polis as a ship that must be steered by expert navigators, guardians trained in the art of governance (Plato, 2008, pp. 488a–489c). For Plato, the guardians use their expertise to overcome the desire of the populace, represented in the metaphor by drunken sailors, and guide the ship safely back to port, back to the solid ground of political order modeled on the unchanging Form of the good polis.[4] If left to their own devices of course, the sailors will wander aimlessly in the fluid and changing medium of the sea, and never arrive on the shores of politics.

For Rancière, by contrast, politics *are* the sea: a fluid, shifting, changeable force, one that is unordered and unpredictable.[5] Every *partage du sensible* presents itself as a solid shore to return to, a fixed Form of the good city where our journey will end. Rancière insists that these shores are always false. They are nothing more than a movie set, a temporary façade that obscures the real *an-arkhê* at the root of human communities. This *an-arkhê*, in the form of democracy, will always reemerge and pull back the curtain. The democratic desires of the drunken sailors will always present themselves and refuse to go along; they will defy the rational wisdom of the guardians and their police order. Rancière insists that no *partage du sensible* is actually the Form of the just city, that no guardians are wise enough to develop a police order that actually does take everything into account.

To this point, Rancière and (Laclau and) Mouffe are in quite close agreement. However, they part company significantly on the question of a new democratic order. Laclau and Mouffe think democracy can be pursued as a hegemonic project, even if they agree with Rancière that such projects are never final or total. However, Rancière does not think democracy can establish any hegemony, even if it is provisional and contested. For Rancière, democracy is by its nature *anti*-hegemonic. It destabilizes all stability, all police orders. Democracy can therefore never be *counter*-hegemonic; it does not seek to establish an alternative order. Democratic eruptions manifest themselves, show the *partage du sensible* to be a sham, and reveal the real ground of society, its fundamental equality and *an-arkhê*. They do not then go on to establish a democratic order. Rather, for Rancière society operates through an ongoing series of events in which democracy disrupts the police, and then a new police forms in response to that disruption. Democracy is very much part of a perpetual process, an ongoing series of eruptions, events, struggles. It

---

[4] It is surely no accident that in the first line of the book Socrates tells us "I went down to the Piraeus," the port of ancient Athens, and that the dialogues in the book take place there, in the borderlands between sea and shore.

[5] There is more than a hint here of Deleuze and Guattari's notion of smooth space and "the real inorganization" of desire (1977, pp. 309, 328).

cannot arrive at an end. He is adamant that democracy is never a destination. "Anything else paraded under this banner," he avers, "is either a trick, a school or military unit" (1995, p. 84). This way of understanding democracy helps us see that all the current talk about places like Egypt and Tunisia carrying out an "orderly transition" to democracy entirely misunderstands what democracy is. Such pronouncements confuse a liberal-democratic state (which is in every way a police order) with democracy as Rancière understands it (for a further development of this argument, see Rose, 2011).

Rancière is so strident in his desire to reject seeing democracy as an end that he is mostly unwilling to consider the possibility of a political sea change, of a breakthrough beyond the *partage du sensible*, in which equality is pervasive but not total and we must perpetually ward off the reimposition of the police order. Here he parts company again with Laclau and Mouffe, but also with Deleuze and Guattari, who envision a breakthrough beyond capitalism and the state, a new land in which flight is generalized as a pervasive condition. Rancière is extremely circumspect about such a possibility. He mostly limits his vision to one in which the *partage du sensible* will always be reinstituted after each eruption of democracy. And yet, despite his circumspection, we can find in Rancière, here and there, a glimmer of more. In an interview in 2000, he suggests that the process of subjectification—through which the part that has no part becomes aware of itself as a part and instantiates a democratic politics—is not always the same. Rather there are degrees of subjectification. A more minor subjectification would see the insurgent part merely taking up its place in a new police order. But he hints here that there could be a fuller degree of subjectification that is capable of more. There is the possibility of "arousing political subjects in the full sense—subjects capable of tracing a connection between all instances of subjectification and attaching them to the great signifiers of collective life" (2000, p. 20). We see an echo here of Deleuze and Guattari's hope that lines of flight can connect with each other and create a breakthrough, more generalized political shift beyond the police order.

But this is just one line in an interview. The bulk of Rancière's work suggests a more modest political program of ongoing disturbance and resettling. The most likely plan of action we would derive from his idea of democracy is to continually reinscribe equality on the body of society, to always act politically *as if* equality were already present. Moreover, we would work to discover and nurture emerging articulations of equality by others. For Rancière, this is what democracy is: never an end, never a state of being in which democracy pervades, but rather an ongoing project to conjure the community of equals by declaring its presence, assuming equality, and forcing politics to occur.

Lefebvre: democracy as the struggle for democracy

Lefebvre would appear to be the most likely to embrace the idea of the end of politics. He is the one, of the scholars discussed here, who works most closely and explicitly with Lenin and Marx, the latter of whom, Lefebvre says, offers a political theory that "aims at the end of all politics" (2009, p. 88). Moreover, Lefebvre insists on the continued relevance of the concept of the dictatorship of the proletariat and the withering away of the state and capitalist social relations (see especially 2009, pp. 70–74). He is clear that he thinks these events are politically necessary. Because of his experience with a deeply Stalinist French Communist Party (as well as both actual Stalinism in the Soviet Union and the extremely powerful French state), he places particular emphasis on the demise of the state. His work on the state is designed to move us decisively beyond the state. Moreover, it is tempting to understand his idea of generalized autogestion as a total solution, as an end of politics. Still another potential item of evidence is the way in *The Urban Revolution* he conceptualizes urban society as an epochal shift beyond the capitalist city, as something that looks to be a utopian vision of a city pervaded by interaction, cooperation, and solidarity.

However, it is precisely in the pages of *The Urban Revolution* that we encounter a Lefebvre who, while he may still feel a lingering temptation to embrace the end of politics, is far too disciplined a thinker to do so. It is in that book that he develops his methodological concept of transduction. He posits urban society as a virtual object, as a horizon toward which we must move but that we can never reach. Urban society is not at all an ideal, a *kallipolis*, a land beyond politics (2003b, pp. 67–68). It is rather an extrapolation in thought of the best qualities of the existing city, the city we already inhabit. It is a way to draw out and magnify the fledgling connections of communal solidarity, the nascent attempts at autogestion. Lefebvre acknowledges that transduction is a utopian approach, but he means "utopian" in a very particular way. It is an approach that "attempts to open a path to the possible, to explore and delineate a landscape that is not merely part of the 'real,' the accomplished....It is a utopian critique because it steps back from the real without, however, losing sight of it" (2003b, pp. 6–7). His approach creates the virtual object of urban society in order to impel us toward it, beyond the limits of the capitalist city that make it currently impossible. It cuts a path out of the "real" and toward the possible, toward urban society, but it does not, and cannot, ever arrive there. In this way, Lefebvre's utopia, his virtual object, is "an illuminating virtuality already present" (2003b, p. 131). It helps us see a present and future urban society amid the blinding light of the industrial city.

Urban society never becomes actual in every aspect; it is rather a perpetual journey we set ourselves on. But unlike Rancière, Lefebvre thinks it is possible for the qualities of urban society (encounter, cooperation, self-realization) to become pervasive, to be generalized throughout urban space. He even hopes these qualities can develop to the point where they occlude and even stifle the features of the capitalist city (segregation, competition, consumption). What he has in mind here is not so much the hegemony of urban society, and still less its dictatorship. It is more that the relations associated with urban society pervade the city. He imagines urban society's fecund growth and spread, burgeoning to the point where it becomes so abundant it overwhelms the capitalist city. The natural metaphor is apt here: a rhizome does not take over a garden in an intentional effort to dominate or kill other plants. It just grows because it possesses a drive to flourish. Similarly, urban society does not grow *in order to* destroy the industrial city; it merely follows its own *physis*, its own will to thrive.

For Lefebvre, the process of autogestion works in very much the same way that urban society does. Autogestion is necessarily embedded in urban society, because the latter involves urban inhabitants managing the space of the city for themselves. But urban society is also embedded in a generalized autogestion, as people everywhere take control again over not only urban space, but all the sites where social relations occur: the factory, the state, the school, the home, the farm, and so on. This interlacing of urban society and autogestion means autogestion is also a virtual object; it is a horizon toward which we move. It is not an end point but a perpetual struggle for autonomous self-management and against heteronomy (Lefebvre, 2009, pp. 134–136). Similarly, Lefebvre hopes that autogestion can grow and spread so much that heteronomy is choked off, to the point that it withers. This is how his idea of the withering away of the state is best understood. It is not that a workers' party seizes the state, abolishes classes, and allows the state to wither away. It is rather that autogestion pervades society: it generalizes itself from below, spreads through the grassroots of society, and makes the state no longer necessary. Generalized autogestion would thus be a breakthrough in Deleuze and Guattari's sense, or a political sea change as in Laclau and Mouffe. But it is never the end of politics. We must always expect the forces of heteronomy—capital and the state first among them—to discover new ways to reassert their control over society. They don't so much wither *away*; they simply wither. And so we must perpetually ward off their reemergence. "There is one path and one practice that may be opposed to the omnipotence of the State," he writes, "that of autogestion" (2009, p. 134). But autogestion, like all human activity, still carries within itself a tendency toward bureaucratization, a latent desire to form routinized structures that concentrate decision-making authority. Autogestion must always "confront a State that, even weakened, even shaken, even withering away in a sense declared by Marx, will always be able to attempt to reassert itself, to consolidate its own apparatus, to turn autogestion into an ideology of the State..." (2009, p. 147). The same is of course true for capitalist social relations: worker-run factories will always be subject to the reassertion of property rights. Autogestion is thus a perpetual struggle. "Far from being established once and for all," Lefebvre says, "autogestion is itself the site and the stake of struggle.... [It] does not provide a model, does not trace a line. It points to a way, and thus to a strategy" (2009, p. 135). It proposes, in short, a path to the possible.

Having established that autogestion is perpetual struggle, Lefebvre then goes on to link that struggle explicitly and closely to democracy. He conceives of democracy in nearly the same terms, as an unending process. "Autogestion must continually be enacted. The same is true of democracy, which is never a 'condition' but a struggle" (2009, p. 135). He speaks of democracy in much the same terms as he does of autogestion in the quote at the end of the previous paragraph. "Democracy," he writes (2009, p. 61),

> is nothing other than the struggle for democracy. The struggle for democracy is the movement itself. Many democrats imagine that democracy is a type of stable condition toward which we can tend, toward which we must tend. No. Democracy is the movement. And the movement is the forces in action. And democracy is the struggle for democracy, which is to say the very movement of social forces; it is a permanent struggle and it is even a struggle against the State that emerges from democracy. There is no democracy without a struggle against the democratic State itself, which tends to consolidate itself as a block, to affirm itself as a whole, become monolithic and to smother the society out of which it develops.

For Lefebvre, democracy, like autogestion, is never a destination but a horizon, a "permanent struggle" toward democracy and away from oligarchy, toward autonomy and away from heteronomy, toward urban society and away from the industrial city.[6]

---

[6] Subcomandante Marcos echoes Lefebvre on democracy: "We are not those who wait, naively, for justice to come from above, when it only comes from below; for liberty, which can only be achieved with everyone; for democracy, which is the ground for all and is fought for all the time" (2001, p. 159).

Deleuze and Guattari: a plane of flows

Like Lefebvre, Deleuze and Guattari have a very complex relation to the question of the end of politics. They are much less willing than Lefebvre to draw explicitly on *The Communist Manifesto* or Marxism-Leninism. With Lefebvre, they reject the state as a temporary vehicle, as a lever that moves society in a radical new direction. However, at the same time, their imagination is explicitly revolutionary. Unlike Rancière, they are not satisfied with periodic upheavals that can only recrystallize into a new social order. They seek a radical transformation of society, advancing a vision of "so many local fires patiently kindled for a generalized explosion" (1977, p. 137). This explosion cannot be contained within the existing order. It is not the substitution of one bloc with another. It is rather the transformation of order-as-such, an uprising to overthrow the operation of control and domination per se.

The new land they aim at is a land paradoxically made up of deterritorialized elements, of flows and escapes. It is a land beyond capitalism and beyond the state, and so in a way it resembles the communist end-of-politics in Marx and Engels. But this land is not an end point, a final resting place for the community. It is rather made up of flight, of becoming. It is literally vibrating with motion. Though they call it a land, they imagine it to be much more like Rancière's sea, rather than a shore. Recall how Deleuze and Guattari imagine that elements of desiring-production, captured in the social order, will detach themselves, deterritorialize, and pursue lines of flight. The most successful of these flights is able to carry a piece of the system off with it as it escapes. "The revolutionary knows that escape is revolutionary... provided one sweeps away the social cover on leaving, or causes a piece of the system to get lost in the shuffle" (1977, p. 277). Lines of flight consist not so much in "running away from the world but rather in causing runoffs, as when you drill a hole in a pipe; there is no social system that does not leak from all directions" (1987, p. 204).

This deterritorialized desire, once free, is impelled to connect with other desires-in-flight; it is driven to stream its flow together with other flows. A large enough flow can overwhelm the system; it can gather enough speed to break out of the socius, to crash through the wall that forms the absolute limit of the social order. "What matters is to break through the wall" (1977, p. 277), to the other side, to the new land. But once they break through, these elements do not rest. They must remain in motion. They cannot consider themselves to have achieved a final victory, to have arrived at their destination. Coming to rest would mean recapture, reterritorialization, reforming a new socius, a new police order. They must always move, always be on the run. They must always be in the process of becoming democratic, never thinking they have achieved a "democracy." As they move, as whole multitudes of fleeing and streamed-together desire travel restlessly, they will begin to trace out a new land. The lines, which they never cease drawing, will become, when taken together, a plane. This new land is not made up of capture, of being, of fixity. It is therefore not a *territory* in Deleuze and Guattari's sense. Properly speaking, escaped elements of desire are not reterritorialized in the new land. They do not adopt a new form of being, a role in a new socius. They do not come to rest at a point, but remain on a line, in flight. A new land made up of unrecaptured autonomous flows of desiring-production. Deleuze and Guattari see Proust as a model for their project:

> The reader always risks stopping at a given plane saying yes, *that* is where Proust is explaining himself. But the narrator-spider never ceases undoing webs and planes, resuming the journey, watching for the signs or the indices that operate like machines and that will cause him to go on further....The narrator continues his own affair, until he reaches the *unknown country*, his own, the *unknown land*, which alone is created by his own work in progress....A new Earth where desire functions according to its molecular elements and flows...an intensive voyage that undoes all the lands for the benefit of the one it is creating (1977, p. 318).

The lands the narrator undoes are territories, whereas the land he is creating is something more like a plane of flows where desire functions according to the impetus it gives itself.

But this unknown country, even if it is on the other side of the wall, even if it is beyond the absolute limit of the state and capital, is always hounded. The forces of heteronomy and oligarchy can never be finally eradicated. Desire can preserve its autonomy in the new land only by connecting to other flows and forming an aggregate of liberated elements so large that they pervade the new land. When heteronomy reasserts itself, liberated elements do not suppress it or dominate it. They do not enter into any relation with it at all. Rather they continually ward it off, flee from it, disengage from it. They remain free by escaping, not by confronting or dominating. The new land therefore involves a process of continuous escape in order to remain free. In that way, it is very similar to Lefebvre's autogestion, in which people must continually struggle to renew their commitment to govern themselves. In neither case is there an end of politics, a once-and-for-all victory. Elements in the new land must always remain in active flight; they must always ward off recapture, the state, and the reformation of the capitalist axiomatic. Desire must "never cease undoing webs and planes"; it must continually reappropriate the new land and reassert its own autonomy.

We should be careful not to let Deleuze and Guattari's imagery overwhelm our thinking here. I think we should read their talk of flight and new lands as metaphors, which is to say we should not understand them as saying we must undertake actual movement, or really become nomads. That is one possible way to do it. But I think we should understand them to mean that we can be in flight, on the line, and constructing a new land even if we remain in the same physical place. That is, to escape the state apparatus of capture does not necessitate wandering in the desert in a land that is not subject to state control (if one even exists). Similarly, Lefebvre is not saying we need to create urban society as a different physical city. Rather, our struggles to forge urban society, or a new land, can very much be, and usually are, a struggle to revolutionize the space we are currently living in. Again, such a reading does not exclude a strategy of actual nomadism and movement, it just affirms that such nomadism would be the exception, that we will almost always flee while staying put.

Conclusion

Chapter 2 proposed that a strong desire for democracy animates the political theory of each of the thinkers we have been examining. Chapter 3 has tried to show that each of them imagines democracy to be a perpetual struggle for (or toward) democracy. They agree that democracy is not an ending place, a *telos* of politics. While I have not addressed Hardt and Negri's position in detail in this chapter, they concur in broad outline that democracy is a process. Their absolute democracy, in which the global multitude forms into a body and governs itself, is not meant as an end state we expect to reach, but as a horizon or "North Star" to move toward (2004, p. 241).

Part of the reason why there is broad agreement that democracy is a process rather than an end state is that such is simply the zeitgeist of the post-Stalinist and post-1968 era. But I think there is another reason, perhaps an even more important one. When we think democracy radically, as these theorists do, when we conceive of it in its fullest form, as the rule of everyone by everyone, we understand the deep difficulty in realizing this radical democracy in practice. *Being* democratic, truly democratic, is too intense an experience to maintain. It is too overwhelming a condition to *be* in. *Becoming* democratic is therefore the only option available to us. Becoming democratic means to be continually fleeing oligarchy and pushing ourselves toward the horizon of democracy. It means to seek and learn to recognize the democratic practices that are already taking place and to nurture them and help them grow.

It is the same with the effort to be autonomous. In *Fundamental Principles of the Metaphysics of Morals*, Kant admits that it is not possible to be purely autonomous (Kant, 2006). He only wants us to *imagine* ourselves in a Kingdom of Ends where we are purely autonomous, where we give ourselves the laws. He then enjoins us to use this image to guide our behavior in the real world. Moreover, autonomy as a pure state is a chimera from the point of view of Nietzsche's individual as multiplicity, which we saw in Chapter 2. If each person (and, by extension, group) is a loose agglomeration of multiple wills that opens out into the world and connects with myriad others, then the distinction between *auto* and *hetero* becomes unavoidably muddy. We cannot any longer imagine a pure autonomy or pure heteronomy. Even so, Nietzsche's conception does not *obliterate* the idea of the self. As we can see in the Jackson Pollack painting, each person still retains some consistency and can still be distinguished from others. There is therefore still a sense in which we can speak meaningfully of autonomy and distinguish it from heteronomy. We can still judge perfectly well between a polity with relatively more autonomous relations and a polity with relatively more heterogeneous ones.[7] But it is impossible to ever be fully autonomous. The political imperative can only ever be to struggle to *become* autonomous, to flee heteronomy and move toward the horizon of autonomy to the extent we can.

This notion of democracy as becoming, as a constant struggle toward democracy, helps diminish the debate between hegemonic and non-hegemonic approaches we saw in Chapter 2, especially that between Laclau and Mouffe and Deleuze and Guattari. That is because everyone in the debate agrees that domination and hierarchy are ineradicable. None is expecting or aiming at a polity in which those relations are permanently absent. Rather, all agree we must engage in a perpetual struggle to move away from domination, heteronomy, and oligarchy, and toward solidarity, autonomy, and democracy. In those rare instances where we achieve a breakthrough, we must continue to ward off the re-formation of oligarchy and heteronomy. Laclau and Mouffe would have us move toward democracy by means of hegemonic struggle, by instituting a new hegemony that moves society in the direction of democracy, rather than in the direction of oligarchy. For Deleuze and Guattari, Lefebvre, and

---

[7] And so it is a red herring for Spivak (1988, p. 71) to worry that any talk of someone speaking or managing their affairs *for themselves* reinstates the sovereign subject of the West and "leads to an essentialist, utopian politics." I have tried to show how we are perfectly capable of rejecting the idea of the independent, atomistic individual and yet still distinguishing meaningfully between autonomy and heteronomy.

Hardt and Negri, democratization must instead be pursued by other, non-hegemonic means (e.g. flight or self-management from the grass-roots). Rancière also rejects embracing hegemonic relations, but he does not offer the possibility of democracy becoming generalized such that it pervades the social body.

But even if we cannot arrive at absolute democracy and the end of politics, even if we cannot *be* democratic, Lefebvre's method of transduction still urges us to imagine democracy in its full-blown form. As we saw in Hardt and Negri, Spinoza's absolute democracy operates as a virtual object that allows us to articulate an idea of the democracy we want to move toward, to imagine a possible beyond what is currently possible. We articulate it by extrapolating from already-existing democratic practices, practices that constitute a present desire for democracy, a real but inchoate absolute democracy. This virtual object helps us better see the democracy that is already here. Democracy can and does emerge and become actual; it can even envelop us for a brief period. There are spectacular examples, like Tiananmen Square in 1989, or Tahrir Square in 2011, but there are also smaller, more everyday cases, too numerous to count, of people taking up their own power again. These examples don't last. They don't form up into a stable absolute democracy with enduring procedures and institutions. They appear, make an impression, and recede. What we must do, as Calvino advises, is to use the virtual object of democracy to help us "seek and learn to recognize" actual democracy when it emerges, whether it is spectacular or more mundane. If we are not looking for it, or are not very good at seeing it, it will pass unnoticed.

So far what I have said in this conclusion aligns with Rancière's democracy, a democracy that emerges, that *may* make a difference to the social order, but then relents and dissipates. But we need to go further than Rancière does. With the other thinkers, we should press for a breakthrough, a generalized democratic explosion. That is the importance of the second part of Calvino's exhortation: "Help them endure, give them space." If we seek a breakthrough, we must help emergent democracy connect with other eruptions so that it is able not just to survive, but to grow and spread. We need to encourage each flow to steam together with others, for each to augment and complement the others. This would mean taking that one glimmer in Rancière, when he wonders about subjectifications connecting with other subjectifications, and multiplying it exponentially. It is not hard to find an example to model this on. In the summer of 2009, Iranians reminded the world what it looks like for people to desire and demand democracy in the face of an authoritarian regime. In 2011, people in Tunisia, Egypt, Libya, Bahrain, Yemen, Oman, Jordan, Syria, and Russia showed similar faith and courage. Also in

2011, people in Spain, Greece, Israel, Chile, Britain, and the United States followed suit in the context of liberal-democratic states under the rule of financial capital.

In all these places, for shorter or longer periods, absolute democracy emerged, took on life, and then exhausted itself. But we should not conclude with Rancière that such exhaustion was inevitable. The way the Arab Uprising spread, quickly, from place to place should be enough for us to realize that the kind of rhizomatic connections that Deleuze and Guattari speak of are possible. We cannot limit ourselves to a horizon that sees democracy as an occasional event that may or may not have an impact on the social order. That horizon, Rancière's horizon, would accept less than we are capable of—less than is possible. It would be akin to heeding pragmatic pronouncements that tell us only some things are possible, that advise us to take certain political goals off the table and banish them from our imagination. This pragmatism is merely laziness. It is giving in to the seductions of heteronomy and oligarchy. It is an excuse to settle for passivity under the guise of being smart, strategic, and pragmatic.[8] Our horizon, our virtual object, should be absolute democracy. Because it is a horizon, we should understand that we will not reach it. But we *can* aim at a breakthrough, a new land, a generalized explosion of becoming-democratic. In 2011 more than ever, in squares all over Europe and the Middle East, we reminded ourselves how much more democracy we are capable of than we thought. This reminder should embolden us to go further, to build on the successes of the Arab Uprising, the Greek and Spanish Revolutions, and the Occupy movement to imagine a far more ambitious virtual object of democracy than we ever have before.

Lastly, perhaps I could just add one more word on behalf of space. Though the other theorists are inconsistent with respect to their analysis of space, Lefebvre is clear that democracy must involve not just the reappropriation of our power but also the reappropriation of our space. And he imagines that reappropriation radically: not just seizing and occupying space, but inhabiting it fully. And not just using existing space, but deciding for ourselves how space is to be produced: a generalized spatial autogestion. The uprisings I mention made great strides, strides toward spatial autogestion, strides no one expected. Without exception, each of the uprisings decided it was essential to draw people together into an important central place, an urban place, in which they could encounter each other, discuss what they wanted, and decide what to do next. Spaces like Pearl, Tahrir, Syntagma, Sol, and Zuccotti were not just metaphors for these movements, they were full participants as well. That is why

---

[8] It is, in short, to think like Barack Obama.

each space was struggled over so acutely. When they were evicted from the Puerta del Sol in Madrid, for example, the Spanish *indignados* felt they absolutely must retake the square. They felt Sol was *necessary* for their revolution. Not only was it a functional space for meeting and discussing, but also the ability to occupy it was a symbolic demonstration of their determination and their power. One of the *indignados'* main messages was "*no nos representan*" or "they [the government] do not represent us [the people]." Presenting themselves in the main square of Madrid, filling it spectacularly with their bodies in a way that seemed to mean that every Spaniard was filling all of Spain, people showed their determination to reclaim Spain, to void the contract, to rise up and begin to decide for themselves. Moreover, beyond that message to Leviathan, the act of gathering in and inhabiting the Puerta del Sol was also a way for *indignados* to find each other, to discover the many others who felt the same way, and to begin to construct their revolution together. To stand in the middle of Sol and be among so many others meant no longer to have to accept suffering as an isolated individual under austerity. It meant to connect with others as participants in a shared project to transform Spain. That was a principal outcome of the experience of Puerta del Sol, and it was the meaning of the sign that hung for a time over the entrance to the Sol metro station: *La revolucion estaba en nuestros corazones y ahora vuela libre in las calles*: the revolution was in our hearts, but now it flies free in the streets.

4

Becoming Active

Whether I shall turn out to be the hero of my own life, or whether that station will be held by anybody else, these pages must show.
— Charles Dickens, *David Copperfield*

Learning how to think really means learning how to exercise some control over how and what you think. It means being conscious and aware enough to choose what you pay attention to and to choose how you construct meaning from experience. Because if you cannot exercise this kind of choice in adult life, you will be totally hosed.
— David Foster Wallace, Commencement Address at Kenyon College, 2005[1]

On its face, Dickens' quote seems absurd. How could somebody other than David Copperfield be the hero of his own life? But Dickens is suggesting that the question is an open one. Moreover, he proposes that the answer lies in how David lives his life, in what choices he will make. David Foster Wallace says something similar. They are both reminding us that the question of whether we will become autonomous and active is an open one, and the answer is up to us.

So let's go back again to the beginning. People are the source of all economic production and all political power. Becoming democratic is therefore a process by which people reclaim their own power. To an extent, that process entails a struggle against an outside power. It involves

[1] Published as Wallace (2009).

The Down-Deep Delight of Democracy, First Edition. Mark Purcell.
© 2013 John Wiley & Sons, Ltd. Published 2013 by John Wiley & Sons, Ltd.

critiquing, resisting, and destroying practices and institutions of oligarchy and heteronomy. But if people are the source of all power, then they must have created these institutions. Something inside them, some element of their self, desired these institutions. And so the struggle of people against oligarchy and heteronomy is also very much a struggle within. It is a struggle to reclaim the power that we also want to give away. We desire to be ruled, to be relieved of the burden of ruling ourselves. We desire inertia, inactivity, passivity, to have someone else make decisions for us. Our desire to be ruled results in our creating structures of heteronomy and oligarchy for ourselves. As we saw in Chapter 1, Deleuze and Guattari (and Foucault, in introducing them) are concerned about this desire within us, our desire for fascism, as they phrase it. Similarly, Giorgio Agamben (2009, p. 23) worries about the rise of

the harmless citizen of postindustrial democracies...who readily does everything that he is asked to do...he leaves his everyday gestures and his health, his amusements and his occupations, his diet and his desires, to be commanded and controlled in the smallest detail by apparatuses.

In the contemporary global North, the desire to be ruled manifests as a taste for the soft, subtle, and seductive oligarchy of liberal democracy and consumer capitalism. That is the oligarchy we live under; that is the fascism we desire to give ourselves to. So the project of democracy, I argue, isn't so much the project to confront a power wielded by malevolent forces beyond our control. Rather, democracy is a struggle against our own desire for oligarchy. It is a struggle to reappropriate our own power by reactivating our desire for democracy. Becoming democratic means to reconnect with our desire to rule ourselves, to nurture it, to help it grow, and to give it space.

To be clear, in taking the position that the struggle is within us, I am not reproducing the neoliberal argument that people should take personal responsibility, that they should work hard and pull themselves up by their own bootstraps. That vision accepts unfettered capitalism as the society in which we can be most free, which is absurd. Instead, I am simply following Hobbes and Marx in accepting that the structures of power that constrain us, especially the state and capital, are necessarily alienated forms of our own power. They can never be a source of power on their own. As a result, then, we must get serious about understanding how is it we come to surrender our power, and we must discover how we can reappropriate it. Of course, it is certainly true that the structures of power, even if they are made up of our own power, can and do take on a life of their own, to an extent. Once our power has been alienated to the apparatuses, they can use it to ensure that we remain willing subjects. Capitalism thus actively seduces us with the idea that capital, rather than labor, is the source of wealth and economic growth. The state actively persuades us that it is identical to the public, that it exists only to serve our interests, that we would descend into chaos without it. Apple actively cajoles us into believing we cannot survive without an iPad. The whole complex of strategies that work to keep us passive, consuming, and governed are what Guy Debord so brilliantly analyzed in *The Society of the Spectacle.*

So, I acknowledge the importance of structures of power and the way they work to prevent us from becoming active. But I want to emphasize that in order to rule us, these structures must connect with a desire inside us, a desire to be ruled, to not be burdened with decisions about production, or about public affairs. Apple can't live if we don't desire their products, and they spend enormous amounts of money to cultivate that desire, to make us believe that we can't live without them. Similarly, the state can't live without our desire to be ruled. It seems to me there are two ways to respond to this problem. The first is to confront the structures on their own terms, with their own forms of power (money, laws, violence, etc.), to smash them, and then to live freely in their absence. The second way would be to recognize that they need us more than we need them. That is, they are dependent on us because we are the source of their power, and so we can, if we choose, starve them of that power so that they wither and die. We can starve capital by refusing to think that we can't live without it. We can starve the state by refusing to think that we cannot govern ourselves. Choosing to engage the struggle within is not a way to *ignore* structures of power, to act as if they did not exist. Rather, it is simply a way to adopt that second response to the problem: to struggle to reappropriate our own power. We do this in order to live well, to become the hero of our own lives. In so doing, we also deprive the structures of power of their source of life. We are perfectly able to live without capital, the state, and the iPad. But it requires becoming active, learning about our own power, reclaiming it, and using it to rule ourselves.

Popular Activation

In *Utilitarianism,* John Stuart Mill explores this question of becoming active, of how we might develop ourselves most fully as human beings. He writes that the

> capacity for the nobler feelings is in most natures a very tender plant, easily killed, not only by hostile influences, but by mere want of sustenance; and in the majority of young persons it speedily dies away if the

occupations to which their position in life has devoted them, and the society into which it has thrown them, are not favorable to keeping that higher capacity in exercise. Men lose their high aspirations as they lose their intellectual tastes, because they have not time or opportunity for indulging them; and they addict themselves to inferior pleasures, not because they deliberately prefer them, but because they are either the only ones to which they have access or the only ones which they are any longer capable of enjoying (1979, p. 10).

Mill is saying that we must actively practice our "capacity for the nobler feelings." In the context of democracy, this means we must keep "in exercise" our desire and ability to rule ourselves. Mill suggests that ability can be actively suppressed by outside forces, but it is even more common for it to atrophy through disuse. As a population, we tend to construct for ourselves oligarchical environments so that we do not need to exercise our democratic faculties, and as a result they wither. In a similar way, all the theorists we have examined agree that democracy requires popular activation. They all imply that people must experience some measure of awakening, a coming into awareness that initiates and sustains the project of governing themselves. Of course, there are differences in how each thinker conceives of what it means to become active, but there is broad agreement that becoming democratic means necessarily becoming active as well.

Gramsci, for example, insists that a party leadership is essential. There must be "a permanently organized and long prepared force," a cadre of informed leaders that pays close attention to changes in the political economy and is ready to act decisively when conditions are ripe (2000, p. 209). As a result, there is in Gramsci an enduring element of heteronomy, a built-in passivity through which people give some of the responsibility for political awareness and judgment over to a small set of leaders they trust. At the same time, Gramsci also insists that the "real movement" is driven by the power of the party membership. For him the real engine of history, of political change, is the spontaneous desire of people. When his "democratic centralism" is functioning well, there is an active energy at the grassroots, strong "thrusts from below" that both energize and direct the movement (1971, p. 188). That energy and direction is critical, he argues, because when it is lacking, when people fail to take an active role in governing the movement, it regresses into "bureaucratic centralism," into an ossified oligarchy in which party leaders rule with impunity (1971, p. 189). The tragedy of the Soviet bloc.

Gramsci gives quite a lot of thought to the consciousness of the masses. He seeks a way to engage their current understanding of the world, what he calls "common sense," in order to produce an understanding that apprehends class relations, what he calls "good sense." For Gramsci good sense already exists, as a "healthy nucleus," inside common sense (1971, p. 328). It is merely a question of drawing it out, of making it more explicit. He thinks education is central to this process. But it is not education where a vanguard comes down off the mountain to give enlightenment to the masses. Rather, education works to "demonstrate that 'everyone' is a philosopher and that it is not a question of introducing from scratch a scientific form of thought into everyone's individual life, but of renovating and making 'critical' an already existing activity" (1971, p. 330).[2] Education is thus a process through which masses and leadership together develop their existing collective intellectual capacity and political awareness. Against the hegemony of bourgeois ideology, in which the good is defined to be what the bourgeoisie considers good, the masses undergo an "intellectual and moral reformation," through which they produce a new psychology, a new way of thinking and feeling specific to the working class (2000, p. 350). That reformation produces a new popular awareness, it gives "a personality to the amorphous mass element. This means working to produce … intellectuals of a new type which arise directly out of the masses, but remain in contact with them to become, as it were, the whalebone in the corset" (2000, p. 340). While there is again an element of oligarchy in this vision, nevertheless Gramsci considers it essential that an awakening produces new kinds of subjects that understand the world differently than they did under bourgeois hegemony. He argues that Fordist capitalism strives to produce nothing less than "a new type of man" whose desire (for drinking, gambling, carousing, etc.) has been strictly controlled (2000, p. 282).[3] This "specific mode of thinking and feeling life" that Fordism inculcates must be transformed, redirected to produce subjects that reclaim control over their own thoughts and feelings. Out of that new psychology can grow a collective will that animates and guides the hegemonic movement, albeit, for him, always in collaboration with the leadership (1971, p. 133).

Laclau and Mouffe again push Gramsci further with respect to the question of activation. They build on his arguments against economism and historical determinism to develop a radical anti-essentialist understanding of politics. For Laclau and Mouffe, there are no pre-given or fixed political identities (especially those around class). Rather, each group's sense of itself must be worked out in the course of its political struggle (Laclau and Mouffe, 2000, p. xvii). Consequently, the agenda

---

[2] It is easy to see here much of Rancière's (2009) argument about the emancipated spectator, which I discuss later in this chapter.

[3] Gramsci here offers an analysis that very much prefigures what Foucault (esp. 1990) would produce many years later.

and desires of each group are also contingent: people do not simply receive their agenda directly from their class position; rather, they must actively work out what they want as they go along. In order to build a hegemonic politics, each democratic struggle must begin to link up with other struggles, each of which is itself working out who it is and what it wants. This process of connecting, of joining up with other groups to make common cause, further defines each group. Moreover, together these groups also construct a sense of themselves as a common entity, they forge together a new collective will or common sense for the hegemonic movement (1985, pp. 67, 181–193). Since for Laclau and Mouffe there is no pre-existing economic base that produces ineluctable forces that move history, then politics must be driven by active, creative actors, actors who are always already struggling, inventing, relating, and defining themselves.

But Laclau and Mouffe don't say much about how these active subjects *become* active, what initiated their struggle and how they maintain its force. These subjects are always already moving when we meet them, already struggling for democracy in their own particular way. Laclau and Mouffe don't much explore the line between action and inaction, between those people that mobilize and those that do not. Mostly they focus on the question of how already-active struggles can link up into hegemonic articulations, and so in their work, activation, and struggle are more assumed than analyzed.[4] Moreover, while Laclau and Mouffe pay great heed to the way mobilized groups relate to each other, they pay less attention to the relations *within* each group. While they do make brief mention of the importance of "true participation by all subjects in decisions about what is to be produced" (1985, p. 178), mostly they treat each group as a black box and don't interrogate the relations between a group's leadership and its base that so concerned Gramsci. As a result of this inattention, they appear to assume by default some form of Gramsci's democratic centralism, conceding that each group will have to have leaders and led in some way, even if the specifics of those relations will be worked out in context. In Laclau and Mouffe, the group is active, but the quantity and quality of activation in each member remains unclear. To be sure, this is not so much a failing in Laclau and Mouffe as it is a lacuna. It just means we need to look elsewhere to understand activation at this more micro scale.

---

[4] Even when they discuss the moment antagonism emerges, when a relation of us vs. them becomes a relation of friend vs. enemy (1985, pp. 153–154), they don't say much about what's happening in the minds of the agents. It is in some ways an almost actorless landscape, one they render in the passive voice, speaking about "relations of subordination which have transformed themselves into sites of antagonisms" and so on.

Deleuze and Guattari, Hardt and Negri, and Lefebvre all go further in investigating the issue of popular activation. For Deleuze and Guattari, desire must become extraordinarily active as it flees the apparatuses of capture, joins up with other deterritorialized flows, and traces out a new land of becoming. In Hardt and Negri, we move toward democracy when the global multitude forms itself into a body, reappropriates its own power, and begins to govern itself. For Lefebvre, the core of democracy, autogestion, occurs when a group actively takes up the project of managing the conditions of their own existence (2009, p. 135). For Lefebvre, the process of becoming democratic is virtually the same thing as the process of becoming active. Becoming democratic, moving toward generalized autogestion, requires a concomitant generalized activation. It requires a political awakening. His "new contract of citizenship" is a starting point, a proposal around which a thorough-going "renewal of political life" can take place (2003a, p. 253). This renewal will awaken and activate people; it will initiate a movement that "transcends ideologies so that new forces can come into action, uniting and exerting pressure on the established order" (2003a, p. 253). It will initiate a perpetual struggle for autogestion, a project of becoming democratic and becoming active.

Of course, all this insistence on activation begs the question: *how* do people become active? And a related question: why aren't they more active already? Why do they accept oligarchy, why do they agree to be ruled? The rest of this chapter addresses these questions. While Lefebvre is eloquent in articulating the necessity for popular activation, he is of very little help in understanding how to bring it about. In *The Urban Revolution*, he contrasts "the organizational activity of the 'decision makers,' supported by those who own and administer the means of production, with the passivity of the 'subjects' who accept this domination" (2003b, pp. 43–44). By the conclusion, he admits he does not have an answer for this difference. "One of the most disturbing problems still remains: the extraordinary passivity of the people most directly involved....Why this silence on the part of the 'users'?" (2003b, p. 181). He offers some well-worn ideas about forces that prevent activation, but he never interrogates what is going on inside users themselves. Four years later in *The Production of Space* (1991, p. 51, see also p. 233), he is still concerned about "the silence of the users of space. Why do they allow themselves to be manipulated in ways so damaging to their spaces and their daily life without embarking on massive revolts?" Much later, in 1990, he has made little progress on this point. An interviewer asks him why over the last two decades since 1968 people have not become more politically active. He says, "The passivity of the people has often intrigued me: the city is changing around them and they accept it, internalize it and bear the consequences" (1996, p. 210). He is pressed by the interviewer: "How in concrete terms can we give inhabitants the means to intervene effectively?" He responds that the "question of people's capacity to participate is crucial. People have been exhorted to participate. They mobilized themselves a little, but the means and the results are not enormous" (1996, p. 211). And then he quickly goes on to more analysis of the problem, of how structures keep people passive, and never addresses the question of how they can become active. Despite his incisiveness as a thinker, at the end of his life Lefebvre had no good answer for this question. Even the tone in the interview seems to imagine people as a passive mass that must be "given the means" to participate, "exhorted" to become active, almost as though they are being prodded like cattle.

In this context, Rancière makes some very helpful arguments in *The Emancipated Spectator*. As the title implies, one thrust of the book is a critique of the Situationist concept of the society of the spectacle (Debord, 1983). As Rancière understands it, the "spectacle" argument is that contemporary consumer capitalism has assembled an extraordinarily effective machine for holding people's attention. The role of the spectators is merely to observe the machine; they are passive recipients of its messages. This implies that the spectator has been dispossessed of her rightful activeness and that our mission is to restore "to spectators ownership of their consciousness and their activity" (2009, p. 7). Rancière, again inspired by Jacotot, proposes that we start from a different assumption, that the incapable are in fact capable. That is, instead of a dispossessed spectator passively receiving stimuli, we should assume instead a capable spectator who is actively making sense of what she sees. More than that, Rancière continues, we should assume that each spectator is connecting with other spectators in a collective effort to make sense of what they have experienced. Understood Rancière's way, the goal is no longer to transform spectators into actors, to activate those who are passive. Rather it is to recognize the activity *already at work* in the spectator (2009, p. 17). Emancipating the spectator means we assume she is already active and we get better at seeing that activity. When each of us makes that assumption about everyone else, we all become better at recognizing and cultivating our already-existing activity. Moreover, Rancière stresses that we must each bring our active interpretations into engagement with the interpretations of others. That second step makes the process collective, projecting it into the body of the political community and, as Lefebvre would remind us, into the space of the city. For Rancière, democratic emancipation does not mean fixating on the intricate architecture of the structures of power and how they keep us from flourishing. Rather it means seeking and learning to recognize the ways we are already active, already managing our own affairs, already ruling ourselves, and then helping that already-existing activity to flourish.

Rancière's intervention is invaluable. It mirrors Lefebvre's insistence that we become aware of the traces of urban society that are already present in the industrial city. However, I don't think Rancière goes far enough. His arguments do not fully apprehend what is at stake, because they don't take into account the dark side of the spectator. That is, every spectator is also capable of passivity. Each also desires to accept images and meaning uncritically, to be carried away, to be entertained. Moreover, Debord is right in a sense: there really *is* an incredibly powerful machine that mines our desire to be passive and trades on that desire, a machine whose job it is to actively inculcate us as passive spectators so that our eyeballs remained fixed on the screen. For example, in 2012, just in the month of June, people watched over *one billion hours* of content on the Netflix site. It was a new record. The CEO of Netflix responded, "when *House of Cards* and *Arrested Development* debut, we'll blow these records away" (Simpson, 2012). So while Rancière is very much right that we must not be blind to the activity already occurring within the spectator, that realization is not enough. We must also realize that becoming-active must take place in the context of a very real and very powerful apparatus that stimulates and feeds our desire to become passive.

But again, that apparatus can only attract and hold our attention by tapping into our desires. It can only survive, then, if some part of us *wants* to watch. Part of us has to want to be passive, to be entertained, to be ruled. When I read the Netflix story, I made a mental note to add it to my book, but part of me also made a note to find out more about the *House of Cards* series, which sounded interesting, like something I would want to watch. Deleuze and Guattari are forced to wrestle with this problem from the outset, because they begin from the position that desire is the source of all production, and so it must produce its own apparatuses of capture. Here again it helps to return to Foucault's introduction to *Anti-Oedipus*:

> the major enemy [in *Anti-Oedipus*], the strategic adversary is fascism.... And it is not only historical fascism, the fascism of Hitler and Mussolini— which was able to mobilize and use the desire of the masses so effectively—but also the fascism in us all, in our heads and in our everyday behavior, the fascism that causes us to love power, to desire the very thing that dominates and exploits us (1977, p. xiii).

The word Foucault uses for power here is *pouvoir*, the power that dominates and captures. It is different from *puissance*, which has to do with potential, the capacity to create something new in the world.[5] Foucault is suggesting, with Deleuze and Guattari, that part of us loves *pouvoir*, that on some level we love to be ruled. Our desire to be passive makes us want to have someone else rule in our place. Deleuze and Guattari go so far as to say that "the fundamental problem of political philosophy is still precisely the one that Spinoza saw so clearly, and that Wilhelm Reich rediscovered: 'why do men fight *for* their servitude as stubbornly as though it were their salvation?'"(1977, p. 29).[6] They go on:

> After centuries of exploitation, why do people still tolerate being humiliated and enslaved, to such a point, indeed, that they *actually want* humiliation and slavery not only for others but for themselves? Reich is at his profoundest as a thinker when he refuses to accept ignorance or illusion on the part of the masses is an explanation of fascism, and demands an explanation that will take their desires into account, an explanation formulated in terms of desire: no, the masses were not innocent dupes; at a certain point, under a certain set of conditions, they *wanted* fascism, and it is this perversion of the desire of the masses that needs to be accounted for (1977, p. 29).

In posing that problem, they are breaking from a long-held assumption in modern political theory, which is that people always prefer freedom to servitude. From Hobbes' claim that "there are very few so foolish, that had not rather govern themselves, than be governed by others" (1996, Chapter 15) to Rousseau's conviction that humans naturally prefer "the most stormy liberty to tranquil subjection" (1987, p. 72),[7] the modern tradition assumes that no one in their right mind would want to be ruled. And yet, as is Deleuze and Guattari's wont, they uncover in that same tradition a different, minority understanding. In Spinoza, otherwise a great admirer of Hobbes, they find the realization that people very much do desire servitude. As a result, a central goal of Deleuze and Guattari's schizoanalysis is to discover why "desire can be made to desire its own repression....[why] an unconscious investment of a fascist or reactionary type can exist alongside a conscious revolutionary investment" (1977, p. 105; see also 1987, p. 215). They emphasize this double nature of desiring-production: it desires to be active and autonomous, to rule itself, but it also desires to be passive, to be ruled in structures of heteronomy. Rancière is right: we desire what nourishes us, what fulfills us, what brings us

---

[5] In Latin, it is *potentia* as opposed to *potestas*, a distinction of Spinoza's that Hardt and Negri emphasize (see Holland, 1998).
[6] They are referring here to Reich's *The Mass Psychology of Fascism* (1970).
[7] This is in the *Discourse on the Origin of Inequality*, Part Two.

delight. But he does not tell us that we also desire what destroys us, what leaves us empty, what brings us despair.

David Foster Wallace

In his fiction and his non-fiction, David Foster Wallace works relentlessly to understand why we desire what destroys us, and how we might desire differently. Throughout his writing, he continually returns to the problem of how hard it is to become active. Like Debord, he offers a masterful analysis of the society of the spectacle, and Wallace is perhaps even more useful than Debord here, given that the spectacle's raw power to hold our attention has grown exponentially since Debord's time. But along with Rancière, Wallace is keenly aware of our active struggle to both make sense of and resist the spectacle. And as with Deleuze and Guattari, he does not shy away from the fact that we desire, very deeply, to fold ourselves up in the spectacle and let it carry us away. Not only does he explore all of these questions, he does so at extraordinary length, with breathtaking intelligence, and in a way that is deeply felt. As the writer George Saunders (2008) put it, when we read his "electrifying, all-chips-in, aware-in-all-directions prose" we are able to feel, if only for a short time, what it might be like to be awake and alive in the world, what it would mean to *pay attention*, in a serious way, to the world and to each other.

Like a good philosopher,[8] Wallace proceeds by stretching the problem to its breaking point. He explores what it might be like if we upped the stakes, if we posed a scenario in which becoming active is utterly necessary, literally a matter of life or death. In the novel *Infinite Jest* (1996), he presents two such scenarios. The first concerns our role as spectators in relation to entertainment. The novel is set in a dystopian near-future in which a film has been produced, an "entertainment" as it is called in the book, that is so compelling, that so stimulates the pleasure centers of the brain, that people are physically unable to stop watching it. Within the first few seconds of viewing, the spectator is rendered helpless, infantile, and must remain watching, permanently. Eventually most spectators simply die of dehydration, or if others care for them, they remain in a catatonic state, unable to survive without the stimulation of the entertainment. The other scenario in the book is drug addiction,

[8] Which he also was: he wrote an undergraduate thesis in philosophy on Richard Taylor's fatalism that was eventually published (Wallace, 2010), and he began graduate study in philosophy at Harvard, though he later changed course to earn an MFA in creative writing. Wallace's other undergraduate thesis, in the Department of English, became his first novel, *The Broom of the System*.

which is more mundane, even if the stakes are the same. Wallace chronicles in great detail the efforts of recovering drug and alcohol addicts to ward off "the Substance," to remain clean and avoid returning to a hellish life of addiction. In both of these scenarios, characters find themselves in a situation where they must actively struggle to retain control of themselves, to manage their destructive desires. If they fail in their struggle, they will almost surely die.

In the first scenario, since even a few seconds of watching the entertainment will result in disaster, it is not a question of finding the strength to pull away. Rather, it is a question of making the choice not to view the film in the first place. People must become aware of the film's existence, to understand the damage it is capable of doing, and then they must choose to abstain. Of course, this requires a collective effort to inform the country about the film. But in the book that process is complicated. Government officials are justifiably unsure whether it is better to inform people or not. They worry that even if people learn what the entertainment does, they will still want to watch it. Even if it will kill them, it will do so by pleasing them so intensely that they don't want to do anything else. The officials are honestly not sure what people will do given that choice. Just the curiosity alone is profoundly compelling: what would that look like, a film so entertaining, so pleasurable, that you are physically unable to stop watching? Wallace seems to say here that government *dirigisme* is insufficient to the task. What is required to avoid an epidemic of catatonia and death is for the whole society together to muster the wisdom and self-worth to care for themselves. They will have to choose, on their own and together, to flourish rather than decay, to live rather than to die. Wallace is very subtle here. One can see in the text, and in other work, that he is very worried we don't have the collective wherewithal to preserve ourselves under such circumstances, even the extreme ones he imagines. At the same time, one can very much feel his profound and abiding hope that we do.

Of course, at the everyday level the stakes are much lower. If I choose to watch TV tonight I won't die. But Wallace wants us to understand the problem in the longer term. As Aristotle stresses in the *Ethics*, our flourishing is not dependent on a single decision. We flourish over the course of a lifetime, by making countless everyday decisions. Wallace is suggesting that in the long run the stakes really are life and death. Over a lifetime, we have to make the choices that cause us to flourish, that help us grow, that allow us to be really alive. And we have to avoid the choices that diminish us. Wallace wants us to understand that it is an everyday struggle, it is very difficult, and it is of the greatest importance.

The addicts in the book face a similar everyday challenge. They are all pursued constantly by their particular substance. Their desire for it visits them every day. One of the heroes of the book, Don Gately, is addicted to painkillers. In a pivotal scene, he has been badly injured and is lying in a hospital bed in excruciating pain. But he can't take any sort of narcotic. He has no choice but to lie there and "abide," to be in pain. He goes in and out of consciousness, and he experiences vivid hallucinations, some of which are of doctors making elaborate arguments for why he should agree to take painkillers. His desire for the substance is so strong that it manifests as actual people, capable of speaking and making compelling arguments for why he should give in, give himself over to the substance. They tell him he is badly injured, that he is in great pain, that it will only be for now, until he heals. The struggle goes on and on in the book, for pages. Wallace describes Gately's every thought, and he specifies Gately's pain in great detail. The reader gets to the point of agreeing with the spectral doctors, that Gately should take the painkillers. We can't see why he would put himself through so much suffering, why he struggles so heroically against the substance.

The answer becomes clear in the last scene of the book. In his hospital bed, Gately relives in his memory what we presume to be his precipitating event, the experience that got him to seek help. It is the most gruesome of scenes, reminiscent of David Lynch's *Blue Velvet*.[9] Gately is getting high with a friend, Fax, in an empty apartment. Fax has stolen hundreds of thousands of dollars from a drug dealer and used it to buy a massive amount of drugs, intending to start his own distribution scheme in another city. But the drug dealer finds out about the theft, and the scheme falls apart. Instead of fleeing, Fax does "what any drug addict in possession of his Substance would do when faced with fatal news and attendant terror," he goes to the apartment he and Gately are squatting and begins to shoot up. Gately discovers him slumped in a corner of the living room, where he has been for days. Telling himself he is only keeping his friend company, Gately joins him in getting high. They stay that way for days, still there in the

> little corner, belts around their arms, arms and noses red from scratching, still at it, the ingestion, on a hell of a tear, cooking up and getting off and eating M&M's when they could find their mouths with their hands, moving like men deep underwater, heads wobbling on strengthless necks, the empty room's ceiling sky-blue and bulging... (1996, pp. 934–935)

They continue on, not moving, getting high, hardly able to speak, with the TV on in the background, always on. They begin to wet their pants and just sit there watching the puddles of urine spread, occasionally

---

[9] Not by accident: Wallace was deeply influenced by the film.

rolling an M&M in the puddle to watch the dye corrode. At some point Gately tries to stand, but he crashes back down to the floor. Eventually, associates of the drug dealer Fax stole from arrive at the apartment. They are a whole entourage. They don't merely kill Fax for his betrayal. They begin to have a party, drinking bourbon, everybody with their own personal bottle of Jack Daniels. They force Gately and Fax to drink with them, to join their party. Gately and Fax are so high that they have to be helped to find their mouths with the bottle. At one point the leader of the crew whispers in Gately's ear that he knows Gately was not involved in the theft. They aren't going to kill Gately, he says, and so all he needs to do is kick back and watch, to enjoy the party and let Fax face his own music. The leader puts on a CD of Paul McCartney's band Wings from which all the tracks have been removed except Linda McCartney singing backup and playing tambourine. Everybody else starts shooting up. So that Fax can feel pain, they inject him with a drug to counteract the effect of the pain-killers he has been taking. Then they sew his eyelids open with needle and thread and begin dropping liquid acid into his eyes. While this is happening, they inject Gately with a pharmaceutical-grade painkiller to render him helpless. As Gately slides into unconsciousness, he watches Fax's face disfigure, his friend's screams mixed with those of Linda McCartney.

This horrific scene is the very last scene in the book. Wallace has taken us through almost a thousand pages, and we have worked long and hard to come with him. And he rewards us with this. It seems cruel. But even though it is the last thing we read, this isn't the last thing that happens to the characters. It is a scene from Gately's memory, something that is helping him to ward off the Substance, to remind himself why he is fighting so hard to remain sober, why he is subjecting himself to so much pain in the hospital. This last scene is therefore incredibly heroic. Gately is struggling courageously to continually renew his determination to stay clean, to not give in to the Substance, to govern himself. Wallace makes clear that Gately must find that courage primarily within himself. He cannot struggle by giving himself up to Alcoholics Anonymous, or to God. To be sure, Gately does draw on the support of others, on his AA sponsors, on Joelle, his developing love interest. But the source of Gately's strength is not located outside of him, in an entity to which he submits. At the same time of course, his desire for the substance, the source of his addiction, is also within him. His desire to stay alive and to govern himself struggles with his desire to submit, to concede, to be governed.

Wallace is clear, both here and in other work, that he thinks this desire to be governed is essentially the desire to return to the care of our mother, to become an infant again. Gately and Fax sit with "heads wobbling on strengthless necks," unable to control their bodily functions or walk on their own, eventually drinking from bottles that have to be held to their mouths. Wallace returns often to this image of the strengthless neck, of how the Substance has the power to make you drop your chin to your chest. The same is true of the entertainment. Near the end of the book, we learn more about the content of this film that is so entertaining you can't stop watching. It is shot from the point of view of an infant, and it shows a beautiful woman in a long flowing white gown leaning over the infant's crib and apologizing over and over. The camera used to shoot the scene was fitted with a lens that wobbled and blurred light in order to mimic how a newborn experiences the world (1996, p. 939). The film is so expertly done, so realistic, that we *fully feel* that we are back in the crib, with our mother tending to us.[10]

In his other work also, Wallace explores how we are made passive, made into infants. In "E Unibus Pluram: Television and U.S. Fiction," a 1993 essay that prefigures many of the themes in *Infinite Jest*, Wallace suggests that what we get from television, what the spectacle trains us to want from it, is reassurance (1997, p. 41). TV invites us "to itself as indulgence, transgression, a glorious 'giving in' [that is] not exactly foreign to addictive cycles" (1997, p. 42). It offers the viewer "an ironic permission slip to do what I do best whenever I feel confused and guilty: assume, inside, a sort of fetal position, a pose of passive reception to comfort, escape, reassurance" (1997, p. 42). He understands that each instance of this "giving in" is itself fairly harmless. TV is like candy: it is a pleasant indulgence, but one that does not nourish us. Each instance of giving in does not hurt us, but as a steady diet it causes our bodies to grow sick. A heavy diet of TV produces mental passivity to the point of "self-conscious catatonia" (1997, p. 64). It "renders my own reality [outside of TV] less attractive (because in it I'm just one Dave, with limits and restrictions all over the place), renders me less fit to make the most of it (because I spend all my time pretending I'm not in it), and renders me ever more dependent on the device...." (1997, p. 75). This becoming-passive is no less true of movies. In "David Lynch Keeps His Head," which also predates *Infinite Jest*, Wallace goes so far as to call movies "an authoritarian medium. They vulnerabilize you and then dominate you. Part of the magic of going to a movie is surrendering to it, letting it dominate you" (1997, p. 169). A "commercial film's goal is to 'entertain,' which usually means various fantasies that allow the moviegoer to pretend he's somebody else and that life is...just more entertaining than a moviegoer's life really is...a commercial movie

---

[10] Wallace drives home the point when another character in the book, Hal, who is struggling with his own addictions, tries to go to a Narcotics Anonymous meeting but instead mistakenly attends a support group to help participants get in touch with their inner infant.

doesn't try to wake people up but rather to make their sleep so comfortable and their dreams so pleasant that they will fork over money to experience it..." (1997, p. 170).

In "A Supposedly Fun Thing I'll Never Do Again," a non-fiction account of his experience on a luxury cruise, Wallace takes great interest in the cruise's brochure, which promises repeatedly to "pamper" passengers beyond their wildest dreams. He can't resist making this explicit: the word is most associated in the United States with a brand of diaper.[11] The ship's staff cuts your food for you, cleans your room, carries your belongings—they do everything a mother does for a child. The ship itself even tucks you in: "in heavy seas you feel rocked to sleep, with the windows' spume a gentle shushing, the engines' throb a mother's pulse" (1997, p. 285). For Wallace, this pampering of passengers' inner infant is the central fantasy the cruise line is selling: it promises to satisfy Wallace's infant, to "sate the part of me that always and only WANTS" (1997, p. 316). But this promise can never be kept:

> I want to believe that this time the luxury and pleasure will be so completely and faultlessly administered that my Infantile part will be sated. But the Infantile part of me is insatiable—in fact its whole essence or *dasein* or whatever lies in its a priori insatiability. In response to any environment of extraordinary gratification and pampering, the Insatiable Infant part of me will simply adjust its desires upward until it once again levels out at its homeostasis of terrible dissatisfaction (1997, pp. 316–317).

Of course, TV, films, and drugs are also "environments of extraordinary gratification" that can never satisfy our Infant that only wants (1997, p. 317).[12] Elsewhere, in an interview, Wallace reflects on what formulaic TV entertainment (like *Law & Order*) offers us. This kind of art "is so *profoundly* soothing....It gives you a sense of order, and that everything's going to be alright. That this is a narrative that will take care of you, that won't in any way challenge you. It's like being wrapped in a chamois blanket and nestled against a big, generous tit..." (Lipsky, 2009, p. 199).

So if the entertainment and the Substance work actively to return us to the crib, what we must do is grow up. We have to leave the chamois blanket and become adults who are no longer helpless, who no longer need our parents to pamper us. We have to develop strength in our necks. But "it is unimaginably hard to do this," Wallace says, "to stay conscious and alive in the adult world day in and day out" (2009). It is not

---

[11] Reading Wallace's descriptions of the scene on the ship, of a great swath of fleshy passengers being "pampered," one can't help but conclude this was the inspiration for the very similar, and brilliant, space-cruiseship scene in *Wall-E*. David Foster Wallace brought to you by Disney Pixar.
[12] On this point, see also Lefebvre (1991, p. 394).

something that just happens as a matter of course, like growing up biologically, because our culture, economy, and polity actively infantilize us. Against this pervasive infantilization, growing up is something that takes tremendous work. Moreover, it also takes work because being an adult often isn't all that *fun*. His later work explores the angst, boredom, and weight of responsibility that attend adult life. In "The Soul Is Not a Smithy," for example, a young boy recounts with stunning perceptiveness the look on his father's face as he arrives home from work every day:

> Turning from the front door while his left hand rose to remove his hat, my father's eyes appeared lightless and dead, empty of everything we associated with his real persona....

> The front door was heavy and difficult to open and close, as if the foyer were somehow pressurized...he had to put his side into the door somewhat in order to make it close all the way, and I would not see his face until he turned to remove his hat and coat, but I can recall that the angle of his shoulders as he leaned into the door had the same quality as his eyes (2004, pp. 103–104).

Seeing his father this way provokes nightmares in the boy about what adult life must be like. The dreams

> always opened with a wide-angle view of a number of men at desks in rows in a large, brightly lit room or hall. The desks were arranged in precise rows and columns like the desks of a...classroom....If there were windows, I do not remember noticing them....Some of the men were older than others, but they were all obviously adults—people who drove, and applied for insurance coverage, and had high-balls while they read the paper before dinner. The...room was at least the size of a soccer or flag football field; it was utterly silent and had a large clock on each wall (2004, p. 103).

> The men's faces [were] puffy and seamed with adult tension and wear and appeared to hang slightly loose, the way someone's face can go all flaccid and loose when he appears to be staring at something without really seeing it...the men's expressions were somehow at once stuporous and anxious, enervated and keyed up—not so much fighting the urge to fidget as appearing to have long ago surrendered whatever hope or expectation causes one to fidget....The overall feeling was that these colorless, empty-eyed, long-suffering faces were the face of some death that awaited me long before I stop walking around (2004, pp. 108–109).

When that story was written, Wallace was already at work on his last novel, *The Pale King*, which remained unfinished at his death.[13] It has

---

[13] And yet published posthumously (Wallace, 2012).

primarily to do with this boredom of adult life, of a middle-class working life, and with the low-level despair and anxiety that life can cause. Wallace's point in this vein is not so much a critique of work under contemporary capitalism, although there is certainly an element of that. His target is more the general condition of adulthood, of the anxiety that comes with the weight of responsibility. For Wallace, it is extremely hard to grow up because we are afraid to experience this anxiety. We want to remain infants, to be passive, to be taken care of. He even suggests that this desire for the crib is stronger than any other desire, even stronger than our desire to stay alive. The entertainment in *Infinite Jest* places us viscerally back in the crib, and it is something we can't pull ourselves away from, even though it will kill us. In the crib, we are freed from the angst and gathering despair of adulthood. We discover how much easier and safer it is to be an infant, to be cared for by our mother, by an entertainment, by a drug, by a corporation. In the same way, it is easier to be politically passive, to let ourselves be ruled. Oligarchy frees us from the anxiety of making decisions, and more, from worrying whether our decisions were the right ones. Democracy, on the other hand, requires that we grow up, that we make our own decisions and live with the consequences. It requires what Marx called "the most damned seriousness, the most intense exertion" (Marx, 1993b, Notebook VI).[14]

At the same time, however, growing up brings with it something else, something Wallace's child narrator does not yet know awaits him: a feeling of accomplishment, of satisfaction—even of joy—at having made decisions for ourselves, at having decided to become the hero of our own life. Lefebvre (1991, p. 137) agrees with Marx that autonomous activity requires "painful effort," but he is quick to add that it also offers "the joy of creation," a feeling of deep delight that so often comes when we achieve a task through a concerted effort. Not a cheap thrill, or a soothing comfort, but a sustained, down-deep delight—a pervasive sense of satisfaction. It is true that we must struggle every day to leave the crib, to ward off our desire to surrender to the structures of power, and to rule ourselves. But even though our becoming-adult and becoming-active must always be a struggle, it is important to know that it also offers a reward, that it always has the potential, if we are doing it correctly, to bring us delight.

Wallace's work helps us understand many things about democracy. One is that the stakes may be higher than we think. He suggests that governing ourselves is necessary in the long term, that it is a question of life and death. We must become active in order to survive. Another is that

---

[14] See also Andy Merrifield's (2011, pp. 152–156) discussion of the question of free working and self-development.

Wallace's exploration of infants and adults helps us see that Plato totally misunderstands and underestimates democracy. *The Republic* would have us believe that democracy is the rule of our inner infant, that it involves the coming to power of the thoughtless mass who, thinking all desires are equal, live out their lives by gratifying the desire of the moment. Already in the *Gorgias*, Plato decries the eternal treadmill that the infant places us on, which is that we will always have many more desires than we can satisfy. In that dialogue, Callicles argues that what it means to be alive is to use all our wherewithal to pursue and satisfy our desires. Socrates counters that this is a kind of hell, like constantly scratching an itch that never abates (Plato, 1998, p. 494).[15] Socrates argues that we cannot let ourselves be ruled by our inner infant. But he mistakes the desire of the infant for desire more generally and quickly concludes that desire is inferior and must be subordinated to reason. He then arrives by analogy at his impoverished understating of democracy: the masses function in the polis like desire does in the soul, and they will do whatever their infant demands. The people, the demos, are therefore inferior, and they must be ruled by a superior guardian class, a class of grown-ups, who are guided instead by reason. The contemporary manifestation of Plato's way of thinking is the idea that we should be wary of having too much democracy, that people are not competent to make decisions for themselves (e.g. Orszag, 2011; Schumpeter, 1947; Macdonald, 2012).

Wallace's exhortation to us to grow up allows us to imagine a much less impoverished understanding of democracy than Plato's. It allows us to see that the people who govern in a *real* democracy are not dependent children but independent adults. To become democratic is to become adult; it is to rule oneself, to struggle every day to be autonomous, to ward off the temptations of oligarchy. Democrats, real democrats, are ruled neither by cold reason nor by the infant part of themselves. They refuse both Socrates' rational man of temperance and Calicles' desiring libertine. Both models diminish us because they reduce the whole human to one of its parts. Instead, the democrat is a *whole* adult who brings the many parts of herself—reasons, desires, emotions, spirits—together to rule collectively. It is therefore not enough to turn Plato on his head and valorize desire over reason. We must push out beyond Nietzsche and Deleuze and Guattari. The democratic adult brings the whole body and all its elements back into play. None of her faculties is more human than any other. All are necessary for a full and healthy human life.[16]

---

[15] As with Gately and Fax in the previous scene.
[16] My argument here parallels and is inspired by Engels' (1996, pp. 47–48) contention that the problem with the industrial capitalist city is that it radically reduces the fullness of human experience to one mode of being—competition and exploitation among self-interested individuals—and it actively suppresses all the other modes of being (e.g. cooperation, love, care) that humans are capable of.

In the same way, all people in a healthy democratic polity come together to rule the polity collectively. They rule themselves without hierarchy, without either an inner infant or a guardian class pulled out of and raised above the rest. The healthy democratic polity uses all its parts, not just a few. It is a polity restored to fullness. The problem with a liberal-democratic state is precisely that raises barriers to that fullness. It creates stable structures whereby a few rule the many. It therefore inhibits our growing up. Its oligarchical structure trains us to be passive, to mind our own business and let someone else do the hard work of making decisions. We fall into the habit of thinking that our governors will provide answers for us, and we slide into a belief that the solution to any current troubles is to simply change governments. That is one reason so many people in the United States came to uncritically equate Barack Obama with "Hope," and why they were quickly disappointed when it turned out that a president cannot solve all our problems—or satisfy all our wants—with a wave of his hand. That is how children think: they look to their parents to take care of the situation. Adults, on the other hand, know that no one is coming to do it for them, that they must rely on themselves. It is in that sense that we must always conceive of becoming democratic as also a process of becoming adult.

In many ways Deleuze and Guattari are exploring a similar line of thinking to Wallace. They are very fond of the line from Artaud (Deleuze and Guattari, 1977, p. 14):

> I don't believe in father
> in mother,
> got no
> pappamummy

They want the schizo (and us as well) to break out of the Oedipal triangle, to open out to the world, to not refer everything back to pappa-mummy-me. They prefer to work with the term *orphan*, with the idea of becoming-orphan, as a way to escape Oedipus. They are essentially exhorting us, with Wallace, to leave the chamois blanket, to move beyond the family and cast our lot out into society more broadly. Deleuze and Guattari insist that the orphan must make connections; he must create a network of alliances throughout society to replace the filiation of the family. But in their work, the nature of these alliances is left quite vague. We do not have a good idea, reading these passages in Deleuze and Guattari, just what our new world beyond the family will look like, or what it would take to construct it. In a sense, they free us from the family but cast us into uncertainty. In Wallace, we are launched out of the blanket, but not into the void. We are delivered instead into our *own* care. Moreover, Wallace shows us what is at stake in the struggle. We are confronted, in that final scene of *Infinite Jest*, with just what will happen if we cannot leave the blanket: a grotesque kind of doom. And Wallace helps us really feel, suffering right along with Gately in his hospital bed, what it will be like, what it will *take*, for us to grow up, for us to become active and adult.

So Then, *How*?

So Wallace shows us why we must become active, what it would take, and to whom we entrust ourselves. But still, *how* do we do it? We are not lying wounded in a hospital bed. What do we actually need to *do* to become active and become democratic? What are the steps? Wallace's model of addiction points to the importance of a precipitating event, something that happens that makes it clear to the addict that he or she needs to get control. In this line of thinking, the first step is awareness; we need to begin by understanding that the addiction—oligarchy and becoming-passive—is a problem.

A vivid example of a precipitating event with respect to oligarchy is provided by Vaclav Havel (1985). He writes about a greengrocer who lives under a totalitarian regime in communist Czechoslovakia. He "places in his window, among the onions and carrots, the slogan: 'Workers of the world, unite!'" He doesn't do it because he agrees with the slogan but "simply because it has been done that way for years, because everyone does it, because that is the way it has to be. If he were to refuse, there could be trouble...he does it because these things must be done if one is to get along in life" (1985, pp. 27–28). The message isn't directed to his customers, or to Czechoslovakians more generally. It is directed above, to his party bosses. The message is: "I am obedient and therefore I have the right to be left in peace" (1985, p. 28). This is not the greengrocer speaking with his own voice; he is not saying things he means or really wants to say. He is, Havel says, "living within a lie" (1985, p. 31). The greengrocer goes on living within the lie, doing what must be done, without thinking. He becomes, to paraphrase Calvino, such a complete part of the lie that he no longer knows it is there. Havel says we are capable of this, of coming to terms with living the lie. He thinks we can succumb to "a profane trivialization of our inherent humanity," merging with the anonymous crowd and flowing comfortably along with it "down the river of pseudo-life" (1985, p. 38).

In this kind of a situation, embedded in an inferno that has become so naturalized that we no longer know it is there, what is required is a radical break. Havel invites us to imagine that one day something in our greengrocer snaps, and he stops putting up the slogans merely to ingratiate himself. He stops voting in elections he knows are a farce. He begins to say what he really thinks at political meetings. And even finds the strength in himself to express solidarity with those his conscience commands him to support. In this revolt the greengrocer steps out of living within the lie. He rejects the ritual and breaks the rules of the game. He discovers once more his suppressed identity and dignity...His revolt is an attempt to *live within the truth* (1985, p. 39).[17]

Of course, the power structure will respond. Agents will come after him; consequences will be imposed. The greengrocer has not liberated society, by any means. What he might do, or rather all that can be hoped for, is for him to touch off a struggle. His snapping

> has broken through the exalted façade of the system and exposed the real, base foundations of power....By his action the greengrocer has addressed the world. He has enabled everyone to peer behind the curtain. He has shown everyone that it is possible to live within the truth (1985, p. 40).

The greengrocer thus provides society with a precipitating event, an opportunity to recognize its addiction, its passive acceptance of Communist Party rule. Lefebvre might say that what the greengrocer has done is to open a path to the possible. Sartre (1963, p. 20) calls it "the moment of the boomerang," when the colonialized person becomes no longer merely subject but capable of reciprocity and autonomous initiative. The greengrocer has given us a glimpse of a different reality, notified (or perhaps reminded) us it exists, and invited us to struggle for it if we choose to do so.

Once we begin to think in terms of such precipitating events, we find no shortage of examples. In Beijing in 1989, the hunger strike of Chai Ling and others helped spark massive popular outrage against the government and helped the events of 1989 become much more than just a student movement (Zhao, 2004, p. 161ff). In Iran in the summer of 2009, a blatantly rigged presidential election caused Iranians of all ages, classes, and genders to flood the streets and voice their chronic dissatisfaction with an authoritarian and mendacious government. In December 2010 in Tunisia, another greengrocer, Mohamed Bouazizi, burned himself in protest in front of the municipal government office. In March of 2011, fifteen Syrian children in Dara'a were arrested for writing anti-regime graffiti. In each of these cases, there is a complex

---

[17] "Attach yourself to what you feel to be true," says the Invisible Committee (2009, p. 65), "begin there."

story to tell. For example, there is quite a lot of question as to just what took place in Bouazizi's case. He was a produce vendor who sold from a mobile cart in the streets of Tunis. His margins were thin. He ran into difficulty with the local authorities, who harassed him for not having the proper permits (or perhaps for not paying the proper bribe). He was slapped by a female official, or he wasn't, there is debate. Some think he felt his manhood had been insulted, others think he was fed up with corruption, others think he was tired of being harassed because he sold in the informal economy. The story is ambiguous, but that is partly its power. What seems clear is that people in Tunisia generally interpreted Bouazizi to have snapped, to have reached a point where he was not going to be intimidated, or humiliated, or ruled anymore by the government, by *this* government. People in Tunisia concluded that the situation had become intolerable to Bouazizi, and he responded by taking perhaps the most dramatic action a person can take. I don't mean that the truth of Bouazizi's story doesn't matter, it does. I mean rather that whatever the truth was, we can interpret surging popular reaction as the result of some affinity of feeling, some idea that Bouazizi felt like we feel, that he said what we have been wanting to say but were afraid to, that *his* act made it okay for *us* to act as well, for us to rise up and say out loud what we are all feeling: enough of humiliation and domination, enough of this government.

Of course, the events in Tunisia sparked other events in turn, in Egypt, Libya, Bahrain, Oman, Yemen, Syria, Jordan, Israel, Chile, Spain, Greece, Russia, and elsewhere. None of this is inevitable cause and effect; events can always unfold otherwise. But there is a very palpable sense that such precipitating events do sometimes un-dam a potential flow, that they can give license to say what one could not say, and do what one could not do. Precipitating events do not *create* this flow—it was already present, already felt. They merely open the gates, allow the flow to flow. If the potential flow is not present, the event won't precipitate anything. Bouazizi opened a crack in the dam, but it was the pressure generated by hundreds of thousands of Tunisians wanting to speak and to act that caused the dam to collapse.

This idea of snapping also has an important place in political theory. For example, Locke relied on it heavily in his insistence on the right of rebellion. He was responding to Hobbes, who argued that the power of the sovereign must be absolute, that any space left for the people to rebel would degenerate quickly into civil war. For Locke though, the real concern was not civil war but the tyranny of an absolute sovereign. He therefore insisted vehemently that the people must retain ultimate right of rebellion, the right to judge when the sovereign has misused the power the people have entrusted to him. To diffuse the Hobbesian objection that such ultimate popular authority would result in continuous upheaval and war, Locke argued that rebellion is rare. "People are not so easily got out of their old forms as some are apt to suggest....It is not an easy thing to get them changed [because of a] slowness and aversion in the people to quit their old constitutions" (1988, Chapter XIX, Section 223). He thinks rebellion only happens after a sovereign repeatedly and arrogantly abuses the people's trust.[18] This abuse must be general, and it must be such that a great majority of people are pushed to the point where they snap. They decide that the situation has become intolerable and that they must void the contract and dissolve the government.

> *Great mistakes...*will be *borne by the people* without mutiny or murmur. But if a long train of abuses, prevarications and artifices, all tending the same way, make the design visible to the people, and they cannot but feel what they lie under, and see whither they are going; it is not to be wondered, that they should then rouse themselves, and endeavor to put the rule into such hands which may secure to them the ends for which government was at first erected...(1988, Chapter XIX, Section 225).

Of course, Locke thinks that after this awakening people will then place their power into the hands of another, more suitable government. He accepts the oligarchy of liberal democracy. But we can democratize Locke by changing "put the rule into such hands" to "put the rule into *their own* hands." Locke's association with liberal government should not cause us to miss the value of his account of how people come to feel their subjection, "rouse themselves," and decide to make a radical break with the present state of affairs.

Even in Plato we find a very similar scenario. In Book 8 of *The Republic*, Socrates theorizes the process by which oligarchy becomes democracy. He describes how an oligarchy works progressively to empower and enrich the few and disempower and impoverish the many. This political and economic inequality grows and becomes more stark and visible, but the oligarchy legitimates itself by pointing to the superior qualifications of the few: they rule because they are said to possess some particular excellence (*arête*). One day, however, a man-of-the-many finds himself, through some chance, to be in close contact with a man-of-the-few. He observes this oligarch, toiling away clumsily, and it becomes plain that his purported excellence is a lie.

> In fact it often happens that a poor man, lean and sunburnt, is stationed in battle alongside a rich man who has had a comfortable upbringing in

---

[18] *Re-bellare* is to make war *again*. Re-bellion for Locke is just the people responding to the state's initial *bellum* or act of war, which is when it breaks the trust.

the shade, and who is carrying a good deal of superfluous flesh. When he sees him wheezing and struggling, don't you suppose he blames his own cowardice for the fact that people like this are rich? Don't they egg one another on when they are alone together? "They're ours for the plucking," they say. "There's nothing to them."... It's like an unhealthy body. It only takes a trivial external cause to tip the balance toward actual illness (2008, pp. 556d–e).

The man-of-the-many snaps. He no longer accepts the logic on which oligarchy rests. He begins to desire, and demand, democracy. Of course, Plato sees this as a move toward sickness, because he holds an impoverished view of democracy. But his account of tipping the balance resonates strongly with the idea of snapping.

In each case, snapping is visceral, more-than-rational. It is a desire, a spirit that causes a body to move, to act, even if that body is not used to acting and has little reason to expect that such action will have desired results. People just act. But then, after people begin to move, after they start to become active rather than passive, something else happens. They become aware of their own body, of their own capacity to move. They realize they were predisposed to do this all along, that they were able to act, to speak, to rule. Tunisia and Egypt are probably the most dramatic examples: people who in the course of a few weeks went from being thoroughly conditioned to believe they could never govern to being entirely confident they could. At the height of the Egyptian uprising, Mubarak refused to step down, saying the Egyptians needed him, that without his strong hand at the helm there would be barbarity. This is a very old ploy: the false choice between authority and turmoil. Whether it is Plato's ship at sea, Hobbes' England, or Egypt in 2011, it has been used forever to legitimate power. It rests on the general agreement that people are incapable of ruling themselves, that without hierarchical authority there will be chaos. This assumption crumbles when people refuse to accept it, when they believe instead they are capable, and then realize their capability by becoming active, by experiencing what it is like to rule, by coming together to manage their own affairs.

Of course, I don't mean to say that people go from being docile subjects to fully functioning, self-governing citizens in three weeks. That certainly did not happen in Egypt, where a military oligarchy took power. I mean instead that when people become active, they can radically increase their estimation of their own abilities. In Tunisia, for example, Amanda Sebestyen (2011) found that "people have started to take control of their lives [and] they are not going to lose that vision. Not all are involved in street confrontations any more: they see a range of strategies for going forwards." In Egypt, people realized they were capable of refusing the regime, of standing together in the square and loudly rejecting Mubarak's false choice. And they could only know for sure the choice was false *after* he left power. So they also learned they had the courage to act against the regime even when they did not know what would happen next. They learned not only that they could become active, but that they had the power to topple a regime that had ruled them for thirty years.

Beyond the monumental accomplishment of toppling regimes, there were also smaller experiments with autogestion in the urban squares of Tunisia and Egypt. During the occupation of Tahrir Square in Cairo, people organized themselves in order to carry out basic functions, like delivering food, water, and medical care to those who needed it. There was even an effective cleaning of the square when Mubarak abdicated and people decided to end their occupation. In addition, in many neighborhoods in Cairo there were neighborhood safety committees that came to the fore during the struggle to help manage the neighborhood's needs and participation in the demonstrations (Janner-Klausner, 2011). We have seen similar kinds of self-management, partly inspired by Tahrir, in the uprisings in Greece and Spain in 2011 as well. In both countries, demonstrators created committees to manage media relations, technology infrastructure, food and water, safety, and the like (Ouziel, 2011). People made a conscious effort to think through how to carry out these functions well, as part of what the movement was trying to accomplish. Not only were they denouncing the collusion of their oligarchic governments with international financial interests, they were also working to prefigure an alternative. They undertook initial but concerted efforts at self-management that could present, to themselves and to the world, another way to live together in the polis.

Clearly the primary concrete political outcome of the Tunisian and Egyptian uprisings was the crumbling of each country's authoritarian regime. That outcome has not occurred (yet) in Spain or Greece or Syria or Iran. The aftermath of each of these uprisings will likely see various reconstitutions of state power. The state will form a new oligarchical structure and recommence its ruling function. But it would be wrong to conclude therefore that the uprisings failed, that because a stable absolute democracy did not come about, everything was for nothing. No. Among many other achievements, what happened in the uprisings in Tunisia, Egypt, Spain, Greece, Syria, and even Iran is that people demonstrated to themselves that they can become active, and that when they come together in the square they can achieve things they never thought they could, things that they thought were impossible. They can make bold new demands on the government, and they can even topple regimes. They can create connections and alliances among people that had been separated from each other. They can take an active role in managing the affairs of their city, region, and country. Today in Egypt, even as the new government makes decisions, people understand that they can go back again to Tahrir to pressure, cajole, or oppose the leadership, and they have in fact done so (Mackey, 2011; Shadid, 2011; Kirkpatrick, 2012). Certainly this is not real democracy, to have to plead with the oligarchy to make different decisions. But it is a very different way to think about political community, a developing common sense within an increasingly activated and connected body of people, people that see themselves playing a radically new role in the affairs of their country. It is this awakening, this growing awareness—this becoming-active—that I think we must stress about the Arab Uprising. It has been an activation of people's growing sense that they both want to and are able to actively manage their own affairs. Even when new crystallizations of state power form, they will no longer be ruling the same populace. They will have to cope with this new popular presence: active, unafraid, and with a taste for something more. The same is true in Spain, where according to Amador Fernández-Savater, the revolution has opened up "a new state of mind," in which, as Marta Sanchez put it, "it is possible to think differently, to feel differently, and to act differently" (Sanchez, 2012). Perhaps evoking Marquez in *One Hundred Years of Solitude*, one *asamblea* in Madrid, Algete y alrededores, characterizes itself this way: "*Dormíamos, despertamos... y ahora tenemos insomnio crónico*," which means, "We were asleep, we woke up... and now we have chronic insomnia" (Taibo, 2012).

So what then? People develop this taste for something more, but it would be a mistake to assume that a taste will be enough to carry us all the way down the path to real democracy. People can also lose the taste. They can forget it almost as quickly as they acquired it. Their desire to be active can become strong, as it did in 2011 in so many places, but it can also become dormant again. Wallace's addict, right after his precipitating event, desperately wants to get clean. But that doesn't mean the desire for the Substance is gone. As Gately lies in his hospital bed, the desire returns, powerful and devious. Desperate to ward it off, he casts himself back vividly to his precipitating event. The book ends with him in the throes of his struggle, fighting desperately to remain sober. The struggle, Wallace is saying, does not end. The addict continues to want the Substance, our inner infant wants to be pampered, people want to be ruled. Our inner desire to "let someone else do it" will always return to seduce us. How much *easier* it would be not to go to the meeting or the demonstration, not to become informed and think through an issue, not to suffer the angst of responsibility that comes with making a decision. Let the oligarchs decide. "You deserve a break today." Our desire to be ruled is strong, at least as strong as our desire to manage our own affairs. The act of becoming aware and becoming active is therefore only a first step. Wallace teaches us that the second step must be to fight like hell. Like Gately, we must fight to stay active, to ward off our desire for heteronomy and oligarchy, and to reaffirm our desire for autonomy and democracy. We must return again to the precipitating event, remember the greengrocer, go back to Tahrir, and continually revive the desire for democracy.

But even this "fight like hell" is not yet enough. It leaves us only with a kind of self-denial, an asceticism that is difficult to maintain in the face of great temptations. We also need to have an idea, and to come to really *feel*, what it is we desire instead. It is not enough to think that oligarchy is soothing and easy and democracy is stressful and hard, to think the choice is between a warm chamois blanket and a cold fluorescent-lit office. We have to also understand that in the active struggle for democracy there is a sense of joy, a down-deep delight that we can discover when we take up the responsibility of managing our affairs together.[19] And the good news is that this delight is not so hard to find if we look for it. In the uprising in Argentina in 2001, for example, people found delight in a sense of self-esteem. Participants in the *piquetero* movement, experimenting with worker-run factories, cooperative bakeries, and neighborhood assemblies, found that "so many years of a politics with state control over the people...generated a lack of self-esteem in us....We didn't feel it was possible for us to fight the politicians. The *piquete* kind of broke that passivity and people [were] able to recover their self-esteem." It created a "change of mood, recovering that confidence in ourselves that we can change things—at least small things—that we couldn't resolve in an office but we can resolve in a *piquete*" (Notes from Nowhere, 2003, p. 474). One woman reflected that

> the system tells you that women...have to be home and take charge of the kitchen and the kids...you can't think, you don't have an opinion...as things change in these movements it comes out that the woman begins to have a voice that can express what she feels...and the MTD[20] woman *feels good* because it's like she found her place where she can be herself, where she can say what she feels *and that is incredible, to find one's place* (Notes from Nowhere, 2003, p. 478, emphasis added).

One can read similar testimony from participants in the Spanish and Greek uprisings of 2011, people who feel a new confidence, almost an exhilaration, in becoming active together with others. So while

---

[19] Foucault in the preface to *Anti-Oedipus*: "Do not think that one has to be sad in order to be militant."
[20] The *Movimiento de Trabajadores Desocupados*, or unemployed workers' movement.

becoming- active can be prompted by the negative motive that oligarchy will destroy us, it must be sustained by a positive motive: democracy can make us feel good, it can bring us to life again, it can generate a down-deep delight.

Coda

I argued in Chapter 3 that democracy must be understood not as a final end beyond politics, but as becoming-democratic, a process by which we move toward the horizon of democracy. It is the same with popular activation. It is neither possible nor desirable to be fully active, to be totally attentive to each and every detail of our lives. That kind of attentiveness would overwhelm us and cause us to shut down. It would require a kind of manic activity, an energy we could not sustain for long. This fact is reflected in how David Foster Wallace thought about his journalism. He conceived of himself as providing a public service, in the sense that he took on the task of paying very close attention to every detail of a particular phenomenon (cruise ships, state fairs, tennis, lobster festivals, etc.), thinking about it very hard over a sustained period, and communicating what he learned to the reader. It was a service because we can't all pay attention like that all the time. It would be counterproductive because it would utterly exhaust us and render us unable to be awake and alive.

Deleuze and Guattari talk about this over-activity in the context of schizophrenia. They make a distinction between the schizophrenic process, by which we can liberate desire from Oedipus and other apparatuses of capture, and the clinical disorder of schizophrenia, which they are at pains to stress they do not wish on anybody. Some of those who have the disorder experience this kind of hyper-attention. They perceive and process details that most other people screen out. They are able to see more, but they are usually not able to function that way for long. Rather than achieve a breakthrough, they suffer a breakdown. So we must figure out how to become active and vigorous enough to ward off torpor, heteronomy, and oligarchy. But we can't take it too far. We can't become so active, aware, and alive that we exhaust ourselves and break down. In Egypt in 2012, for example, when the courts dissolved the newly elected Egyptian Parliament, activist Hossam Bahgat posted on Twitter: "Egypt just witnessed the smoothest military coup. We'd be outraged if we weren't so exhausted" (Bahgat, 2012).

I don't want to suggest something like a homeostasis here, a non-descript safe zone between oligarchy and democracy. That is a resting place, a state of inertia or inactivity. Instead, becoming-active means to insistently push out further toward activity, awareness, and democracy, radically so. We don't want a balance or equilibrium, we want democracy. But we want it and push for it with the understanding that to actually reach it is to go too far. Democracy and activity are, as Lefebvre says, a *horizon*. They are something we aim at and struggle toward, a destination we want desperately to reach, even though we know we never can.

It is a tricky project: flee, not as fast as you can go, but as fast as you can sustain. Marshall your strength so you can remain in flight. It isn't easy. But it can help to share the task, to connect up with others in flight. Much of this chapter has talked about becoming active in the context of one person, about the kinds of choices each of us must make. That internal struggle is vitally important, but of course the struggle to become active must also be collective. When we become active together we will be stronger in our flight, and we can also help each other recognize when we are going too fast, when we need to slow down or rest. So, becoming-active and becoming-democratic require also that we make connections. They require us to associate with others in a collective project. How we should do so, what those connections should be like, is the subject of Chapter 5.

5

Revolutionary Connections

The Ornithology of Collective Action

If you are in Rome at dusk, you may have the opportunity to see the
starlings in flight. They rise together into the air, a black mass of perhaps
50,000 birds, to hunt insects for their dinner. The flock is cohesive, but
it is constantly changing shape as the birds move about in pursuit of
prey. At times it looks like a funnel cloud, then it seems to flex like a
great hand, then it is a wide ribbon, undulating purposefully. You are
aware the flock is a multitude of individual birds, but it seems you are
watching a single coherent thing, a pulsing life-form with an obvious
intelligence, efficiently carrying out the task of finding, catching, and
ingesting food. Scientists tells us that there is no leader, that the flock
makes decisions without any centralized system of command (Hayes,
2011). They call this emergent organization, which sounds inefficient
and slow. It isn't. The flock doesn't take flight or turn or change shape
gradually. Despite its great mass, it can change direction in less than a
second—so fast you catch your breath. The flock seems not only to have
a collective mind, but also to be able to change that mind in an instant.
Another thing: the mass can also change color or transparency almost
instantly. When the flat of their wings is facing you, the flock is solid
black. But as they fly toward you or away, as they show you their wings'
blade-edge, the mass changes, through dark gray, to silver, and then it
even sometimes disappears entirely. The whole flock, 50,000 birds, disappears in an instant. And then before you can process what you are
seeing, it reemerges again as fast as it vanished. All of this is true. You
can see it on YouTube.

The Down-Deep Delight of Democracy, First Edition. Mark Purcell.
© 2013 John Wiley & Sons, Ltd. Published 2013 by John Wiley & Sons, Ltd.

In *Invisible Cities*, Marco Polo tells Kublai Khan of many fascinating places, but perhaps the most breathtaking is Marozia. Marco tells us that it consists of two cities. The present city, the city of rats, is marked by oppression, domination, and competition. But

> if you move along Marozia's compact walls, when you least expect it, you see a crack open and a different city appear. Then, an instant later, it has already vanished. Perhaps everything lies in knowing what words to speak, what actions to perform, and in what order and rhythm; or else someone's gaze, answer, gesture is enough; it is enough for someone to do something for the sheer pleasure of doing it, and for his pleasure to become the pleasure of others: at that moment, all spaces change, all heights, distances; the city is transfigured, becomes crystalline, transparent as a dragonfly. But everything must happen as if by chance, without attaching too much importance to it, without insisting that you are performing a decisive operation, remembering clearly that any moment the old Marozia will return and solder its ceiling of stone, cobwebs, and mold over all heads (1974, p. 155).

Perhaps, Marco suggests, the answer is to invent new words and a new way of speaking. Or maybe it is merely to live, to act for the sheer pleasure of it, and to transmit that pleasure to others. But Marco says we cannot seek this pleasure, this possible Marozia, through a revolutionary act. We cannot burst through the crack and force urban society to arrive all at once. Rather we must encourage it to emerge on its own. We must allow events to unfold, Marco says, because in the midst of the city of rats "a new century is about to begin in which all the inhabitants of Marozia will fly like swallows in the summer sky...tracing with their wings' blade the curve of an opening horizon" (1974, p. 154). Marco proposes that both the Marozia of rats and the Marozia of swallows "change with time, but their relationship does not change; the second is the one about to free itself from the first" (1974, p. 155). Like Lefebvre, Calvino sees in the midst of the infernal city something like urban society struggling to emerge, a city of swallows searching for a way to take flight together.

So many naturalistic metaphors. But are they even metaphors? Are we more creatures of the natural world than we like to assume? Aristotle famously defines humans as the *zoon politikon*, the political animal. A person who does not engage in the affairs of the polis, he argues, is either beast or a God (1998b, p. 1253a). As we saw in Chapter 2, for Aristotle politics means engaging in the affairs of the polis, and we do that by using reason and speech (*logos*) to discuss with fellow citizens what the good polis means. For Aristotle, a good polis brings people together to ensure that each of them can flourish, so that each comes as close as possible to reaching his or her human potential. The polis is thus an association whose purpose is to create an environment in which its members can thrive. Taking only a little liberty, we might say that for Aristotle politics is the act of coming together to articulate and achieve what in *The Communist Manifesto* Marx and Engels call "an association in which the free development of each is a condition of the free development of all" (Simon, 1994, p. 176).[1]

It is not surprising then that in Chapter 2, it was clear that thinking about democracy very quickly raises the question of how we are going to relate to each other in a self-governing society. What kind of connections should we form with each other in the process of becoming democratic and becoming active? These questions occupy Gramsci, Laclau and Mouffe, and Deleuze and Guattari in particular. Democratic connections must help create some sort of solidarity, commonality, and consistency among people. But they must also be such that they ward off the formation of oligarchy and heteronomy. The connections must bring people together to form a body politic that resembles what Deleuze and Guattari call a body without organs (BwO). The BwO is an assemblage that gathers people into meaningful relations with each other, so that each is not merely an autonomous monad. The assemblage thus has enough consistency to hold together, to function in some meaningful way as a body politic, as a coherent polis. But at the same time, even as it creates some meaningful consistency, the body must also be without organs. That is, it must not form fixed centers that perform particular functions. Socially, this means the body lacks enduring hierarchical differentiation. Spatially, the body lacks strong centralization of its governing functions. For Deleuze and Guattari, the BwO has a "real inorganization"; it presents a permanent refusal to be organ-ized, either socially or spatially (1977, p. 39). Lacking organs, this body must function by producing concentrations of intensities, zones of thickening that emerge from the undifferentiated mass to operate, to carry out a function, even if it is only temporary. The body must function, and so the BwO does not resist all concentrations. Rather, it resists the routinization of the concentrations, it refuses their formation into fixed nodes, institutions, and organs. Following this line of thinking, we could say that becoming-democratic requires that people join together into collective bodies that function the way a flock of starlings does. It must form a BwO, a leaderless and decentralized mass that nevertheless possesses an emergent coordination that enables it to act at a moment's notice. Not an easy task, to be sure, but one the starlings do every day.

---

[1] For Aristotle "all" here would mean only all *citizens*. For Marx and Engels "all" means everyone.

Gramsci: Beyond Welding

The common-sense way to understand political alliance is to imagine a number of discrete groups, each of which has its own distinct identity, that join together into a common political movement. A good metaphor to describe this conception would be to say that the groups are welded to each other: they attach themselves together firmly into a larger body, but in doing so they don't substantially change their previous characteristics. They can detach themselves from the larger body and be basically the same as they were before they joined it. Gramsci uses the term *welding* more than once when talking about political alliance (2000, pp. 220, 348).[2] Nevertheless, when we dig into his thought a bit more, we can find it quite helpful in unsettling this common-sense welding imagination.

Recall that Gramsci insists adamantly on the importance of political alliance. He argues that society is plural and that no group can rule on its own. He begins from the assumption that there are some broad categories in society: the bourgeoisie, the proletariat, the peasants, the clergy, petty bourgeois, soldiers, and so on. While these groups are themselves the product of political struggle, for the purposes of his analysis Gramsci typically assumes them to already exist and to be guided by a set of interests, even if these are contingent and liable to change. Unlike many Marxists of his time, Gramsci rejects the idea that the proletariat can dissolve other elements of society into "one big union." But he also tries to move beyond the welding metaphor, beyond the idea that each group is unchanged when it joins with others. Instead, he expects that the process of joining politically with others will alter the agenda and worldview of each group. For Gramsci, such alteration is in fact essential to the process of forming a specifically *hegemonic* movement. As it connects with others, he suggests, each group is altered because it takes on board some elements of the agenda and identity of other groups. Each group comes to partly adopt the interests of others as its own. Gramsci is not saying here that each group is *entirely* changed, that it loses itself by dissolving into a homogenous unity. Each group is only *partly* transformed. Each also remains distinct and partly autonomous from the larger group. For Gramsci, the key example is the northern Italian industrial proletariat joining with the southern peasantry. He argues that the workers cannot merely add the peasantry as a strategic and temporary ally, as a convenient

---

[2] Although on p. 200 he writes of two groups being "welded into a new organism," a strange mixing of metaphors that seems to hint at his struggle over just how these groups should relate to each other.

partner that will help them realize proletarian goals. He argues instead that the concept of

> hegemony presupposes that account be taken of the interests and the tendencies of the groups over which hegemony is to be exercised, and that a certain compromise equilibrium should be formed—in other words, that the leading group should make sacrifices of an economic-corporate kind (1971, p. 161).

As the workers incorporate the peasants' struggle into their own, he is saying, they must sacrifice some of their narrow self-interest (what Gramsci calls "economic-corporate" interests in the quote). The peasants must reciprocate, as must all groups who join a hegemonic formation. Each group therefore takes on board new political goals, and each lets go of some old ones. A good contemporary example of this way of thinking can be seen in the strategy of an organization called the Miami Workers Center. Their executive director, Gihan Perera, says,

> We're trying to build this environmental/labor/community coalition, [and] there is a low road and a high road.... The low road is labor wants jobs; the environmentalists want green buildings; the community wants houses. Traditional organizing theory is, "Just match up those self-interests and there you've got your coalition." But I feel like we are at the end of being able to operate at that low level of self-interest because if we don't adopt each other on a higher plane, the coalition is going to be limited to that self-interest. So, for example, if the environmentalists are happy that they are building green houses but don't understand the importance of supporting the African American community's political power, it will not be a solid coalition. Once that project is over, if the threat to the African American community still continues, those concerned about environmental issues may not be there with support. So our job is to keep the conversation going. Yes, you're here for green buildings, but you also have to be doing this to actually build the power of a black community....That has to be central to their consciousness as environmentalists (Heller and Perera, 2007, pp. 24–25).

Perera's "high road" on which allied groups "adopt each other on a higher plane" is very much what Gramsci thinks must happen in a hegemonic alliance. Environmentalists must take on the agenda of black community empowerment and make it a central element in the environmental agenda.

Even though Gramsci insists that each group remains partly autonomous (1971, p. 161), nevertheless he is also clear that together the groups must forge a collective will that guides the hegemonic formation's struggle for a broader societal alternative (2000, pp. 220, 348). For Gramsci, this will is built up through ideological, cultural, and educational struggle. The alliance must actively develop a set of shared intellectual, moral, and cultural assumptions that frame how it interprets the world. When managed and shaped, these shared assumptions can become a "hegemonic principle" that forms the basis of the collective will. Education, conceived by Gramsci in the broadest sense, serves to develop the existing consciousness of people toward a new collective will. As we saw in the last chapter, for Gramsci, education aims to produce nothing short of a new psychology, a new way of thinking and feeling proper not just to a specific class, but to the wider hegemonic group. It entails the active and conscious production of particular types of subjects whose ways of thinking and being resonate with the wider logics of the new hegemonic formation.

We can see in this formulation that Gramsci takes cohesion and coordination very seriously. While he moves away from a concept of a movement that entirely dissolves each group into a unitary whole, he is also wary of each group's autonomy, because he very much fears that groups will drift in and out of the movement and the larger hegemonic project will not cohere. We saw this fear in his idea of democratic centralism in Chapter 2: he insists on a strong and disciplined party leadership that can help the coalition move when the political time is right. His concern for a collective will is part of that same instinct. He wants very much to make sure that the movement remains coherent politically, and so he stresses the need for a strongly shared ideology and culture. Again, more than other Marxists of his time, he accepts a measure of autonomy for each part of the coalition, but his instincts tend to favor coherence more than autonomy. He fears the disorganization and dissolution of the movement more than he fears the danger of some groups being coerced to think or act in a particular way.

Gramsci's preference for cohesion can also be seen in his understanding of the relations among groups in a hegemonic formation. While each must partly be remade by the others, and each must genuinely adopt a measure of the others' agendas, nevertheless in Gramsci's imagination the working class is typically prioritized over the other groups. Even if workers must sacrifice their self-interest to some extent, they are, for Gramsci, "the leading group," a position that casts everyone else as followers. Even though Gramsci argues one class is not able to rule society on its own, he retains the idea that one class can and should be *leading* in a hegemonic formation.[3] This idea of a leading role for the

---

[3] The word Gramsci often uses here is *dirigente*, present participle of the verb *dirigere*, to lead, to direct, to be at the head of, to guide.

working class is certainly born of Gramsci's life-long involvement in socialist and communist struggles. In his pre-prison writings, which are closer to traditional Marxism, he privileges the working class more nakedly. In the Lyons Theses, for example, he argues "in the capitalist countries, the only class which can accomplish a real, deep social transformation is the working class" (2000, p. 142). The working class is "a class which aims to lead the peasants and intellectuals." It can only win "if it is aided and followed by the great majority of these social strata" (2000, p. 174). Such language appears less frequently in the *Prison Notebooks*, written later in his life, although even there he has phrasing like, "The combination of national forces which the international class [the proletariat] will have to lead and develop" (1971, p. 240). A hegemonic class, he explains, "leads the classes which are its allies, and dominates those which are its enemies" (1971, p. 57). While he maintains that the proletariat absolutely must ally with other groups to achieve a wider transformation of society, nevertheless Gramsci consistently sees the former as "the leading class" (1971, p. 240). I think it is reasonable to conclude that these leader/follower roles stem from a deeper conviction in Gramsci that the proletariat and the bourgeoisie are the two "fundamental productive classes" (1971, p. 116) in society, an idea sometimes rendered as "fundamental social group" or "'essential' social group" (1971, pp. 5–6). They are fundamental for Gramsci because they are constituted at the level of the relations of production. He emphasizes that although the working class must make economic-corporate compromises in building hegemony, there is "no doubt that such...compromises cannot touch the essential; for though hegemony is ethico-political, it must also be economic, must necessarily be based on the decisive function exercised by the leading group in the decisive nucleus of economic activity" (2000, pp. 211–212). For Gramsci, therefore, a hegemonic formation must be led by one of the fundamental classes. In the French Revolution, which Gramsci studied very closely, the bourgeoisie was the leading class. In the transformation to come, he imagines the proletariat will take up that role.

Laclau and Mouffe: Equivalence

The idea of the leading class in Gramsci is what Laclau and Mouffe (1985, p. 85) call his "last redoubt of class reductionism." Given the language Gramsci uses, we might go one step further and call it a last redoubt of essentialism as well. Laclau and Mouffe take much inspiration from Gramsci, but they are determined to lay siege to this last redoubt. Their notion of a hegemonic formation insists that there is no privileged point of departure for politics, no essential characteristics around which politics must be framed. Political identities, agendas, and relations are always the result of political struggle, and they can always be renegotiated through politics. That is why Laclau and Mouffe see their idea of pluralism as a *radical* extension of Gramsci's pluralism, because Gramsci retains the idea of an untouchable "essential," and assigns leading roles to particular economic groups. As a result, for him the collective will that organizes the hegemonic formation must derive from the fundamental class. While other elements must help construct the collective will, in doing so they take their lead from the fundamental class. As Laclau and Mouffe put it, for Gramsci "there must always be a *single* unifying principle in every hegemonic formation, and this can only be a fundamental class" (1985, p. 69). Laclau and Mouffe's radical pluralism does away with a class-derived unifying principle. When groups connect with each other in an effort to form a larger political body, they are operating without any fixed ground, and therefore without any leading class.

So in this free-floating environment, without any essential ground, how do they imagine groups connect with each other to form viable hegemonic movements? Laclau and Mouffe use the term "articulation" to capture these connections. Each group articulates with the others, which, as in Gramsci, involves partly remaking itself in a complex negotiation of values and interests. Unlike in Gramsci, however, this articulation does not have any primary origin in a "fundamental class." Rather it flows from multiple points, as many different groups simultaneously seek to articulate with many others. For Laclau and Mouffe, a hegemonic articulation is produced collectively by groups acting "on an equal footing" with all the others (1985, p. 87). This shift away from a concept of a leading class helps make their approach a radical-democratic one. They imagine a hegemonic articulation in which each group is radically equal to every other. Their rejection of Gramsci's idea of a leading class thus leaves them with a hegemonic articulation in which leadership must emerge, in which some groups and locations can come to the fore in particular situations to chart a direction for the whole, but they cannot remain there, in a permanent leadership position. They must always fall back into the mass. Laclau and Mouffe thus also move beyond Gramsci's concept of democratic centralism, because they reject the argument that a party apparatus must occupy the center of the articulation and act as "a permanently organized and long prepared force" that gives direction to the spontaneous desire of the mass of people.

Although Laclau and Mouffe reject a permanent leadership, they do retain Gramsci's idea that the hegemonic articulation must develop a collective will (1985, pp. 72, 87). They argue that the groups in a hegemonic articulation must construct together a collective will that is distinctly different from, and yet rooted in, the individual wills of the groups. That new political understanding is forged around what Mouffe calls an articulating principle (1979, p. 193). This is quite similar to Gramsci's "hegemonic principle," in that it connotes a complex worldview, an interlocking system of values that organizes one's way of understanding the world and conducting oneself in it. However, Mouffe's articulating principle is not derived from the experience and agenda of a privileged element of the formation. Rather it is the creative product of collaboration among the many groups, each of which is equal to every other. Moreover, an articulating principle is not a pre-existing idea waiting to be discovered. It is instead the result of an intentional act of creation. It is *produced* by groups who, engaging each other on equal terms, consciously decide to construct a shared common sense, a collective way to see the world and to move forward together.

Of course, this act of connection and collective construction remakes each group to an extent. Although no group comes to the articulation with an essential character, nevertheless each possesses a history and a sense of itself that has been developed in the course of past struggles. That historical sense of itself is remade through the act of joining with others to form a hegemonic articulation and a collective will. But that historical sense is only *partly* remade; the group's history is never wholly defined by its participation in the hegemonic articulation. It retains significant autonomy to define itself and its political desires. Moreover, each group is always also constituted by a variety of engagements outside of its participation in the hegemonic formation. Each part of a hegemonic formation, then, engages the others in relations of simultaneous dependence and independence, and simultaneous commonality and particularity. Each of those conditions continually prevents the other from being fully realized. They remain in irresolvable tension. Consequently, the identity and subjectivity of each group in a hegemonic articulation is simultaneously shared with and distinct from the other elements. In Laclau and Mouffe's phrasing, each element is never entirely interior or exterior to the articulation, and any one element is never entirely interior or exterior to any other (1985, p. 111). They are mutually imbricated in each other, they bleed into each other and yet retain a measure of their own integrity.

That condition of simultaneous commonality-and-particularity is what I have called "equivalence" in the past (Purcell, 2008). Laclau and Mouffe argue that a hegemonic articulation for radical democracy would necessitate multiple struggles for democracy linking up with each other into what they call "chains of equivalence" (2000, p. xviii). That is, each group is similarly disadvantaged by the dominant order of neoliberal capitalism, but each is disadvantaged in a particular way. Two things that are equivalent are not identical, not entirely the same. But the term clearly denotes significant similarity, some measure of a common position in the social field and a shared understanding of the world. The concept resonates with one instinct in Gramsci's democratic centralism, which for him involves "the critical pursuit of what is identical in seeming diversity of form and on the other hand of what is distinct and even opposed in apparent uniformity, in order to organize and interconnect closely that which is similar" (1971, p. 189). Equivalence is also quite similar to what Michael Hardt has called "mutual adequation," which for him is how the various groups on the global left should engage each other in the contemporary era. They should

> reveal and address not only the common projects and desires, but also the differences of those involved—differences of material conditions and political orientation. The various movements across the globe cannot simply connect to each other as they are, but must rather be transformed by the encounter through a kind of mutual adequation….not to become the same, or even to unite, but to link together in an expanding common network (Hardt, 2004, p. 232).

It is a fair characterization of the structure of Laclau and Mouffe's hegemonic articulation: an expanding common network with an emergent leadership in which each group engages the others in relations of equivalence.

Deleuze and Guattari: Relentless Connection

While Hardt's idea of mutual adequation resonates with Laclau and Mouffe's idea of equivalence, his way of conceiving the larger whole, as an "expanding common network" rather than as a hegemonic articulation, moves us closer to the way Deleuze and Guattari understand the formations that are produced when mobilized groups connect with each other. We saw in Chapter 2 how Deleuze and Guattari are searching for ways desiring-production can free itself from the apparatuses that capture it. Elements of desiring-production draw lines of flight as they deterritorialize themselves and work to remain free. In the language of this book, people attempt to escape an oligarchical apparatus by becoming active and pursuing a perpetual project of becoming democratic.

But perhaps as much or more than any of the other thinkers I have been considering, Deleuze and Guattari stress that when elements pursue lines of flight, they must link up with each other in order for their escape to be successful. If they are not able to forge connections, they will almost certainly end up being recaptured. If they push their flight too far or too fast, they will lose touch with others and give in to schizophrenia or catatonia or career off into death. So, the goal of connections among lines of flight is to create a kind of mutual-aid network through which escapees help each other remain in flight. For example, Deleuze and Guattari advise us on how to escape two apparatuses of capture—the body and self—by dismantling ourselves as organisms and as subjects. Here is where they urge us to become a Body without Organs, to disarticulate our understanding of ourselves as material bodies organized into discrete wholes and instead become aware of our material connections to our outside, to others and to our habitat. Similarly, we should dismantle our self, our ego, by letting go of the idea that we are self-contained and independent psychic monads, and we should, again, open ourselves out onto the world and come to know our myriad emotional and affective connections to others.

"Where psychoanalysis says, 'Stop, find yourself again,' we should say instead, 'Let's go further still, we haven't found our BwO yet, we haven't sufficiently dismantled our self' " (Deleuze and Guattari, 1987, p. 151). But Deleuze and Guattari warn us not to undertake this dismantling too fast. "You don't reach the BwO...by wildly destratifying....Staying stratified [captured]...is not the worst that can happen; the worst that can happen is if you throw the strata into demented or suicidal collapse" (1987, pp. 160–161). Going too fast results in death for the organism. "Dismantling the organism," they argue, "has never meant killing yourself, but rather opening the body to connections that presuppose an entire assemblage" of material and energy (1987, p. 160).

Similarly, we must tear consciousness away from the subject, but not so as to induce catatonia or schizophrenia. They are saying, in short, that we must undertake our flight cautiously, thoughtfully, and soberly.[4] And as we saw in Chapter 2, we are ultimately aiming at a wider breakthrough, a revolution that causes the apparatuses (or socius or strata) to collapse onto themselves. But all this must be done carefully. We must always make sure our flight is not so harried that it causes us to lose our bearings.

This caution emerges most clearly in the middle parts of A Thousand Plateaus, and it is relevant here because it reiterates the importance of connection. The danger of going too far and too fast, or its opposite, the

---

[4] We can see this idea of dismantling the self-as-monad quite clearly in Deleuze and Guattari's modern heirs, The Invisible Committee, who argue that we *are made up of* our attachments to others. As a result, they argue, we should not understand freedom to involve an atomistic individual severing his constraining ties to others. Rather freedom is a process by which each of us actively works on our connections, weaving ourselves into the world according to our desires (2009, pp. 19–20).

danger of a flight being recaptured, are mostly dangers of solo flights. The best way to modulate one's speed, to introduce caution and thoughtfulness into one's flight, is to flee in association with others. It is to connect up with other flights flowing in complementary ways. By connecting with others, "decoded and deterritorialized flows boost one another, accelerate their shared escape, and augment or stoke their quanta...." (1987, p. 220). They thus increase their own power to both ward off the apparatuses of capture and to remain in motion, to continue their project of becoming, to successfully trace out a new land. A successful flight is thus necessarily a collective project. For Deleuze and Guattari, becoming democratic, becoming autonomous, and becoming active, if they are to be done effectively, must be done in association with others. If they are not, if they are undertaken by solitary agents, they will result either in a reinscription of oligarchy or in exhaustion and self-destruction (e.g. Deleuze and Guattari, 1987, pp. 229–231).

The good news, as we saw in Chapter 2, is that one of the defining features of desiring-production is that it is driven to make connections. Part of what it rediscovers when it regains its proper autonomy is this capacity to connect. But what kind of connections? What is the nature of the relations among the various lines of flight and deterritorialized flows? Deleuze and Guattari have various names for the associations that form among elements in flight. They call them minoritarian aggregates, assemblages, rhizomatic blocs, war machines. On the one hand, these aggregates must create what Deleuze and Guattari (1987, p. 473) call "revolutionary connections": they must gather enough elements that together have enough consistency that they are able to create a breakthrough, to form a new land beyond capital and the state. But on the other hand, these connections cannot be too rigid; the new land must not become organized in the sense that certain centers take on set roles, as with organs in a body. Inspired by William Burroughs, Deleuze and Guattari imagine a body in which "no organ is constant as regards either function or position, ... sex organs sprout anywhere,... rectums open, defecate and close, ... the entire organism changes color and consistency in split-second adjustments" (Deleuze and Guattari, 1987, p. 153; they take the quote from Burroughs, 1966, p. 8).[5] In other words, the aggregate body functions, it carries out necessary acts (like sex or defecation), but it does not assign particular organs to always carry out those functions. Necessary organization emerges, the body acts, but then that organization dissolves back into an undifferentiated BwO.

---

[5] Burroughs' *Naked Lunch* provided a great deal of the inspiration for the concept of the body without organs.

In this discussion of emergent organization, both in Deleuze and Guattari and beyond, natural metaphors are common: the ant hill, the beehive, the termite mound, the bird flock, the wolf pack. Perhaps Deleuze and Guattari's most memorable natural image is the rhizome. They propose that deterritorialized elements of desire can arrange themselves like a rhizomatic plant. Instead of a tree, which is arranged hierarchically in the sense that all parts branch out from a single trunk, a rhizome is a non-hierarchical system of equal roots that spreads horizontally, underground. Each element of the rhizome can connect to any other. Each stem is "superficial," and the connections they make are contingent: no connection is more important than any other and the loss of one connection does not disrupt the system to any great degree (1987, pp. 2, 7). Unlike in a tree, where one is connected only and permanently to one's hierarchical superior or inferior, in a rhizome every element has multiple connections, each of which is to a peer. Each element can disconnect at any time from any other element, and it can make new connections with others (1987, p. 21). These superficial connections, taken together, can nevertheless create a coherent (or even a strong) aggregate because the connections are so numerous. In addition to this lack of hierarchy, rhizomes also lack centralization. They do not have a more-important cluster of connections, a node through which a higher volume of traffic or communication or nutrients must flow (1987, p. 21). So, how do rhizomes decide and act? How do they coordinate their various roots? Deleuze and Guattari approach this question by asking another: "Is a general necessary for n individuals to fire in unison? The solution without a General," they argue, "is to be found in an acentered multiplicity possessing a finite number of states with signals to indicate corresponding speeds...without any copying of a central order" (1987, p. 17).

That appears to be a pretty vague solution, especially for anyone who takes seriously Gramsci's insistence that the movement must have a well-organized leadership that is ready to act when the time is right. To clarify the situation, it is helpful to go beyond the rhizome image in thinking about democratic connections. The idea of corresponding speeds in the quote helps remind us that the rhizome metaphor can only take us so far. The agents in question are not relatively static *points* connected in an immobile (or slow-growing) net or mesh, but aggregates of *lines*, of fleeing elements of desiring-production. They are deterritorialized flows that are streaming themselves together into a larger flow and moving in a common direction. So, "corresponding speeds" makes sense in that context. Nevertheless, the idea that the "signals" just exist and will allow a large mass of people to act effectively in concert seems a bit of wishful thinking. Here again we can turn to nature, to realize that this is almost precisely how a flock of starlings operates, at least as we currently understand it (see Hayes, 2011). For starlings, there is no point of central command, and yet flocks of thousands of birds can very much act effectively, such as when they turn on a dime to avoid predators or pursue food. The scientists' research suggests that this cohesion is achieved by each individual following a simple algorithm: (1) avoid hitting other birds, (2) stay connected to the flock, and (3) match the speed of others nearby. When each follows the algorithm, the whole can act in concert. Similar characteristics of emergent organization can be seen in swarms of bees, ant hills, and termite mounds. Shouldn't it be possible for humans to self-organize as well? Hobbes argued that we cannot. In order to defend his argument that we need Leviathan, he rejects the possibility of emergent human self-organization. He has little choice, because if we can self-organize, if we can form a successful cooperative society without an overarching authority, then his frightening state of nature, the war of all against all, is a red herring and his Leviathan is unnecessary. So, in Chapter 17 of *Leviathan* he gives a long list of reasons why self-organization is impossible: competition, reason, free will, language, and so forth. Each of these reasons is rooted in the premise that humans are individual monads, that each of them has an individual will and individual interests that can vary from the interests of the whole community. Each of us can decide individually to not follow the algorithm, and so we can't operate like starlings or ants, each of which is unable to decide for itself.

To some extent, Deleuze and Guattari's campaign to dismantle the organism and the subject that we saw previously is a response to this gambit of Hobbes. They very much want us to unsettle the idea that we are self-contained individuals that can make independent and conscious choices outside of our embeddedness in a network of others. Since Hobbes argues his Leviathan is necessary precisely because of the free will of individuals, Deleuze and Guattari explore how we might pull those individuals apart. If we are not self-contained monads, but are instead extremely complex assemblages that are embedded in a network of millions of other such assemblages, and if the many elements held together in our assemblage are subject to continual reshuffling, with elements always joining and leaving (Deleuze and Guattari, 1987, pp. 341–342), then it becomes harder to imagine a lone individual making choices independently of the group. If each assemblage-self is constantly exchanging matter, ideas, emotions, and affects with many other assemblage-selves, then none can function completely independently from the others. Each decision that we think of as being made by an individual is actually being made by an assemblage-self that is in large part made up (physically and psychologically) of its connections to others.

Hardt and Negri help make Deleuze and Guattari's line of thinking still more relevant to the question of emergent organization by considering the human brain. They contend that according to contemporary neurobiology, the human brain operates much more like Deleuze and Guattari's assemblage than like a discrete, self-contained organ. The brain

> does not function according to a centralized model of intelligence with a unitary agent. Thought is better understood, the scientists tell us, as a chemical event or the coordination of billions of neurons in a coherent pattern. There is no one that makes a decision in the brain, but rather a swarm, a multitude that acts in concert. From the perspective of the neurobiologists, the one never decides (2004, p. 337).[6]

The flock of starlings, the brain, the human body, the masses of people in the squares of Europe in 2011: these are all multitudes. For Deleuze and Guattari, the naturalism objection misses the mark. Unlike Hobbes, they consider humans to be very much part of the natural sphere. They contend that we are all qualitatively the same sort of thing, made out of the same sort of stuff as an ant hill or a flock of starlings. This move is a radical break from Hobbes and most modern political theory. It means there is little difference between trying to get n soldiers to fire in unison without a general and trying to get a single soldier to do so. Either way, a nearly uncountable multitude of elements must be coordinated with no central intelligence and no unitary agent. It is therefore not an implausible fantasy, because it happens all the time. Every time what we think of as "a person" makes a decision, or a flock of starlings turns, or an unplanned crowd gathers: n soldiers without a general have been organized to fire in unison.[7]

So then for Deleuze and Guattari, connections among elements should be such that they are conducive to emergent organization. They use yet another image, that of the wolf pack, to further explain those relations. As with the rhizome and the flock, their wolf pack operates as a band of equals with no central intelligence. For each wolf, it is imperative to remain with the pack, for wolves must live together to survive. However, each wolf must also avoid being drawn into the center of the pack, where it will be destroyed. "In becoming-wolf," they tell us, "the important thing is the position of the mass, and above all the position of the subject

---

[6] For the source of the neuroscience, they refer the reader to Damasio (2003).

[7] Of course, I don't mean to strictly equate aggregates of all sizes here. It is certainly possible that self-organization becomes more difficult as populations get larger. I just mean to say that self-organization at the individual level is already extremely complex and involves the coordination of huge numbers of elements, and yet it happens successfully all the time. And so, perhaps, self-organization at larger scales is much less far-fetched than we tend to believe.

itself in relation to the pack or wolf-multiplicity" (1987, p. 29). They recount the dream of a girl called Franny:

> *I am on the edge of the crowd, at the periphery; but I belong to it, I'm attached to it by one of my extremities, a hand or foot.* I know that the periphery is the only place I can be, that I would die if I let myself be drawn into the center of the fray, but just as certainly if I let go of the crowd. This is not an easy position to stay in, it is even very difficult to hold, for these beings are in constant motion and their movements are unpredictable and follow no rhythm. They swirl, go north, then suddenly east; none of the individuals in the crowd remains in the same place in relation to the others. So I too am in perpetual motion; all this demands a high level of tension, but it gives me a feeling of violent, almost vertiginous, happiness (1987, p. 29).

Deleuze and Guattari approve: "A very good schizo dream. To be fully a part of the crowd and at the same time completely outside it, removed from it: to be on the edge, to take a walk like Virginia Woolf..." (1987, p. 29). It is hard not to see the starlings in their description of the swirl. The flocks have a very similar structure. The density of birds is much greater on the *edges* than in the middle, precisely the opposite of how a cluster forms through a force like gravity (Hayes, 2011). Just by following their algorithm (avoid collisions, stay together, match speeds), the birds tend to move nearer to the edge, and thus they avoid both getting drawn into the middle and losing touch with the flock.

Clearly this sort of imagination, of non-hierarchical and acentered relations within aggregates, contrasts with Gramsci's notion of a movement with an organized leading group. Deleuze and Guattari specify that relations between liberated flows should be connections rather than what they call conjugations. That is, flows should come together in a way that is mutually affirming, that accelerates their shared escape. When flows are conjugated, on the other hand, one is subordinated to another. Conjugation "indicates their relative stoppage, like a point of accumulation that plugs or seals the lines of flight, performs a general reterritorialization, and brings the flows under the dominance of a single flow capable of overcoding them" (Deleuze and Guattari, 1987, p. 220). This rejection of a "single flow" that overcodes others means that Deleuze and Guattari are expunging any remnants of Gramsci's "leading" class, a more important group that conjugates other flows into its own. Instead, flows should relate through affinity, solidarity, or what Hardt calls mutual adequation. Deleuze and Guattari imagine lines of flight that are mutually immanent to each other, such that none is transcendent, each is at work within the others (1987, p. 205). They also talk about these relations in terms of love. Liberated elements try to create "a nonsubjective, living love in which each party connects with unknown tracts in the other without entering or conquering them" (1987, p. 189).

Recall that the entities connecting here are not discrete monads but assemblages of partially dismantled bodies and subjects. They are multitudes that hold together but are by no means independent, homogenous, or self-contained. Thus when they connect, parts of one assemblage can connect with parts of another. And since each assemblage has millions of pieces, it can make many such connections with many other assemblages. This way of thinking greatly expands the potential for connection. Deleuze and Guattari enjoin us to multiply these connections, to make as many links as possible, to connect almost obsessively. We should always push ourselves toward the horizon of the fully rhizomatic assemblage in which every element is connected to every other.[8] Each one of these connections is superficial, temporary, non-specific, and contingent. Each is quite weak, but because there are so many they can form a strong mass when taken all together. Deleuze and Guattari are moving us away from a Freudian familial model in which we make a few deep, enduring, specific, and necessary connections. They urge us to become starlings, to become wolves, to always remain in the pack by making multiple connections that shift and adapt as the pack changes shape or changes direction. This way of connecting is extremely dynamic and requires great energy and attention. We must be constantly vigilant. It is hard and stressful. We are always in danger of losing touch or of being drawn into the center. But this way of connecting also has a tangible reward. We will know when we really have it right, Franny tells us, when we feel delight, when we are visited by a "violent, almost vertiginous, happiness."

All these images of wolves and rhizomes and brains are evocative, but it is also useful, I think, to relate all this to actual human communities. Beginning in the summer of 2011 in Spain, a large and changeable mass of people rose up to challenge the dominant political-economic arrangements in the country. The uprising of *indignados* has been unexpected, diverse, and in many ways spontaneous. It is not unreasonable to see it as a minoritarian aggregate of loosely affiliated people who are indignant about the state of affairs in Spain for many different reasons. Students worry about economic future, pensioners worry about their benefits, public employees worry about their jobs. Some want reform of the

---

[8] It is perhaps worth pointing out that this is precisely how Hobbes saw relations among people subject to Leviathan. Unlike Locke, he argued that people were a multitude rather than a single body. As such, in creating Leviathan each person has to contract with each and every other person in society. Each contract is an agreement between two people that they will both yield their power to the sovereign. Hobbes' social contract is thus actually made up of millions of social *contracts*. It is much like a rhizome in which every element contracts (rather than connects) with every other. The difference is that Hobbes did not see this rhizome as a democratic horizon to move toward, but as an imagined starting point from which Leviathan was born.

system, some want to return to the good old days before the crisis, some insist that the larger economic system is broken and must be swept away (Wall, 2011). All are appalled by the Spanish government, and most are dissatisfied with the influence of the international financial oligarchy (the so-called "troika" of the European Central Bank, the IMF, and the EU). Some of the latter experimented with alternative forms of leaderless social organization, such as protest camps, deliberative peoples' assemblies (*asambleas*), and democratic committees (European Revolution, 2011; Sitrin and Moreno-Caballus, 2011). Each person who has chosen to participate in this assemblage is herself an aggregate; parts of her connect up with other parts in other people, then disconnect and reconnect with others. The uprising has been fluid, it has surged and waned, and it has responded to events as they have occurred. Occupying the squares in Madrid and other Spanish cities has been a key strategy, as have long marches through the countryside, called *marchas populares indignas*. These tactics tend to be only partially organized and planned, and often people participate without having fully worked out their desires beforehand. To a great degree, people have come to know why they are upset and what they want to see only by taking action and interacting with others. Traditional organs, like unions, NGOs, and political parties have participated, but they have played distinctly minor roles. While leaders have emerged and had an effect, mostly the uprising has occurred without a centralized and hierarchical leadership structure. As is fast becoming the norm, social media like Twitter, Facebook, and various blogs have played an important role in organizing action and spreading information.

Despite this non-traditional structure, the movement has been quite able to act effectively. For example, it has occupied important spaces in Spanish cities, and even occupied space in the main square in Madrid, Puerta del Sol, for an extended period. It has done so with large demonstrations that extended into the radial streets that meet at the plaza, as well as by camping overnight and holding popular assemblies and other sorts of encounters in which participants can discuss the political-economic situation and what they might do to change it. In the early morning of August 2, 2011, police evicted a small group of campers (less than a hundred) who were staffing the information tent, which was both the logistic and symbolic center of the occupation. After the eviction, cleaning crews arrived to erase all traces of the camp. *Indignados* who contribute to the blog "Take the Square" reported the eviction under the headline "Sol has been evicted, but we know the way back" (Carolina, 2011b). The next day, tens of thousands of people returned to reclaim the square. They were prevented from entering the square by a small army of police with armored vehicles.

When they realized they couldn't take the square, the protesters quickly dissolved into a dozen side-streets and regrouped on a number of key locations: Cibeles, Atocha and Congreso, among them. For hours now, protesters have been blocking all the main traffic arteries in the city center. The mass protest is now reported to be headed back towards Sol for a second time, in another attempt to take back the square (Roos, 2011a).

The actor here was not so much a cadre of leaders, but rather the whole mass of people. They reacted and decided spontaneously, much like a flock of starlings. The alternate squares became bases of operation for this mass as they searched for ways to return to Sol. Eventually, four days later, they were able to retake the square, apparently with the unofficial support of police, who were not as rigorous as they might have been in carrying out a government order to hold the square. The crowd's first act was to begin to reconstruct the information tent. There was incredible joy and celebration.

Certainly this brief account is only evocative. The *indignados* are not reducible to an example of Deleuze and Guattari's vision. They are not a completely acentered and non-hierarchical mass. They are differentiated, and some people do emerge to act as leaders. But these are relative distinctions. As opposed to the police that tried to channel them, as opposed to a more traditional labor march organized by a party and led by union officials, this mass was relatively without leaders and without hierarchy. They often rose spontaneously—sometimes within twenty-four hours— and they reacted collectively in response to conditions that changed by the hour. They communicated both in person and online. In a very real way, they were a multitude that was able to decide and to act effectively. They wanted Sol back, and they took intentional action to satisfy that desire. On the night of the reconquest, when the people again controlled the square, the headline was very different: "The sun rises: *indignados* take back Puerta del Sol" (Roos, 2011c).

A very similar story could be told about events in Greece that same summer. Or Egypt and Tunisia in the winter of 2011. Or Buenos Aires in 2001.[9] Or Tiananmen Square in 1989. In the case of Beijing, diverse student groups initiated action against the government, demanding more freedoms and democratic rights. There were many leaders, none of whom had control over the larger mass. One group decided to launch a hunger strike, and as that wore on, it touched off a spontaneous mass mobilization. As a military convoy approached the city to evict the students from the square, waves of regular people went to block the troops and make it impossible for the trucks to get to the square (Zhao, 2004, p. 184ff).

[9] And of course these events are not unconnected. The chant voiced in Argentina, for example, "Que se vayan todos!" ("They should all go!"), was repeated verbatim in the Puerta del Sol.

The convoy was turned back. There were leaders here and there urging the mass in particular directions, but the mass also was able to act on its own, to fill the streets, fend off the army, and defend the square. Again, such examples do not prove that this approach to mobilization is better or more effective than a traditional one. Rather, they should be seen as glimpses, as fleeting instantiations of a more fully democratic way to connect, to act collectively, and to be political. These events can teach us, or perhaps remind us, that we are capable of more, that we can go farther down the path toward democracy, autonomy, and activity than we think.

Conclusion

It is so easy to wave away this kind of vision, to call it utopian, and then in a flanking argument, to decry its naturalism, to judge it inapplicable to human society. But when we look at history, *human* history, through its lens, we start to see something new, something other. And we see it over and over again. It turns out this sort of mass thought and action is not only possible, it is common. To be sure, it may be *more* common to see regimented mass action, action by groups organized oligarchically with clear leaders and institutional organization. But still, people *do* make the kinds of connections Deleuze and Guattari advocate. Or, more precisely, since what Deleuze and Guattari are presenting is a horizon, a full-blown image of a rhizome or a wolf pack or a BwO, what people have in fact achieved is great strides in the direction of the rhizome, heroic tries at becoming-wolf. In the language of Lefebvre's method of transduction, the wolf pack is a virtual object, an image in thought extrapolated from actual practices: Tiananmen, Tahrir, Sol. It is an image of a network of people without a center and without a hierarchy in which each element is connected to every other element. It is a collective body, a multiplicity that acts effectively to ensure its own growth and flourishing, a body that manages its own affairs. But it does so without leaders. The whole body organizes and coordinates itself. It is Lefebvre's urban society, in which every inhabitant is connected to every other, and they deliberate collectively about what kind of city they want to create together. Again, for Lefebvre this virtual object, this urban society (or this total rhizome), is not an end goal that we can reach. It is not conceived as an ideal society beyond politics. It is rather a horizon, a destination that is not specific. It is not a point; it is unspecified, a line. But even though it is unspecified, it still points in a direction. We can know when we are moving toward this horizon and when we are moving away from it (2003b, pp. 16–18).

What happened in Tiananmen, in Tahrir, in Sol—among so many other things—is a certain kind of insistent, creative, and remarkable work. It is the work of a multitude struggling to remove the obstacles—physical and psychological—that currently make the rhizome impossible, that make urban society impossible. It is the coming together of people, drawing themselves together into an encounter, to engage their differences and work out their future together. It is the work of cutting open a path to the possible, of becoming aware of the horizon, and understanding how to walk toward it. In the most spectacular of cases, it even involves walking quite a ways down that path. The crowds in the squares of Egypt and Tunisia and Spain and Greece and New York and other US cities have refused the industrial city, they have refused to be separated, stored, and ruled in isolation. They have taken flight from the heteronomy and oligarchy of their societies, and have sought each other out. Together they have explored their own capacity for autonomy. To be sure, they didn't rid the world of oligarchy forever. They didn't establish a pure democracy or a stable communist society. But they fled, they voiced their indignation at being ruled, and they walked down the path a long way, as far as they could go for the time being. And they discovered that they were far more capable of managing themselves without leaders than they (or anyone) thought they were. With Lefebvre and Calvino, our task, the task of everyone, of anyone at all, is to seek this democracy out, to recognize it when we see it, and to help it, however we can, to develop on its own terms.

6

Conclusion

Objections

Certainly this way of thinking about democracy has its critics. Some take a Platonic line, which is an oligarchic one: you can't have a polis in which people rule themselves, because people are no better than adolescents. They act according to whatever whim strikes them. They are not good enough at governing to govern themselves. The main variant of this line is Hobbes, who argues that without a transcendent "power able to overawe them all," people will turn to war and destroy each other (1996, Chapter 13). Some combination of these objections has been the stock-in-trade of power for centuries. In Argentina, workers in a self-managed factory reported bosses asking, "Do you lazy slobs really think you can run a company?" (Colombo and Mascarenhas, 2003, p. 459). At the height of the Egyptian uprising, Hosni Mubarak declined to leave office, saying, "If I resign today there will be chaos." He also reported telling President Obama, "You don't understand the Egyptian culture and what would happen if I step down now" (Amanpour, 2011).

This objection assumes that people have a certain essence, that they are either capable of democracy or they are not. But that is wrong. People are neither essentially capable nor incapable of democracy. They can grow and change. They can go from being adolescents to adults, or from adults to adolescents. Moreover, democracy itself entails a process of growing up. Becoming-democratic involves deciding to take up responsibility in the world, to refuse infantilization and accept the hard work of self-government. It requires that people nurture their desire for democracy, autonomy, and activity, and ward off their desire for oligarchy,

The Down-Deep Delight of Democracy, First Edition. Mark Purcell.
© 2013 John Wiley & Sons, Ltd. Published 2013 by John Wiley & Sons, Ltd.

heteronomy, and passivity. It requires that they constantly become-adult. But in the contemporary era, we are being infantilized every day by a political and economic oligarchy. The state and capital nurture our adolescent passivity. To say we are too immature for democracy and therefore we must be ruled by an oligarchy—that would be to cure the disease with the germ that is making us sick. Reinscribing oligarchy will not help. Plato is right to decry a polis run by adolescents. That would be at best a David Lynch film and at worst Hobbes' state of nature. But that polis is not at all a democratic polis. Democrats are adults, or at least they are engaging in a conscious effort to grow up, to become-adult and become-democratic.

Many on the left, ironically, raise an objection very similar to Plato's. They tell us our movement against capitalism (and neoliberalism) needs leaders. Even today, they say we need a disciplined party organization, because otherwise we will not be able to act effectively when the time is right. If we rely on self-organization, on some sort of collective intelligence to just emerge, they worry, we will ensure inaction and our irrelevance as a movement. This argument assumes that people are incapable of success on their own, that they need leaders. Even Gramsci, despite his hostility to vanguardism, was sympathetic to this critique. Sometimes this insistence that we need leaders is overt, as when Slavoj Zizek argues that the movements in Greece and Spain were not enough to "impose a reorganization of social life. To do that, one needs a strong body able to reach quick decisions and to implement them with all necessary harshness" (Zizek, 2011). Or when Jodi Dean (2011), in a much more thought-out argument, advocates a return to party organization as a way to create the stable solidarity needed to confront capitalist domination. Or when Oisín Giollamóir (2011) complains that when movements arise outside of established institutions (like unions), they come and go quickly and leave little in their wake. Or when Immanuel Wallerstein (2011) raises concerns about the process in Egypt, because he does not see the kind of institutions on the left (parties, unions, etc.) that he thinks are necessary to carry the revolution forward. Typically, this way of thinking imagines political success to mean gaining institutionalized state power, and so when it encounters democratic movements that aim at something more, it judges them to be failures.

In other cases, the assumption that there must be leaders and followers is implicit, as when the head of the British union Unite said of his organization: "Our beliefs are the core values of working people and we're their voice. We have to raise the consciousness of people and their confidence" (Power, Wainwright and Calderbank, 2011). Or James O'Nions (2011) writing about the rioters in the United Kingdom in 2011, opined that sometimes "the howls of protest from the oppressed...have political direction, and sometimes they don't." Those that lack proper direction, of course, need to be led, an argument Daniel Harvey (2011), also writing about the rioters, was eager to make: "We have to radicalise them further, we have to politicise them and turn them against the *real* targets of our alienation and poverty...the faltering capitalist regime" (emphasis added). This modern vanguardism imagines politically knowledgeable leaders and organizers acting upon directionless adolescent masses who are energetic and active, but who need correction and guidance. It imagines that some arrangement of rulers and ruled is necessary for achieving any *real* political success.

This old-left objection is important because it gets to the heart of what is at stake if we are to truly embrace democracy as our political vision. Everyone mouths the word democracy. It is a near-universal political value. But truly embracing democracy as a political vision means deciding that political success no longer entails a revolution that installs *our* oligarchs in place of *their* oligarchs. For democrats, such an outcome is a failure. It may very well be a kind of improvement, but it is only ever a tactical move to mitigate some of the more egregious ills of capitalist oligarchy. To be sure, such revolution can make people's lives materially better in a very real way, and that is an achievement we should take seriously. But it is not nearly enough. The goal is not merely greater material equality or working-class empowerment. The goal is democracy. A new oligarchy can never be our principal aim. The minute we hear a union leader, no matter how earnest, profess to speak for the working class, or yearn to "raise people's consciousness," we should get the itch to flee. They are proposing oligarchy, and we must ward them off. Embracing democracy means committing ourselves to the struggle for democracy, it means continually fighting off oligarchy as we move down the path toward democracy. We cannot arrive at the end, but we can move in its direction. We cannot be led by oligarchs toward democracy. We must walk that road ourselves. All of us together.

These are important critiques, but there is an even bigger and more insidious one out there, a critique that is so pervasive as to be common sense. It is the liberal-democratic objection to utopia.[1] Liberal democrats present themselves as the reasonable ones, the ones who inhabit "reality." They say that this "real democracy" you propose is idle fantasy. It is simply impractical to hope that people can rule themselves. Unlike Plato, liberal democrats do not so much think people are adolescents as that they have other things to do. People may have other preferences, other

---

[1] This paragraph presents a composite argument that I intend to represent what a whole number of theorists and commentators would say. Important texts that provide the ground for these arguments include Mill (1991), Acton (1955), and more recently Rawls (1993) and Nye (2002).

pursuits. Or they may not have the time, or energy. On top of that, there is a problem of scale. There are too many people; we cannot get all members of the nation together to make a collective decision, even using our ever-improving arsenal of communications technologies. Liberal democrats might even concede that real democracy is preferable, but they are adamant that it is not humanly possible. So instead, they tell us soberly, we need institutions, representatives, an agreed-upon system whereby a few rulers specialize in the work of governing (e.g. Petit, 2011). They say we should make this system as democratic as possible by balancing powers, upholding the rule of law, letting people elect their representatives, and so on. But that is really the best we can do. Anything more is starry-eyed overreaching; it is setting people up to fail, and, eventually, to slip into chaos.

Transduction

Seek and learn to recognize

It is in the face of this liberal-democratic objection that Lefebvre's method of transduction is so valuable. Lefebvre defines a different project than the one the liberal-democratic critics attack. They assume that democracy is conceived as an end point, that it proposes a stable system in which everyone rules. Since that end point is impractical, they claim, we must settle for some other system, one that is practical. But for Lefebvre, that argument misses the point. He agrees entirely that democracy as an end point is impractical. He even makes clear that it is impossible. Full-blown democracy, "real" democracy must always be understood as a horizon that we are always moving toward but that we can never reach. As a result, any democratic project we might engage in is always a process. We can never *be* democratic, we can only ever be in the process of *becoming* democratic. Democracy can only ever be the struggle for democracy, the journey down a path toward more democracy, autonomy, and activity (Lefebvre, 2009, p. 61). Liberal-democratic institutions work to stall this struggle. They bring the struggle to rest in a stable, relatively-more-democratic form of oligarchy. Really what they offer is a warmed-over version of Aristotle's "polity," a mixture of oligarchy and democracy that tries to balance the two in the name of establishing a regime whose principal strength is simply that it is stable (Aristotle, 1998b, pp. 1296b–1297a). Aristotle thought this was the most practicable constitution, but he didn't think it was the best, the one that was most likely to lead to human flourishing. The democratic project I advocate here refuses to settle into what is practicable. It insists that we must always push democracy further, that we must go beyond the purported best-we-can democracy offered by liberal democracy. We must continually remind ourselves we are capable of more.

As we have seen, transduction helps us down this path. It proceeds by paying very close attention to already-existing democratic practices and then augmenting them in thought, extrapolating them into their full-blown form, into a virtual object. It is important to be aware that this extrapolation can vary by circumstance. In some cases, it can require lots of effort and imagination. For example, in *The Urban Revolution* Lefebvre uses Jane Jacobs to illustrate inchoate urban society emerging in the industrial city. He is inspired by her modest example in which inhabitants use the street actively, they know each other, and they look out for the block. He sees this as an important example of reappropriating urban space. For him it shows that it is possible for people to manage the city for themselves, that "use and use value can dominate exchange and exchange value" (2003b, p. 19). In this case, urban society emerges quietly and faintly, such that we have to be very attentive and look very hard for it. But there are also relatively more apparent appropriations. For example, Italian cities have a long tradition of squatted and self-managed social centers, such as Leoncavallo in Milan, as do cities in the Netherlands, Spain, and Germany. Reappropriated residential dwellings are common as well, both in Europe and Latin America. More organized examples include the occupations of unused spaces and buildings by the Brazilian Homeless Workers' Movement, such as Quilombo das Guerreiras in Rio, or João Cândido near Sao Paolo. These are an urban extension of the actions of Landless Workers' Movement, which occupies and inhabits underused farm land in rural areas. A relatively more spontaneous occupation and reappropriation is the "Tower of David" in Caracas. It is an unfinished high-rise office building occupied by about 2,500 squatters (Romero and Diaz, 2011). Of course, the most obvious and important example of people appropriating space for their use has been the explosion of squatter settlements in cities all over the global South. Following transduction, we should not see these examples as ideal models to copy. They are not pure manifestations of Lefebvre's urban society. Rather we should seek in them glimmers of urban society. In each case, we can find inhabitants actively appropriating space for their use. We must be attentive to those glimmers, learn them, and discover how they can flourish more fully.

And sometimes these glimmers do more than glow. Sometimes they flare up and blaze brightly. Events like Tahrir in 2011, or Paris in 1968, or the *indignados* in 2011, or Buenos Aires in 2001, or Tiananmen in 1989 are cases where the desire for democracy explodes into the city and rushes headlong toward the horizon, if only for a few days. In these cases, urban society is very easy to see, or at least its effects are very apparent. And so we must be searching for both the spectacular events and the quotidian ones as well. Urban society emerges in multiple ways, each of which is evidence of the desire of urban inhabitants to become active, to become connected, and to take up the project of managing the city themselves.

It is also important to remember that Lefebvre's example of a virtual object, urban society, is only one kind of virtual object. We must also imagine, for example, a virtual object of popular autonomy in the midst of the heteronomy of the state apparatus. We must seek ways out of the Hobbesian contract and toward the withering away of the state. Or, if we think in terms of capitalism, we must search for practices of economic self-management (autogestion) in the midst of capitalist class relations and property rights. We must discover little worlds where self-management is the norm, where people are becoming familiar with its joys and struggles (Gibson-Graham, 1996). Or, with David Foster Wallace, we can seek in our everyday lives the virtual object of activity in the midst of passivity; we can discover the struggle to become grown-up in a society that sends out constant stimuli designed to infantilize us. My own focus in the book has been to imagine the virtual object of democracy, to seek out democratic practices in the midst of a pervasive oligarchy. Of course, each of these ways to think about virtual objects is bound up with the others; autonomy, activity, democracy, and urban society are nearly always interwoven in practice and in thought.

In all the ways we practice it, however, transduction is affirming. It is affirming because when we begin to look carefully for these emerging practices, we begin to see examples everywhere. That is good for our psyche, because it makes the world seem quite a lot less dark, especially when compared to a method like critical political economy that focuses intently on cataloguing, often meticulously, the many forms of oppression and apparatuses of capture.[2] But transduction also sharpens our senses. It makes us better able to perceive alternative practices, which helps us see more examples, which further sharpens our senses, and so on. As we gain experience perceiving the alternatives, we have more opportunity to examine them, and to know what to make of them when we find them. This process is very important, and it is tricky. The UK riots of 2011, for example, prompted a storm of interpretation and debate about how to make sense of the whole thing. Much energy was spent debating how best to interpret what took place. Transduction offers a very clear approach. It starts from the assumption that an event like the riots involves many different people, each with multiple wills operating simultaneously, and so the event is constituted by a cacophony of drives,

---

[2] See Andy Merrifield's (2011, p. 88) excellent critique of this way of thinking.

desires, and voices. As a result, we should decline to paint the event all with one brush. We should refrain from judging the riots as a whole to be political or not, progressive or not, good or not. Rather transduction would urge us to seek out, amid the cacophony, the many desires for democracy, for autonomy, and for active participation in society. Those desires are present, though in differing degrees, in all events. They exist alongside all sorts of other desires: the desire to be ruled, to punish, to take revenge, and even to destroy—to follow a pure, cold line of abolition, as Deleuze and Guattari say (1987, p. 230). All of this was certainly present in the UK riots, or the Los Angeles uprising of 1992, or in Detroit in 1967. In the various uprisings in 2011, democracy has been far more prominent and abolition much less so. Each event presents a unique composition of wills. Transduction enjoins us to acknowledge that multiplicity, and then learn to patiently sift through the many wills, to become better able to recognize the desire for democracy, to articulate it, to emphasize it, and to protect it so it can grow on its own terms.

For example, in the factory occupations in Northern Italy in 1920 we can discover that workers are in fact able to take, hold, and manage factories effectively on their own (Kohn, 2003, p. 61). We also discover the police will retake the occupied factories by force, reminding us that whatever else the state is, it is always very much a means of violence that protects capitalist property rights. In 2001, similar occupations in Argentina reiterated both those lessons. In Tiananmen, we can see that through occupying and inhabiting the center of the city, it is possible to both ward off the state apparatus and experiment with new forms of autonomous social organization. Similar lessons are apparent in the Spanish *indignados* movement of 2011, as well as the Occupy Wall Street movement in the United States in the same year. Or, in the years leading up to the Iranian uprising in 2009, we can learn that even when people appear inactive, it may be instead that they are living under repression, that their desire for democracy is steadily building up over the course of many years of popular demands and state repressions, and that a single incident (in this case the rigged election) can cause a great release of that desire, an extremely rapid becoming-active that spills out into the streets and transforms the city. In 2011, we see a similar dynamic in other repressive states like Tunisia, Egypt, Syria, Yemen, Bahrain, and Oman. Iran in 2009 can also teach us that people have the capacity for extraordinary bravery: they can continue to demand control over their own affairs even in the face of a state using pitiless violence to intimidate them. Certainly events in Syria in 2011 reiterate that lesson powerfully. And Bahrain in 2011 reminds us that people sometimes back down in the face of such violence, as fear and self-preservation (quite understandably) can outweigh a desire for democracy, at least for the moment.

In each of these cases, more was taking place than my brief narrative suggests. Other desires were at work. In Bahrain, for example, a largely Shiite population is ruled by a Sunni government, and so religious and ethnic politics were very much part of the story as well. My purpose here is not to give a comprehensive empirical account of becoming democratic. It is rather to propose a method by which we can construct a lens that seeks out democratic practices and pays attention to them in an effort to gather material for the project of building the virtual object of democracy. Each new lesson—squatting or workers' autogestion or occupy-the-square or active citizens simmering under the surface—adds to and reshapes that virtual object, which in turn helps us to discover democratic desires in other struggles.

In particular, I think transduction is a productive way to make sense most effectively of the Arab Uprising of 2011. For moments of varying length in Tunisia, Egypt, Libya, Bahrain, Yemen, and Syria, what was visible was a breathtakingly clear view of democracy. Lefebvre suggests (as in the Jane Jacobs example) that we are used to seeing democracy as a "shadow in the light of the rising sun" (1996, p. 148). But these events were like high noon, or a long lightning flash in which democracy was plainly visible. It was not the sanitized liberal democracy we are used to seeing. It was raw democracy, democracy at the bone. It was a democracy without representatives or elections or leaders. There were no parties, no state, no laws, no corporations. It was a democracy that did not stand still, that *moved* all throughout the brief time it lasted. It would not take orders or be organized. It was cacophonous, kaleidoscopic, and unruly. It was the most powerful thing on earth, and yet it was extremely fragile. What transduction helps us do, I think, is to see this manifestation of democracy on its own terms. To really look at it. To refuse to project onto it an image of how we are trained to think democracy should look. To refuse to see it as a prelude to an endgame, as merely the beginning of a transition to a liberal-democratic state. Transduction would have us apprehend its heterogeneity, feel its disorder, listen to its cacophony. Rather than judge it lacking in disciplined leadership, we can watch how it operates without leaders. Rather than expecting it to produce a bullet-point list of demands to the state, we can watch as people work out together what their desires are. And of course rather than suppress it or try to kill it, we can nourish it and help it grow.

Help them endure, and give them space

But once we develop our ability to seek and learn to recognize democracy, how do we help it endure? What would it mean to "give it space"? What techniques do we use? Let me return again to Calvino's prescription:

"Seek and learn to recognize who and what, in the midst of inferno, are not inferno, and help them endure, give them space." As I say in Chapter 1, I have been somewhat creative with the translation. The Italian is *"cercare e saper riconoscere chi e cosa, in mezzo all'inferno, non è inferno, e farlo durare, e dargli spazio."* In the original translation, the last six words are rendered in English as "then make them endure, give them space" (original, 1993; translation, 1974). I have phrased it instead as "and help them endure, and give them space."[3] That is because the first crucial thing about transduction is that the "them" in question—democratic struggles, urban society, Calvino's those-who-are-not-inferno—are active and alive. They are *already* going about the work of becoming-democratic, of exploring their capacity to govern themselves. They operate according to their own desire to endure, their own impulse toward self-preservation and self-realization.[4] So it is not possible to *make* them endure. They are already doing that on their own. The only thing we can do is *help* them do what they are already doing. The other problem with the translation is that the pronoun *them* suggests that whoever is acting is someone else, someone that is not us. But by definition *anyone at all* can participate in the struggle to become democratic. Everyone is eligible to become not-inferno. That is the path the virtual object of democracy urges us down: everyone struggling together to become democratic and active. If I were given free rein to translate the sentence, I might make it something like "seek and learn to recognize those things, both in society and in yourself, that in the midst of inferno are not inferno, and nurture those things, give them space and help them flourish on their own terms." That probably undermines the artistic power of Calvino's Italian. But it tries to articulate a key principle of transduction that must guide the practice of becoming-democratic: the desire or will to become democratic, autonomous, and active already exists in us, and it is struggling to endure. Whatever actions we take for democracy should merely seek to help it to do what it is already doing.

Of course, Calvino's "give it space" suggests that there is a need to shelter this will, to protect it from threat. Indeed, there are numerous forces that will work relentlessly to capture, govern, lead, infantilize, institutionalize, and otherwise control our desire to manage our own affairs. So we need ward off those forces, to carve out and defend a space in which becoming-democratic can grow. On the one hand, that space is literal: we need ways to create physical space for democracy. This requires techniques of conquest, ways to "take the square" as *indignados* have it. There are many different tactical strategies here, and I don't want

---

[3] I am not criticizing Weaver's translation, which is excellent.
[4] Their own *conatus sese conservandi*, as Spinoza had it (Spinoza, 1996, esp. Part 3).

to go into great detail, but I do want to make a case for a broad allegiance to non-violent conquest. It is easy to think of conquest in military terms, as ways to engage in armed struggle. But the project of democracy as I have outlined it is one that affirms growth, life, and development. Its primary strategy is not to confront and violently destroy oligarchy, but to help democracy flee from oligarchy, and to nurture democracy so that it grows everywhere. Becoming-democratic does require a vigilance against our desire for oligarchy, but I think the best way to be vigilant is to continually reaffirm our desire for democracy. In the same way that we cannot be led by others toward autonomy, I think we cannot nurture our desire for democracy by using violence against oligarchy. Rather, I think the *indignados* have it right. When they faced a line of police in riot gear who wanted to remove them from the square, they raised their hands and chanted *"estas son nuestras armas"*—"these are our arms." They confronted the threat of violence with the insistent desire of a multitude of bodies to inhabit the square. They returned over and over to present their bodies and their desire. There is no guarantee that the police will relent in the face of this desire, but in the Spanish case, they did.

Once physical space is taken over for democracy, there is very often a need for techniques of physical defense, because the authorities will seek to reclaim that space. These techniques include the famous barricades of the Paris commune, the *piquetes* of Argentina, the camping occupations of 2011, and people simply blocking access routes with a swarm of bodies, as the Chinese did to defend Tiananmen. These strategies are designed not to confront and defeat the state, but simply to hold the space, to create a cordon around the space so people can inhabit it, so that room is made for people to practice democracy. So, even if defensive tactics are sometimes necessary, the goal is not to confront the state, but rather to hold the space so that we can *use* it, so that we can get a *polis* up and running. We use the space to become active and democratic, to encounter each other and debate among ourselves what we want the polis to be. This use of space can take many forms: often people arrange spaces for popular assemblies, communications, food distribution, waste disposal, and the like. These are tactics of inhabiting the space, of people getting on with the work of governing themselves, no matter how briefly. Not just taking and holding the square, but using it to live, using it to become democratic.

In a way, taking the square is a speech act: it is people articulating a message aimed at both the present system and at themselves. In the context of the Spanish case, Carlos Frade has called this a politics of "presentation" as opposed to re-presentation (Frade, 2011). People gathered in the square, he argues, to present "the people" physically to the government. That presentation demonstrates clearly in physical space the gap between government representatives and those who are represented, between oligarchy and democracy. In Tunisia (and Egypt, Greece, Spain, Syria) the message being conveyed to the government by the seas of people in the square was: *we* are Tunisia, not you. That is one reason national flags were so prominent, at least in Tunisia, Egypt, Greece, and Libya. Tired of seeing the regime operate under the symbol of the nation, claiming to represent the nation, to *be* the nation, the crowds were reclaiming the nation for its people (Kouvelakis, 2011). The *indignados* were articulating the same gap when they chanted "*no nos representan*"—"*they* do not represent *us*." A similar message has been repeatedly voiced in the demonstrations across Europe, as well as in Wisconsin, where people insisted, "*We* will not pay for *your* crisis" (Announcements, 2011). The starkest has been the U.S. Occupy movement's "We are the 99%." Taking the square is thus a way to denounce the state's cold lie, as Zarathustra called it (Nietzsche, 2005, p. 44). When it says "I, the state, am the people," people respond, "No you're not. We are."

But occupying space is not only about talking to the powers that be, it is also about talking to each other. It is about drawing ourselves together into an encounter, to listen to and learn about each other, to understand our commonalities and differences, and to work out together what our desires are. It is coming to learn what student activists at Santa Cruz learned in 2009: that "there is no power to which we can appeal except that which we find in one another" (California Student Occupation Movement, 2009). These kinds of encounters are instantiations of Lefebvre's urban society. A more traditional demonstration consists of organizers speaking to the crowd or the crowd chanting its slogans, which are usually aimed at the state. But in Greece and Egypt and Spain, as well as in Argentina and Tiananmen, people also actively turned toward each other to solve their problems. They deliberated together about what kind of society they wanted to create, both in the square and into the future (Sitrin and Moreno-Caballus, 2011). As the first people's assembly in Syntagma put it:

> For a long time decisions have been made for us, without consulting us.... We are here because we know that the solutions to our problems can only be provided by us. We call on all residents of Athens, workers, unemployed and youth, to come to Syntagma Square, and all of society to fill the public squares and to take their lives into their own hands. In these public squares we will shape our claims and our demands together (People's Assembly of Syntagma Square, 2011).

Many movements even went so far as to establish working groups to consider the best way to conduct popular assemblies (Carolina, 2011a). They were exploring how to be and to act together outside the existing political and economic system. In that same vein, the Spanish made an effort to bring together their urban-centered uprising into an encounter with people in rural places. These *marchas populares* through the countryside were a tactic inspired by the *Columna Durruti*, the revolutionary columns that marched from Barcelona to Madrid in 1936 in an effort to liberate rural villages during the Spanish Civil War (Roos, 2011b). They were also inspired by the Zapatistas, who marched to Mexico City as a way both to call attention to their struggle and to connect with others with similar desires.[5] For the Zapatistas, as for the *indignados*, the march was not designed to liberate or to lead others, but to encounter them, to exchange ideas and stories, to build commonalities and become aware of differences. It was an attempt to establish the kind of rhizomatic connections I discuss in Chapter 5.

But such physical, spatial strategies are only a part of what is needed. As we saw particularly in Chapter 4, becoming democratic and becoming active is very much an interior struggle as well. If our own popular power is not to be found "out there" but already within us, then we require strategies to help ourselves understand and mobilize that power. We need techniques to nurture our desires for democracy, autonomy, and activity. Here Deleuze and Guattari's technique of schizoanalysis is particularly useful (1977, pp. 273–382). It is a kind of self-study, an examination of one's desires, both conscious and unconscious. Schizoanalysis first involves a negative task, which is to recognize and unthink certain assumptions that limit one's desire. In terms of democracy, for example, we would need to emphatically reject the Hobbesian choice between state power and chaos, reject the common sense that liberal democracy is the best we can do, and reject the fascist within us, our desire to be ruled by someone else. These assumptions place limits on what we can do; they assume we are incapable and so prevent us from discovering what we are capable of. This first negative task of schizoanalysis is quite similar to Lefebvre's injunction that we clear away the obstacles—like pragmatic reformism or ungrounded utopianism—that cloud our imagination and thus block a path toward a possible democracy (2003b, p. 17).

But Deleuze and Guattari stress that schizoanalysis is primarily a positive move, rather than a negative one. Its goal is to discover our own power, our capacity for flight, connection, autonomy, activity. Through schizoanalysis we seek to discover our own *conatus*, our own desire to grow and flourish (Spinoza, 1996). Our flourishing is the primary goal of schizoanalysis. Even the negative task of clearing away obstacles is not done for the pleasure of destroying; it is done in order to set our own power free, to make it so that our desire can act of its own accord. For Deleuze and Guattari, that positive task proceeds pragmatically, almost

---

[5] And of course Gandhi is an inspiration here as well.

as a kind of tinkering (1987, p. 109). They tell us to become attentive to the apparatuses of capture, to learn their contours, and then to launch little escapes, tentative flights that teach us what it is like to be in flight, how the apparatus will try to recapture us, and how we might connect up with others (1987, p. 161). These escapes are their "many local fires patiently kindled" (1977, p. 137). We experiment in this way, learning a little bit each time, carrying away a little bit of the apparatus with each escape, until we grow strong enough, and weaken the apparatus enough, to achieve "a generalized explosion," a great surge down the path toward democracy (1977, p. 137).

We can also tinker in this way with the act of connection. For Deleuze and Guattari, this would involve learning how to construct a new kind of relation, a relation of affinity in which we link up with others through multiple, non-specific, and shifting connections. That relation is not easy, nor is it something we have experience with. It takes practice. We need to practice being in groups like a wolf or a starling, on the edge, remaining connected but never getting drawn into the center. In terms of Lefebvre's vision of urban society, we need to practice being with others in a collective discussion of what the polis should be. We need to learn how to engage in politics as Aristotle understood them: how to speak and listen to others on an equal footing in an effort to develop common understandings of a good community and to engage seriously with different understandings. Deleuze and Guattari use the term "pragmatics" to describe this tinkering. They are invoking the philosophical position of pragmatism, as people like James, Peirce, and Dewey conceived it: a method of inquiry, of politics, and of living by which we learn continuously through experimentation. It is not meant to suggest crude pragmatism in the sense of an incrementalist and reformist approach, in which we are satisfied with small victories because it is the best we can do. Lefebvre explicitly rejects this kind of "short-term realism" (2003b, p. 75), saying it systematically reduces the possible "to the triteness of what already exists" (1991, p. 357). Similarly, Deleuze and Guattari's repeated insistence on revolution leaves little doubt about their position on reformism. Instead, their pragmatics are a practicable way to struggle relentlessly, in ways both big and small, for democracy.

There is something like Deleuze and Guattari's pragmatics going on today in Spain. As the *indignados* have continued their efforts past the heady early days of mass mobilization and protest, they have begun to experiment with new practices, new concrete modes of connection and common action. For example, under the slogan "*Toma los Barrios,*"[6] they have taken the *asambleas* they were conducting in the Puerta del Sol

---

[6] Take (or reclaim) the neighborhoods.

back out into the neighborhoods of Madrid (Sanchez, 2012). They are trying to reinvigorate a long tradition of neighborhood assemblies in Spain. The idea is for the neighborhood *asambleas* to be not merely the smallest scale of government, but for them to remain independent of the state and the formal economy, to create forms of autonomous organization for local inhabitants. They are constructing an arena in which to make neighborhood decisions, one created and controlled by the neighbors themselves. *Asambleas* are also providing some measure of social services, organizing to stop evictions, monitoring human rights of immigrants, planting community gardens, and creating of "time banks," which are a system of sharing resources and meeting local needs outside the market sphere. The *asambleas* therefore manifest some amount of institutionalization. They tinker with how to routinize practices and create rules of conduct. Some even have commissions to adjudicate disputes (Sanchez, 2012, and see for example the asamblea in La Concepcion at http://asambleapopularlaconce.wordpress.com/). But with Deleuze and Guattari and Lefebvre, we should not read this sort of experimentation as the movement maturing into a "real" movement that moves "beyond protest" and gets down to the important work of influencing decisions in the corridors of power. No. That would mean only the death of the revolution. Rather we should be attentive to the extent to which these initiatives are searching attempts to continue the struggle to become democratic, to find ways to live that are not just protest, not just indignation, not just mass demonstrations, but are also efforts to forge positive alternatives, to invent democratic collectives that can think and act outside the state and outside the market. These collectives may tinker with institutions, with rules, with leaders; they will try them out, see how they work. But becoming democratic means they will never settle down into those institutions. They will always renew their commitment to become active by continually remaking the structures they create, always disassembling institutions, recalling leaders, and reaffirming that it is the active participation of people themselves that constitutes the community and the movement. Like a wolf, they will continue to try the difficult trick of remaining on the edge of the pack, never getting drawn into the center, and never losing contact with the others.

The Down-Deep Delight of Democracy

To reiterate, none of these techniques *create* the desire for democracy. They are all merely strategies we can use to shelter and encourage a desire to become democratic that is already there. That desire has its own will to grow and thrive. We merely have to help, to create favorable conditions for it. And so, let's return again to Lenin's question, "What is to be done?" What is to be done is not to *make* democracy happen, to create a vanguard that leads a passive population of spectators toward democracy. We should not lament the dull glow on the face of the spectator watching TV. We should instead search tirelessly for the light inside that spectator, for the active thinking she is doing. We should search for the struggle to become democratic that is going on all around us, that is alive in the body and mind of the recovering addict, and the consumer, and the urban inhabitant, and the citizen of the liberal-democratic state, and the multitude in Egypt.

But still, how do we know when we are on the right track? How do we know this struggle, this not-inferno, when we see it? I think perhaps at this point, more than anything, we need to rely on how it feels. Recall Franny's "violent, almost vertiginous happiness" when she was on the edge of the wolf pack. She says it is extremely hard to remain on the edge, but she knows it is right because she feels this unmistakable feeling. Hardt and Negri write about the "irrepressible lightness and joy" the multitude can discover when it is able to govern itself (2000, p. 413). Deleuze and Guattari often phrase it in terms of enjoyment (*jouissance*). Nietzsche, for his part, talks about the *delight* we can feel when we discover our own strength and our ability to discharge it into the world (1989a, Section 19). Nietzsche contrasts that delight in our own strength with the feeling of *ressentiment*, which we feel when we are dominated by others and can only resent and criticize their power. In *ressentiment*, our only option for self-affirmation is negative: they are bad, and because we are not them, we must be good by disassociation. Nietzsche worries that *ressentiment* can grow to eat up all other modes of thought, leaving us capable of feeling only spite, bitterness, anger, and envy. Such feelings mean we are on the wrong track, that we are trapped in *ressentiment*, that we are obsessed with oligarchy, that we are not discovering our own proper power and our desire for democracy. It means we are speaking only in the voice of critique, mockery, and irony. Those tools destroy, they clear the path. Even if they are necessary, even if we must constantly remove the obstacles and ward off the apparatuses of capture, *ressentiment* can never be primary. It is merely the "voice of the trapped who have come to enjoy their cage" (Hyde, 1955). The negative task is only the first step. We do not become democratic by endlessly criticizing oligarchy. We become democratic by developing our own productive desire, by relentlessly struggling to move down the path toward democracy. When we are developing that desire, we won't feel resentment. We will feel delight. It will make us happy. Foucault's reminder should always be in our heads: we do not have to be sad to be militant. In fact, we should amend him to say that it is alright to be sad sometimes, but not most of the time. What we are looking for mostly is delight. The struggle for democracy is a positive one, a struggle to live, to grow, to flourish. Becoming democratic unleashes our own power; it mobilizes our better angels. It should fill us with delight.

And maybe just one more thing on delight. Franny's kind of happiness, a violent vertiginous happiness, isn't quite right. It helps us know we are on the right track, but it isn't a long-term option. We can't always be travelling down the path toward democracy feeling a happiness that makes us dizzy. We need to discover instead a steady pace, a kind of happiness that we can sustain, that we can keep up over the long term. This happiness can perhaps start out as, or be punctuated by, a vertiginous feeling, a rush through our bloodstream. When Mubarak stepped down or the *indignados* retook the Puerta del Sol, the feeling was no doubt vertiginous, and that is good. But that feeling has to eventually settle down into our bones and then radiate outward. It needs to be in our marrow, to offer a slow burn of feeling that can energize us over the long haul. What I am trying to say is that we need to discover the down-deep delight of democracy. We need to learn what the delight feels like and what we can do to help ourselves feel it. And we need to get better at returning to it, at remembering to continually come back, so that when we wander into *ressentiment*, we know how to come back to delight. We need to always know the way back to Tahrir, to Sol, to Syntagma, to Tiananmen. We cannot become democratic only by a sort of asceticism that warns us off oligarchy, heteronomy, and passivity, that slaps us on the wrist when we sin. Our primary strategy is not so much to run *from* oligarchy but to run *toward* the horizon of democracy. We must increasingly come to want, even to crave, the deep delight it offers us. We need to feed off this delight, to relish it, and to flourish by living within it.

References

Acton, J. (1955 [1862]) Nationality. *Essays on Freedom and Power*. Edited by G. Himmelfarb. Cleveland, Meridian Books, pp. 141–170.

Agamben, G. (1993 [1990]) *The Coming Community*. Translated by M. Hardt. Minneapolis, University of Minnesota Press.

Agamben, G. (2009) *What Is an Apparatus?* Translated by D. Kishik and S. Pedatella. Stanford, Stanford University Press.

Agamben, G., Ed. (2011) *Democracy in What State?* New York, Columbia University Press.

Amanpour, C. (2011) Mubarak: 'If I Resign Today There Will Be Chaos'. *ABCNews.com*, September 12.

Ames, M. (2008) The Summers Conundrum. *The Nation*, November 24.

Announcements (2011) We Will Not Pay for Your Crisis! Workers Unite! *Defend Wisconsin*, http://www.defendwisconsin.org/2011/08/19/we-will-not-pay-for-your-crisis-workers-unite/. Accessed on 16 November 2012.

Anonymous (1921) The Turin Factory Councils Movement. *L'Ordine Nuovo*, March 14, probably written by Antonio Gramsci.

Arendt, H. (1998 [1958]) *The Human Condition*. Chicago, University of Chicago Press.

Aristotle (1998a) *The Nicomachean Ethics*. Translated by D. Ross, J. Ackrill, and J. Urmson. Oxford, Oxford University Press.

Aristotle (1998b) *The Politics*. Translated by C. Reeve. Indianapolis, Hackett Publishing Company, Inc.

Astor, M. (2011) Ebadi Details Iran Injustice in Book. *Seattle Times*, May 9.

Badiou, A. (2006) Democracy, Politics and Philosophy. Lecture at European Graduate School. Saas Fee, Switzerland, http://www.egs.edu/faculty/alain-badiou/articles/democracy-politics-and-philosophy/#. Accessed on 16 November 2012.

Badiou, A. (2008) The Communist Hypothesis. *New Left Review* 49(Jan/Feb), pp. 29–42.

The Down-Deep Delight of Democracy, First Edition. Mark Purcell.
© 2013 John Wiley & Sons, Ltd. Published 2013 by John Wiley & Sons, Ltd.

Bahgat, H. (2012) Egypt Just Witnessed the Smoothest Military Coup. We'd Be Outraged If We Weren't So Exhausted. June 14, Tweet @hossambahgat.

Bakunin, M. (1972) *Bakunin on Anarchy*. Translated by S. Dolgoff. New York, Knopf.

Bakunin, M. (1973) *Michael Bakunin: Selected Writings*. Translated by S. Cox and O. Stevens. London, Jonathan Cape.

Bookchin, M. (2002) The Communalist Project. *Communalism: International Journal for a Rational Society* 2(November).

Brenner, N. and S. Elden (2009) Introduction. *State, Space, World: Selected Essays by Henri Lefebvre*. Edited by N. Brenner and S. Elden. Minneapolis, University of Minnesota Press, pp. 1–48.

Brenner, N. and N. Theodore, Eds. (2003) *Spaces of Neoliberalism*. Malden, MA, Blackwell.

Bukharin, N. and E. Preobrazhensky (2007 [1920]) *The ABC of Communism*. London, Merlin Press.

Bukowski, C. (1993) The Laughing Heart. *Prairie Schooner* 67(3), p. 168.

Burroughs, W. (1966) *Naked Lunch*. New York, Grove Press.

California Student Occupation Movement (2009) October Occupation Statement. *We Want Everything*, October 16, http://wewanteverything. wordpress.com/2009/10/16/october-occupation-statement/. Accessed on 16 November 2012.

Calvino, I. (1974) *Invisible Cities*. Translated by W. Weaver. New York, Harcourt Inc.

Calvino, I. (1993 [1972]) *Le Citta Invisibili*. Verona, Mondadori.

Carolina (2011a) Quick Guide on Group Dynamics in People's Assemblies. *Take the Square*, July 31, http://takethesquare.net/2011/07/31/quick-guide-on-group-dynamics-in-peoples-assemblies/. Accessed on 16 November 2012.

Carolina (2011b) Sol Has Been Evicted but We Know the Way Back #Spanish-revolution #Nopararemos #Nofear. *Take the Square*, August 2, http://takethesquare.net/2011/08/02/sol-has-been-evicted-but-we-know-the-way-back-spanishrevolution-nopararemos-nofear/. Accessed on 16 November 2012.

Castoriadis, C. (1988) *Political and Social Writings*. Translated by D. Curtis. Minneapolis, University of Minnesota Press.

Chang, H.-J. and O. Gilmore (2011) The Revival – and the Retreat – of the State? *Red Pepper*, June.

Colombo, P. and T. Mascarenhas (2003) We're Nothing: We Want to Be Everything. *We Are Everywhere: The Irresistible Rise of Global Anticapitalism*. Edited by Notes From Nowhere. New York, Verso, pp. 458–463.

Crane, S. (1972) *The Complete Poems of Stephen Crane*. Edited by J. Katz. Ithaca, Cornell University Press.

Daley, S. (2011) Economist Named to Lead Greek Unity Government. *New York Times*, November 11.

Damasio, A. (2003) *Looking for Spinoza: Joy, Sorrow, and the Feeling Brain*. New York, Harcourt.

Davis, M. (2006) *Planet of Slums*. New York, Verso.

Dean, J. (2011) The Communist Horizon. New York, Lecture hosted by The Public School and Not an Alternative, July 28, see http://vimeo.com/27327373. Accessed on 16 November 2012.

Debord, G. (1983 [1967]) *Society of the Spectacle*. Detroit, Black and Red.

Deleuze, G. and F. Guattari (1977 [1972]) *Anti-Oedipus: Capitalism and Schizophrenia*. Translated by R. Hurley, M. Seem, and H. Lane. New York, Penguin.

Deleuze, G. and F. Guattari (1987 [1980]) *A Thousand Plateaus*. Translated by B. Massumi. Minneapolis, University of Minnesota Press.

Deleuze, G. and F. Guattari (1994 [1991]) *What Is Philosophy?* Translated by H. Tomlinson and G. Burchell. New York, Columbia University Press.

Deleuze, G. and A. Negri (1990) Control and Becoming: Gilles Deleuze in Conversation with Antonio Negri. *Futur Anterieur* 1(Spring).

Dicken, P. (1998) *Global Shift*. New York, Guilford.

Dickens, C. (2012) *David Copperfield*. New York, Vintage.

Dikec, M. (2005) Space, Politics, and the Political. *Environment and Planning D: Society and Space* 23, pp. 171–188.

Elden, S. (2004) *Understanding Henri Lefebvre: Theory and the Possible*. New York, Continuum.

Engels, F. (1996 [1845]) The Great Towns. *The City Reader*. Edited by R. LeGates and F. Stout. New York, Routledge, pp. 46–55.

European Revolution (2011) Three Months of Struggle: An Overview of the #15m Movement and the #Spanishrevolution. *Take the Square*, August 20, http://takethesquare.net/2011/08/20/three-months-of-struggle-an-overview-of-the-15m-movement-and-the-spanishrevolution/. Accessed on 16 November 2012.

Feuerbach, L. (2008 [1841]) *The Essence of Christianity*. New York, Cosimo, Inc.

Forgacs, D. (2000) Introduction to Part One, Section III. *The Antonio Gramsci Reader*. Edited by D. Forgacs. New York, New York University Press, pp. 76–78.

Foster, J., B. Clark, and R. York (2010) *The Ecological Rift: Capitalism's War on the Earth*. New York, Monthly Review Press.

Foucault, M. (1977 [1972]) Preface. *Anti-Oedipus*. Translated by R. Hurley, M. Seem, and H. Lane. New York, Penguin.

Foucault, M. (1980) *Power/Knowledge: Selected Interviews and Other Writings, 1972–1977*. Collection edited by Colin Gordon. New York, Pantheon.

Foucault, M. (1990 [1976]) *The History of Sexuality: An Introduction*. Translated by R. Hurley. New York, Vintage.

Frade, C. (2011) Events in Spain. The Rise of the Indignant: Spain, Greece, Europe. Conference at Birkbeck Institute for the Humanities, University of London, June 22.

Friedman, M. (1962) *Capitalism and Freedom*. Chicago, University of Chicago Press.

Fukuyama, F. (1992) *The End of History and the Last Man*. New York, Free Press.

Gibson-Graham, J. K. (1996) *The End of Capitalism (as We Knew It)*. Oxford, Blackwell.

Giollamoir, O. (2011) Unhappy Economies: Greek Debt, PIIGS and the Eurozone Crisis. *The Commune*, August 4, http://thecommune.co.uk/2011/08/04/unhappy-economies-greek-debt-piigs-and-the-eurozone-crisis/. Accessed on 16 November 2012.

Gramsci, A. (1971) *Selections from the Prison Notebooks*. Translated by Q. Hoare and G. Smith. New York, International Publishers.

Gramsci, A. (2000) *The Antonio Gramsci Reader: Selected Writings 1916–1935*. Edited by D. Forgacs. New York, New York University Press.

Guattari, F. and A. Negri (1990 [1985]) *Communists Like Us*. Translated by M. Ryan. New York, Autonomedia.

Hardt, M. (1993) *Gilles Deleuze: An Apprenticeship in Philosophy*. Minneapolis, University of Minnesota Press.

Hardt, M. (2004) Today's Bandung? *A Movement of Movements: Is Another World Really Possible?* Edited by T. Mertes. New York, Verso, pp. 230–236.

Hardt, M. (n.d.) "Reading Notes on Deleuze and Guattari, *Capitalism & Schizophrenia*." http://www.duke.edu/~hardt/Deleuze&Guattari.html. Accessed on 16 November 2012.

Hardt, M. and A. Negri (2000) *Empire*. Cambridge, MA, Harvard University Press.

Hardt, M. and A. Negri (2004) *Multitude: War and Democracy in the Age of Empire*. New York, Penguin.

Hardt, M. and A. Negri (2011) *Commonwealth*. Cambridge, MA, Belknap Press.

Harvey, D. (2005) *A Brief History of Neoliberalism*. New York, Oxford University Press.

Harvey, D. (2011) Don't Moralise, Don't Judge, Don't Take Pictures – It's Time for the Riot to Get Some Radical Politics. *The Commune*, August 8.

Havel, V. (1985 [1978]) The Power of the Powerless. *The Power of the Powerless: Citizens against the State in Central-Eastern Europe*. Edited by J. Keane. Armonk, NY, M.E. Sharpe, Inc., pp. 23–97.

Hayek, F. (1994 [1944]) *The Road to Serfdom*. Chicago, University of Chicago Press.

Hayes, B. (2011) Flights of Fancy. *American Scientist* 99(January–February), pp. 10–14.

Heller, C. and G. Perera (2007) *The Right to the City: Reclaiming Our Urban Centers, Reframing Human Rights, and Redefining Citizenship*. San Francisco, Tides Foundation.

Hoare, Q. and G. Smith (1971) Introduction. *Selections from the Prison Notebooks*. Edited by Q. Hoare and G. Smith. New York, International Publishers, pp. xvii–xcvi.

Hobbes, T. (1996 [1651]) *Leviathan*. New York, Cambridge University Press.

Holland, E. (1998) Spinoza and Marx. *Cultural Logic* 2(1).

Holloway, J. and H. Wainwright (2011) Crack Capitalism or Reclaim the State? *Red Pepper*, April.

Hyde, L. (1955) Alcohol & Poetry: John Berryman and the Booze Talking. *American Poetry Review*, October.

Janner-Klausner, T. (2011) Egypt: 'Democracy, Social Justice and Human Dignity' – but When, and How? *The Commune*, June 17.

Judt, T. and T. Snyder (2012) *Thinking the Twentieth Century*. New York, Penguin.

Kant, I. (2006) *Fundamental Principles of the Metaphysic of Morals*. Translated by T. Abbott. Saddle River, NJ, Prentice Hall.

Kautsky, K. (2010 [1910]) *The Class Struggle (Erfurt Program)*. Translated by W. Bohn. Charleston, SC, Nabu Press.

Kirkpatrick, D. (2012) Military Warns against Threats to Egypt's 'Higher Interests'. *New York Times*, June 22.

Kohn, M. (2003) *Radical Space*. Ithaca, Cornell University Press.

Kolbert, E. (2006) *Field Notes from a Catastrophe*. New York, Bloomsbury.

Kouvelakis, S. (2011) Insurrection in Greece. The Rise of the Indignant: Spain, Greece, Europe. Conference at Birkbeck, University of London, June 22.

Krause, R. and M. Rolli (2008) Micropolitical Associations. *Deleuze and Politics*. Edited by I. Buchanan and N. Thoburn. Edinburgh, Edinburgh University Press, pp. 240–254.

La Boetie, E. (1975 [1548]) *The Politics of Obedience: The Discourse of Voluntary Servitude*. Translated by H. Kurz. New York, Free Life Editions.

Laclau, E. (2000) Identity and Hegemony: The Role of Universality in the Constitution of Political Logics. *Contingency, Hegemony, Universality: Contemporary Dialogues on the Left*. Edited by J. Butler, E. Laclau, and S. Zizek. New York, Verso, pp. 44–89.

Laclau, E. and C. Mouffe (1985) *Hegemony and Socialist Strategy: Towards a Radical Democratic Politics*. London, Verso.

Laclau, E. and C. Mouffe (2000) Preface to the Second Edition. In E. Laclau and C. Mouffe, *Hegemony and Socialist Strategy*. New York, Verso, pp. vii–xix.

Lefebvre, H. (1970) *La Révolution Urbaine*. Paris, Editions Gallimard.

Lefebvre, H. (1976–1978) *De L'etat: Les Contradictions De L'etat Moderne*. 4 vols. Paris, Union Generale de l'Editions.

Lefebvre, H. (1990) Du Pacte Social Au Contrat De Citoyennete. *Du Contrat De Citoyennete*. Edited by Groupe de Navarrenx. Paris, Editions Syllepse et Editions Periscope, pp. 15–37.

Lefebvre, H. (1991 [1974]) *The Production of Space*. Translated by D. Nicholson-Smith. Oxford, Blackwell.

Lefebvre, H. (1996) *Writings on Cities*. Translated by E. Kofman and E. Lebas. Cambridge, MA, Blackwell.

Lefebvre, H. (2003a [1990]) From the Social Pact to the Contract of Citizenship. *Henri Lefebvre: Key Writings*. Edited by S. Elden, E. Lebas, and E. Kofman. New York, Continuum, pp. 238–254.

Lefebvre, H. (2003b [1970]) *The Urban Revolution*. Translated by R. Bononno. Minneapolis, University of Minnesota Press.

Lefebvre, H. (2009) *State, Space, World: Selected Essays*. Edited by N. Brenner and S. Elden. Translated by G. Moore, N. Brenner, and S. Elden. Minneapolis, University of Minnesota Press.

Lenin, V. (2009 [1917]) *The State and Revolution*. New York, Penguin.

Lipsky, D. (2009) *Although of Course You End up Becoming Yourself: A Road Trip with David Foster Wallace*. New York, Broadway Books.

Locke, J. (1988 [1689]) *Two Treatises of Government*. New York, Cambridge University Press.

Lummis, C. (1997) *Radical Democracy*. Ithaca, Cornell University Press.

Macdonald, N. (2012) The Problem with Too Much Democracy. *CBC News*, January 8.

Mackey, R. (2011) Protesters Return to Cairo's Tahrir Square. *The Lede*, June 29, http://thelede.blogs.nytimes.com/2011/06/29/protesters-return-to-cairos-tahrir-square/. Accessed on 16 November 2012.

Marx, K. (1970 [1843]) *Critique of Hegel's Philosophy of Right*. Edited by J. O'Malley. Translated by A. Jolin and J. O'Malley. Cambridge, Cambridge University Press.

Marx, K. (1976) The Poverty of Philosophy. *Collected Works of Karl Marx and Friedrich Engels, 1845–48*, Vol. 6. New York, International Publishers.

Marx, K. (1993a [1867]) *Capital*, Vol. 1. New York, Penguin.

Marx, K. (1993b [1857]) *Grundrisse: Foundations of the Critique of Political Economy*. New York, Penguin.

Marx, K. (1994 [1844]) Economic and Philosophic Manuscripts. *Karl Marx: Selected Writings*. Edited by L. Simon. Translated by L. Easton and K. Guddat. Indianapolis, Hackett Publishing Company, Inc.

McCaffrey, L. (2012 [1993]) An Expanded Interview with David Foster Wallace. *Conversations with David Foster Wallace*. Edited by S. Burn. Jackson, University Press of Mississippi pp. 21–52.

Merrifield, A. (2011) *Magical Marxism*. London, Pluto Press.

Mill, J. (1979 [1861]) *Utilitarianism*. Indianapolis, Hackett Publishing Company, Inc.

Mill, J. (1991 [1861]) *Considerations on Representative Government*. Amherst, NY, Prometheus Books.

Mouffe, C. (1979) Hegemony and Ideology in Gramsci. *Gramsci and Marxist Theory*. Edited by C. Mouffe. London, Routledge & Kegan Paul, pp. 168–204.

Mouffe, C. (1993) *The Return of the Political*. London, Verso.

Mouffe, C. (1999) Deliberative Democracy or Agonistic Pluralism? *Social Research* 66(3), pp. 745–758.

Mouffe, C. (2002) *Politics and Passions: The Stakes of Democracy*. London, Center for the Study of Democracy.

Mumford, L. (1937) What Is a City? *Architectural Record* 82(November).

Ness, I. and D. Azzellini, Eds. (2011) *Ours to Master and to Own*. Chicago, Haymarket Books.

Nietzsche, F. (1954) *The Portable Nietzsche*. Edited by W. Kaufman. New York, Penguin.

Nietzsche, F. (1989a [1886]) *Beyond Good and Evil*. Translated by W. Kaufmann. New York, Vintage.

Nietzsche, F. (1989b [1887]) *On the Genealogy of Morals*. Translated by W. Kaufmann. New York, Vintage.

Nietzsche, F. (1999 [1872]) *The Birth of Tragedy and Other Writings*. Edited by R. Geuss and R. Speirs. Translated by R. Speirs. Cambridge, Cambridge University Press.

Nietzsche, F. (2005 [1883]) *Thus Spoke Zarathustra*. Translated by C. Martin. New York, Barnes & Noble Classics.

Notes from Nowhere, Ed. (2003) *We Are Everywhere: The Irresistible Rise of Global Anti-Capitalism*. London, Verso.

Nye, J. (2002) *The Paradox of American Power: Why the World's Only Superpower Can't Go It Alone*. Oxford, Oxford University Press.

O'Nions, J. (2011) Riots: The Left Must Respond. *Red Pepper Blog*, August 10.

Orszag, P. (2011) Too Much of a Good Thing: Why We Need Less Democracy. *The New Republic*, September 14.

Ouziel, P. (2011) Spain's 'Indignados': Vanguard of a Global Nonviolent Revolt against Neoliberalism. *Global Research*, August 6.

Patton, P. (2005) Deleuze and Democracy. *Contemporary Political Theory* 4, pp. 400–413.

Patton, P. (2008) Becoming-Democratic. *Deleuze and Politics*. Edited by I. Buchanan and N. Thoburn. Edinburgh, Edinburgh University Press, pp. 178–195.

People's Assembly of Syntagma Square. (2011) Vote of the People's Assembly of Syntagma Square. Athens, May 27, http://en.wikipedia.org/wiki/File:Vote_of_the_People%27s_Assembly_of_Syntagma_Square.svg. Accessed on 16 November 2012.

Petit, P. (2011) Republican Reflections on the 15-M Movement. *booksandideas. net*, September 20.

Plato (1998) Gorgias. *Ethics: The Classic Readings*. Edited by D. Cooper. Translated by W. Hamilton. Oxford, Blackwell, pp. 11–28.

Plato (2008) *The Republic*. Edited by G. Ferrari. Translated by T. Griffith. Cambridge, Cambridge University Press.

Popper, K. (1945) *The Open Society and Its Enemies*. London, Routledge.

Power, N., H. Wainwright, and M. Calderbank (2011) New Life in the Unions? Red Pepper Interviews Union Leaders Len Mccluskey of Unite and Mark Serwotka of PCS. *Red Pepper*, September 9.

Purcell, M. (2008) *Recapturing Democracy: Neoliberalization and the Struggle for Alternative Urban Futures*. New York, Routledge.

Rancière, J. (1991 [1981]) *The Ignorant Schoolmaster*. Translated by J. Ross. Palo Alto, Stanford University Press.

Rancière, J. (1995 [1992]) *On the Shores of Politics*. Translated by L. Heron. New York, Verso.

Rancière, J. (1999 [1995]) *Disagreement: Politics and Philosophy*. Translated by J. Rose. Minneapolis, University of Minnesota Press.

Rancière, J. (2000) Literature, Politics, Aesthetics: Approaches to Democratic Disagreement. Interviewed by S. Guenoun and J. Kavanagh. *SubStance* 92, pp. 3–24.

Rancière, J. (2001) Ten Theses on Politics. *Theory and Event* 5(3).

Rancière, J. (2004 [2000]) *The Politics of Aesthetics: The Distribution of the Sensible*. Translated by G. Rockhill. New York, Continuum.

Rancière, J. (2009 [2008]) *The Emancipated Spectator*. Translated by G. Elliott. New York, Verso.

Rawls, J. (1993) *Political Liberalism*. New York, Columbia University Press.

Reich, W. (1970) *The Mass Psychology of Fascism*. Translated by V. Carfagno. London, Souvenir Press.

Romero, S. and M. Diaz (2011) A 45-Story Walkup Beckons the Desperate. *New York Times*, February 28.

Roos, J. (2011a) Eviction of Puerta Del Sol Backfires—Big Time! *Roar Magazine*, August 2.

Roos, J. (2011b) La Lucha Sigue: The Struggle of the Indignados Continues. *Roar Magazine*, July 27.

Roos, J. (2011c) The Sun Rises: Indignados Take Back Puerta Del Sol. *Roar Magazine*, August 6.

Rose, M. (2011) Commentary on Egypt. *Blog of Environment and Planning D: Society and Space*, July 18, http://societyandspace.com/2011/07/18/commentary-on-egypt-by-mitch-rose/. Accessed on 16 November 2012.

Rousseau, J. (1987) *The Basic Political Writings*. Translated by D. Cress. Indianapolis, Hackett Publishing Company, Inc.

Roy, A. and A. Ong (2011) *Worlding Cities: Asian Experiments and the Art of Being Global*. New York, Routledge.

Sanchez, M. (2012) Losing Strength? An Alternative Vision of Spain's Indignados. *Reflections on a Revolution*, June 23.

Sartre, J. (1963) Preface. *The Wretched of the Earth*. Translated by C. Farrington. New York, Grove Press.

Saunders, G. (2008) Wake-up Artist. *Five Dials* 10, p. 15.

Schumpeter, J. (1947) *Capitalism, Socialism, and Democracy*. New York, Harper and Brothers.

Sebestyen, A. (2011) Dispatches from Tunisia. *Red Pepper*, May.

Shadid, A. (2011) Not Satisfied, Protesters Return to Tahrir Square. *New York Times*, July 12.

Simon, L., Ed. (1994) *Karl Marx: Selected Writings*. Indianapolis, Hackett Publishing Company, Inc.

Simpson, C. (2012) Congratulations, We Wasted a Billion Hours on Netflix in June. *The Atlantic Wire*, July 4.

Sitrin, M. and L. Moreno-Caballus (2011) The Camp Is the World: Connecting the Occupy Movements and the Spanish May 15th Movement. *Take the Square*, November 23, http://takethesquare.net/2011/11/23/the-camp-is-the-world-connecting-the-occupy-movements-and-the-spanish-may-15th-movement/. Accessed on 16 November 2012.

Spinoza, B. (1996 [1677]) *Ethics*. Translated by E. Curley. New York, Penguin Classics.

Spinoza, B. (2000 [1677]) *Political Treatise*. Translated by S. Shirley. Indianapolis, Hackett Publishing Company, Inc.

Spivak, G. (1988) Can the Subaltern Speak? *Marxism and the Interpretation of Culture*. Edited by C. Nelson and L. Grossberg. Basingstoke, Macmillan Education, pp. 66–111.

St. Thomas Aquinas (1989 [1265–1274]) Law and Grace. *Summa Theologica: A Concise Translation*. Edited by T. McDermott. London, Eyre and Spottiswoode, pp. 276–306.

Stepan, A. (2011) Tunisia's Election: Counter-Revolution or Democratic Transition? *The Imminent Frame*, December 17, http://blogs.ssrc.org/tif/2011/12/17/

tunisia%E2%80%99s-election-counter-revolution-or-democratic-transition/. Accessed on 16 November 2012.

Subcomandante Marcos (2001) *Our Word Is Our Weapon*. Edited by J. Ponce de Leon. New York, Seven Stories Press.

Taibo, C. (2012) El 15-M De Algete Y Alrededores, En Madrid, Se Autodefine Con Gracia: 'Dormíamos, Despertamos...Y Ahora Tenemos Insomnio Crónico'. June 18, Tweet @carlos_taibo.

The Invisible Committee (2009 [2007]) *The Coming Insurrection*. Los Angeles, Semiotexte.

Tucker, E. (2012) Spinoza's Absolute Democracy. Spinoza Symposium. University of Washington, Seattle, March 2 and 3.

Urry, J. (2011) *Climate Change and Society*. Cambridge, Polity Press.

Vaneigem, R. (1974) *De la Grève Sauvage à L'autogestion Généralisée*. Paris, Éditions 10/18.

Wall, I. (2011) Anger and the Streets. The Rise of the Indignant: Spain, Greece, Europe. Conference at Birkbeck Institute for the Humanities, University of London, June 22.

Wallace, D. (1996) *Infinite Jest*. New York, Little, Brown, and Co.

Wallace, D. (1997) *A Supposedly Fun Thing I'll Never Do Again*. New York, Little, Brown and Co.

Wallace, D. (2004) *Oblivion: Stories*. New York, Little, Brown and Co.

Wallace, D. (2009) *This Is Water: Some Thoughts, Delivered on a Significant Occasion, About Living a Compassionate Life*. New York, Little, Brown and Co.

Wallace, D. (2010) *Fate, Time, and Language*. New York, Columbia University Press.

Wallace, D. (2012) *The Pale King*. New York, Back Bay Books.

Wallerstein, I. (2011) Wallerstein on the Arab Revolts. *Against the Grain: a Program about Politics, Society and Ideas*. Pacifica Radio, May 31.

Zhao, D. (2004) *The Power of Tiananmen*. Chicago, University of Chicago Press.

Zizek, S. (2011) Shoplifters of the World Unite: Slavoj Žižek on the Meaning of the Riots. *London Review of Books Online*, August 19.

Index

Wallace, David Foster, 21–2, 26–7,
        92, 102–12, 118–19, 120, 148
    "A Supposedly Fun Thing I'll Never
        Do Again", 107
    Infinite Jest, 102–6, 109, 112
    The Pale King, 108–9
    "The Soul is Not a Smithy", 108
welfare state, 4–7, 9–10, 10n, 12,
        14, 17

wolves, wolfpack, 134, 136–8, 141,
        155–7
will, 44, 135, 151
will to power, 13
workers' councils, 14, 39, 40, 57

Zizek, Slavoj, 29, 144